B

NORTH BAY TRAILS

OUTDOOR ADVENTURES IN MARIN, NAPA, AND SONOMA COUNTIES

David Weintraub

WILDERNESS PRESS
BERKELEY

All photos © 1999 by the author
Book design by Margaret Copeland—Terragraphics
All maps © 1999 by National Geographic Maps, with trails added by the author
Cover photos © 1999 by David Weintraub
Cover design by Larry B. Van Dyke

Library of Congress Card Number 99-055952
ISBN 0-89997-236-5

Manufactured in the United States of America
Published by: **Wilderness Press**
1200 5th Street
Berkeley, CA 94710
(800) 443-7227; FAX (510) 558-1696
mail@wildernesspress.com
www.wildernesspress.com

Contact us for a free catalog

Cover photos: View northwest from China Camp State Park—Trip 3
Watercolorists on summit of Mt. Tam (inset)—Trip 16

♻ Printed on recycled paper, 20% post-consumer waste

Library Of Congress Cataloging-in-Publication Data

Weintraub, David, 1949-
    North Bay trails : outdoor adventures in Marin, Napa, and Sonoma counties /
David Weintraub.— 1st ed.
        p.   cm.
    Includes bibliographical references and index.
    ISBN 0-89997-236-5 (alk. paper)
    1. Hiking—California—San Francisco Bay Area—Guidebooks. 2.
Trails—California—San Francisco Bay Area—Guidebooks. 3. San Francisco Bay
Area (Calif)—Guidebooks. I. Title.
    GV199.42.C22 S2697   1999
    917.94'60453—dc21   99-055952
                                                                       CIP

View from Mt. Tam's East Peak extends from MMWD lands all the way to the Point Reyes area. In the foreground are Bon Tempe Lake and its smaller neighbor, Lake Lagunitas.

Table Of Contents

Acknowledgments

Although hiking, for me, is generally a solo activity, many people contributed to this book. Park personnel were generous with their time and expertise. Friends were recruited to walk with me so I could add human interest to my scenic photographs. A number of park rangers looked over my manuscript and added their comments and corrections. A few high-tech gurus helped me understand computer mapping. My thanks to all.

We have our parklands to enjoy thanks to the daily efforts of people working in federal, state, and local government agencies, and in non-profit organizations. Many of these people are park rangers working in the field, maintaining the trails we love to hike, bike, and ride. In my exploration of the North Bay, I was lucky to have the help of Ron Angier, Natalie Gates, Ane Rovetta, Denis Odion, Diana Roberts, Klytia Nelson, Ralph Ingols, Milan Pittman, Angela Nowicki, Lynda Doucette, Paul Larson, Al Vosher, Willard Wyman, Elizabeth Beale, Charles Potthast, Ronessa Duncan, Dawn Kemp, Marla Hastings, Cleve Dufer, Kevin McKay, and Bill Cox.

Many of the happy hikers pictured in this book are friends who have learned over the years how to be excellent photographic models. My thanks to Ken Kobre, Betsy Brill, Steve Gregory, Vickie Vann, Laura Wood, Barry Low, Mary Lou Mackin, Lea Redmond, Otto Schutt, John Macchia, Paul Ash, Elena Ash, Silvia Fernandez, Lee Eisman, Jay Tennenbaum, Jordan Tennenbaum, and Carla Palmer.

The following people deserve thanks for reviewing my manuscript and making many helpful suggestions: Patrick Robards, China Camp State Park; Gale Lester, Marin Headlands; Mia Monroe, Muir Woods National Monument; Bill Michaels, Point Reyes National Seashore; Casey May, Marin Municipal Water District; Scott Rasmussen, Marin County Open Space District; Glenn Ryburn, Mt. Tamalpais State Park; Fred Lew, Olompali State Historic Park; Carlos Porrata, Tomales Bay State Park; Landon Waggoner, Samuel P. Taylor State Park; Bill Grummer, Bothe-Napa Valley State Park; Cheryl Lawton, Sugarloaf Ridge State Park; Rich Lawton, Sonoma Coast State Beach; Val Nixon, Annadel State Park; Greg Hayes, Jack London State Historic Park; Bill Trunick, Sonoma County Regional Parks; and Martha Wise, Napa County Land Trust.

I am grateful to the folks at National Geographic Maps, including Matt Heller, Mike Dyer, and Dan Braun, for helping me learn TOPO!, their interactive mapping software, and for spending many hours with me to make sure I could create the maps for this book.

A book is more than text, photographs, and maps. The people at Wilderness Press are experts at turning an author's vision into printed form—thank you all!

Finally, I want to thank Maggi, my wife, for her love and support.

◆ Introduction ◆

THE NORTH BAY

If this were a novel instead of a guidebook, its leading characters would be named Marin, Napa, and Sonoma. How best to describe them? Marin has a split personality, torn between its sophisticated, upscale, high-tech half, and its laid-back rural and agricultural other half. Napa is beautiful, full-bodied, rich, and pleasantly tart. Sonoma is big, brawny, bountiful, and bold. Although a guidebook doesn't really have a plot, these three leading characters form a story line that is woven through everything that follows.

Marin, at 521 square miles, is the smallest North Bay county but has the most parkland and open space, about 220 square miles in federal, state, and local lands. Hikers, bicyclists, and equestrians are in heaven here, enjoying hundreds of miles of trails that wind through public land. The county's terrain includes rugged Pacific shoreline, redwood groves, forested valleys and ridges, open grassland, chaparral, and salt marsh. Some of Marin's place names, such as Mill Valley and Corte Madera ("a place where wood is cut") are clues to its lumber-producing past. Others, like San Rafael and Sausalito ("little willow grove") tell of Franciscan missionaries and Mexican ranchos. Still others—Tamalpais, Olompali—are derived from Marin's original inhabitants, the Coast Miwok people.

Often foggy and windy, the rural areas of West Marin are dominated by cattle and dairy ranches. It is here that you find most of Marin's public land, in a long swath running from the Golden Gate to the tip of Tomales Point. The jewel in the crown is Mt. Tamalpais, at 2571 feet the highest North Bay peak near the coast. Low on its southern slope lies Muir Woods National Monument, one of the last remaining groves of old-growth coast redwoods. Fronting San Francisco and San Pablo bays, you find a more suburban, residential Marin, where open space, including wooded areas, grasslands, and salt marsh, is tucked between towns and housing developments. Industry here includes movie and video production, computer software, communications, and manufacturing. This part of Marin, usually sheltered from the fog, is often 10 to 20 degrees warmer than coastal areas, including San Francisco.

Napa needs no introduction. Thanks to its world-class wines, Napa's reputation is well known and well deserved. At 758 square miles, it ranks between Marin and Sonoma in size, but offers the least amount of public land for hiking. The land here is devoted to growing grapes, and nearly every tillable acre is taken up with that pursuit. Only two state parks—Bothe-Napa Valley and Robert Louis Stevenson—offer hiking and riding trails. Unlike Marin and Sonoma, Napa County operates no county parks, and in 1992 Napa voters rejected a plan to create an open-space district. The City of Napa, however, has about 40 parks, some of which have hiking trails, and a volunteer group operates Skyline Wilderness Park, a paradise for hikers, bicyclists, and equestrians. In the days before wine became queen, Napa had, at various times, large ranchos, fruit and nut orchards, and mines that produced gold, silver, and cinnabar. Before the coming of Europeans, the narrow valley bordered by the Mayacmas Mountains to the west and the Vaca Mountains to the east was inhabited by the Wappo people. Today, especially on weekends, the valley is inhabited by tourists, whose cars move at a snail's pace up and down Highway 29.

Sonoma is the largest of the three North Bay counties, about 1600 square miles. It is also the most varied, stretching from the volcanic highlands of the Mayacmas Mountains to the wave-washed Pacific shore. Along its northern coast and in the Russian River area are found some of the North Bay's most beautiful and remote parks. The area's tallest peak, Mt. St. Helena (4339'), is just inside the county line at the edge of Napa and Lake counties. Sonoma has some of the finest hiking, bicycling, and horseback riding in the North Bay, in state parks such as Annadel, Armstrong Redwoods/Austin Creek, Jack London, Salt Point, Sonoma Coast, and Sugarloaf Ridge. The county maintains its own system of regional parks, which offer hiking and riding, camping, swimming, picnicking, fishing, and sports.

For thousands of years, the area's natural resources supported three Indian tribes—Coast Miwok, Pomo, and Wappo. Prized by early European and American settlers, Sonoma has seen six flags raised over its soil, those of England, Spain, Russia, Mexico, the US, and the Bear Flag Republic. Rich in history, Sonoma was home to some of California's most colorful personalities, including General Mariano G. Vallejo and author Jack London. Today, the county supports dairy farming, cattle and sheep ranching, fishing, timber harvesting, and tourism. Sonoma has several wine-growing regions, including the Sonoma Valley, the Valley of the Moon, the Alexander and Dry Creek valleys, and the Russian River area. The Sonoma Valley and its northward extension, the Valley of the Moon, are divided from Napa County on the east by the Mayacmas Mountains, and are bordered on the west by the Sonoma Mountains.

For this book, I have defined the North Bay to include all of Marin and Napa counties, and Sonoma County north to a line stretching from Mt. St. Helena to Salt Point State Park. Most of the trailheads are within an hour to an hour-and-a-half drive from San Francisco, Oakland, and Berkeley. If you are visiting a park along the Russian River, on the Sonoma coast, or in the northern Napa Valley from more than an hour or so away, it is a good idea to stay overnight. Camping is available in Austin Creek State Recreation Area, Sonoma State Beach, Salt Point State Park, and Bothe-

Napa Valley State Park. Comfortable motels can be found in Guerneville, Bodega Bay, and Calistoga.

The parklands described in this book are managed by seven government agencies and one volunteer organization. These are: National Park Service (NPS), California State Parks (CSP), California Department of Fish and Game, Marin County Open Space District (MCOSD), Marin Municipal Water District (MMWD), Sonoma County Regional Parks, City of Napa Department of Parks and Recreation, and Skyline Park Citizens Association. In these pages, I often use the agency's initials instead of its full name.

Climate and Weather

Most of the North Bay is blessed with an ideal climate: not too cold in winter, not too hot in summer. Compared with other parts of the US, we live in an area that is almost perfect for year-round outdoor activity. Nature's own air-conditioner, the Pacific Ocean, provides cool relief from summer's heat, offering us fog-shrouded hills and shady redwood groves. In winter, the ocean provides a moderating influence, keeping temperatures near the coast above freezing. Snow, except on the highest peaks, is rare. Aren't we being contrary, then, when we curse the fog, rail at the wind, complain about the rain, and bemoan the heat? Not really. These have to do with weather—daily atmospheric conditions—and not climate. Our climate is great, but it's the weather that keeps us guessing!

In our area, the dry season generally lasts from May through October, giving us about 180 rain-free days for hiking and other outdoor activities. The summer months are characterized by fog at the coast, but generally clear and warm conditions elsewhere. Grassy hillsides turn brown and seasonal creeks dry up. When the rains arrive, usually in November, it doesn't take long before brown hillsides turn green, and dry creek beds flow with water. A fall or winter storm sweeping down from the Gulf of Alaska usually leaves in its wake a few cold but exceptionally clear days. This is perhaps the best time to experience the North Bay's highest peaks, such as Mt. Hood and Mt. St. Helena. In the dead of winter, our manzanitas begin to bloom, decorating chaparral areas with delicate white-and-pink flowers. Other shrubs and the earliest wildflowers begin their show in late winter or early spring, and by the time April rolls around, especially after a wet winter, the floral display is usually fantastic.

The farther inland you go, the less pronounced is the moderating influence of the ocean. Temperature differences—the daily highs and lows for any given location—widen as you leave the coast. Each successive range of coastal hills blocks more and more Pacific moisture, creating a rain-shadow effect. This can be seen dramatically in the Napa Valley, the most inland area in the North Bay and the state's most famous wine-growing region. The valley opens onto San Pablo Bay, allowing some marine air to penetrate. The farther up the valley you go, the hotter and drier it becomes. This changes the flavor of grapes grown in different parts of the valley, and affects the wine that is made with them. Another example can be seen in the distribution of our coast redwoods. These giant trees depend on fog-drip to keep them watered during our generally rainless summers. Hence they are found only along the coast and in nearby valleys tributary to coastal rivers.

A fine hike can easily be spoiled by high winds or a sudden squall. The National Oceanic and Atmospheric Administration (NOAA) broadcasts continuous weather information, including special advisories and warnings, over a network of radio stations around the country. You can listen to these broadcasts on small, inexpensive receivers available at Radio Shack, outdoor stores, and other outlets. Anyone planning to spend time outdoors will find one of these radios useful.

Geology

The North Bay lies within the northern Coast Ranges, the name given by geologists to the complex system of ridges and valleys that extend from Arcata south to San Francisco Bay and inland to the edge of the Central Valley. These ridges and valleys trend northwest to southeast, paralleling the San Andreas and other faults. South of the Golden Gate, the ridges and valleys continue as the southern Coast Ranges, extending south almost to Point Conception. The highest elevation in the northern Coast Ranges is Solomon Peak (7581') in Trinity County. The tallest peak in the North Bay is Mt. St. Helena (4339'), at the corner of Sonoma, Napa, and Lake counties. Other prominent North Bay summits include Mt. Hood (2730'), Mt. Tamalpais (2571'), Sonoma Mountain (2295'), and Mt. Wittenberg (1407').

The major river in the North Bay, the Russian River, gets its start near Cloverdale, on the border of Sonoma and Mendocino counties. It flows southeast for about 40 miles, makes several abrupt twists and turns near Healdsburg, runs south to Forestville, and then trends southwest through a deep gorge to reach the Pacific Ocean at Jenner. On the southern edge of our area another river—actually the combined waters of the Sacramento and San Joaquin rivers—empties into the ocean through the Golden Gate. San Francisco and San Pablo bays are the mouth of this river system, which was flooded as sea levels rose at the end of the last Ice Age. The Petaluma River, Sonoma Creek, and the Napa River drain North Bay valleys and empty into San Pablo Bay.

Where we see a stunningly beautiful landscape, geologists see "a nightmare of rocks." How did the Coast Ranges arise? For years, geologists struggled with confusing evidence, some of it contradictory. Finally a scenario emerged that was both simple and elegant. The world's continents and ocean floors are not fixed in position. Instead, they move as a result of geological forces deep within the earth, and sometimes meet head on. This happened along what is today the West Coast of North

America. As the floor of the Pacific Ocean collided with the western edge of North American continent, the ocean floor was dragged under the continent. This process scraped material from the ocean floor and piled it higher and higher on the continent's edge, creating the Coast Ranges in what is now California.

Most of the rock found in the northern Coast Ranges is called the Franciscan Formation, consisting generally of sedimentary shale and sandstone. In places a gray-green rock called serpentine, California's state rock, has intruded into the Franciscan rocks. Serpentine forms a soil that is toxic to many plant species, but some have adapted to it. Among these are Sargent cypress, leather oak, and a variety of uncommon wildflowers. Young volcanic rock caps the Mayacmas and Vaca mountains bordering the Napa Valley, but none of the original volcanoes remain. A geothermal area on the border of Sonoma and Lake counties gives proof that violent forces are still at work underground.

The other lead player in the Coast Range saga is the San Andreas fault. Some of the coastal bluffs and headlands in the Coast Ranges contain rocks matching those found hundreds of miles to the south. The Point Reyes peninsula and Bodega Head, for example, contain granite from the co-called Salinian Block, which was formed near the southern end of the Sierra Nevada and shifted northward during the last 25 million years by slippage along the San Andreas fault. During the 1906 earthquake, the earth moved 21 feet in Olema Valley. The Earthquake Trail at Point Reyes National Seashore runs through San Andreas fault and offers lessons in its geology. Interestingly, the fault marks the western limit of coast redwoods in Marin County, perhaps because of the granitic soil west of it. The fault runs though Bolinas Lagoon, Tomales Bay and Bodega Bay before moving offshore north of Bodega Head. It makes landfall again about 2 miles south of Fort Ross and then stays about 2 to 5 miles inland before finally heading out to sea north of Point Arena.

Plant Communities

California has more than 5,000 native plant species and an estimated 1,000 introduced species. Of the native plants, about 30 per cent occur nowhere else—these are called endemics. Among the most common endemics are many types of manzanita (*Arctostaphylos*) and monkeyflower (*Mimulus*). The state also has some of the oldest species, in terms of evolution, and also some of the youngest. For example, coast redwoods date back to the dinosaurs, whereas certain species of tarweed (*Madia*) have evolved within the past several thousand years. Botanists divide the plant kingdom into several major groups: flowering plants, conifers, ferns and their allies, mosses, and algae. The members of these groups that grow together in a distinct habitat are a plant community. For this guidebook, I relied heavily on *Plants of the San Francisco Bay Region*, by Eugene N. Kozloff and Linda H. Beidleman. They sort the principal plant communities found in the region into 14 categories as follows.

Valley and Foothill Woodland

The dry hills of Napa County, untouched by fog except in winter, are characteristic of this community, which is found at elevations between 300 and 3500 feet. Common trees and shrubs found in this generally open woodland, sometimes called a savanna, include various oaks, California buckeye, gray pine, California bay, buckbrush, toyon, coffeeberry, snowberry, and poison oak. Especially with oaks, slope aspect and elevation determine which species occur where. Among the oaks in our area are valley oak, Oregon oak, black oak, blue oak, canyon oak, interior live oak, and coast live oak.

Interior live oak favors hot, dry areas.

Riparian Woodland

Members of this moisture-loving community are usually found beside rivers and creeks. Among the most common are bigleaf maple, white alder, red alder, California bay, various willows, California rose, poison oak, California wild grape, elk clover, and giant chain fern. Trails that run along Ritchey Creek in Bothe-Napa Valley State Park, and along Coast Creek in Point Reyes National Seashore, give you opportunities to study this community.

Redwood Forest

Coast redwoods are the world's tallest trees and are among the fastest-growing. Redwood groves once formed an extensive coastal forest that stretched from central California to southern Oregon. Commercially valuable, they were heavily logged. The remaining old-growth coast redwoods in the North Bay are confined a few areas, most notably Muir Woods National Monument and Armstrong Redwoods State Reserve. Associated with redwoods are a number of plant species, including tanbark oak, California bay, hazelnut, evergreen huckleberry, wood rose, redwood sorrel, western sword fern, and evergreen violet.

Closed-cone Pine Forest

Unlike other pines, whose cones open when their seeds are mature, closed-cone pines retain their seeds until heat, usually from fire, opens the pitch-glued cones and releases the seeds. There are three closed-cone species in the North Bay: Monterey pine, bishop pine, and knobcone pine. Monterey pine has been planted in our area, but is native only in a few places farther south on the central California coast. Bishop pine is found along the Marin and Sonoma coasts, and can best be viewed along the Jepson Trail in Tomales Bay State Park. Stands of knobcone pine can be seen on the upper reaches of Mt. Hood and Mt. St. Helena. Growing with bishop pine may be coast live oak, manzanita, coyote brush, coffeeberry, poison oak, and evergreen huckleberry. Knobcone pine usually forms almost pure stands, but nearby may be plants of the chaparral community.

Knobcone pine is found on poor soils in hot, dry areas.

Douglas fir, with its distinctive cones, is easy to identify.

Douglas-Fir Forest

In many areas of the North Bay, Douglas fir is the "default" evergreen, easily told by its distinctive cones, which have protruding, three-pointed bracts, sometimes called rat's tails. Douglas fir and coast redwood are California's two most important commercial trees. Some of the common plants associated with Douglas fir are the same as those associated with coast redwood, namely California bay, tanbark oak, and western sword fern. Others include blue blossom, coffeeberry, and poison oak. The Mt. Wittenberg Trail in Point Reyes National Seashore climbs through a beautiful Douglas-fir forest.

Chaparral

This fascinating community is made up of plants that thrive in poor soils under hot, dry conditions. Chaparral is very susceptible to fire, and some of its members, such as various species of manzanita, survive devastating blazes by sprouting new growth from ground-level burls. Despite the harsh environment, chaparral can be beautiful year-round, with certain manzanitas blooming as early as December, and other plants continuing into spring and summer. The upper slopes of Mt. Tamalpais are cloaked in chaparral. The word itself comes from a Spanish term for dwarf or scrub oak, but in the North Bay it is chamise, various manzanitas, and various species of ceanothus that dominate the community. Other chaparral plants include mountain mahogany, yerba santa, toyon, chaparral pea, and poison oak.

Blue-eyed grass is one of the North Bay's most common spring wildflowers.

Hill and Valley Grassland

Few if any grasslands in the North Bay retain their native character. Human intervention, in the form of farming and livestock grazing, along with the importation, mostly inadvertent, of non-native grasses like wild oat, have significantly altered the landscape. Gone from most areas are the native bunchgrasses, perennial species that once dominated our area. Remaining, thankfully, are native wildflowers, which decorate the grasslands in spring and summer. Among the most common are bluedicks, California poppy, owl's-clover, checkerbloom, lupine, and blue-eyed grass.

Coastal Prairie

Lacking protection from trees and shrubs, these windswept grasslands extend inland from coastal cliffs, offering a toe-hold for hearty perennial grasses and wildflowers. Generally flat and smooth, coastal prairies are marine terraces that have been lifted above sea level by geological forces. Perfect for farming and grazing livestock, many of these terraces were cleared of trees and shrubs, creating man-made prairies. Fine examples of this community can be found at Point Reyes and along the Sonoma coast.

Coastal Scrub

Often called soft chaparral, this community consists mostly of shrubs and grasses growing near the coast. Among the most common members are California sagebrush, coyote brush, toyon, bush monkeyflower, and various brooms. The Point Reyes area is an excellent place to find coastal scrub.

Coastal Forest

Near San Francisco Bay, woodlands dominated by coast live oak often alternate with areas of coastal

Coffeeberry is a shrub found throughout the North Bay.

scrub to form a coastal forest, some of whose other members include California bay, hazelnut, blue elderberry, coffeeberry, blackberry, and poison oak. Angel Island State Park is a good place to enjoy a coastal forest.

Vernal Pools

Filling with rainwater during the winter and soon drying after the rains cease, these depressions in the landscape are home to unusual plants, some found nowhere else. Hidden Lake, a large vernal pool on Burdell Mountain, is home to at least 10 species of rare plants, including white water-buttercup, pale navarretia, and yellow linanthus. Other plants associated with vernal pools including maroonspot downingia, yellowray goldfields, and Douglas meadowfoam.

Freshwater Marsh

Edging many lakes, ponds, and shallow creeks are cattails, bulrushes, and sedges, the main components of a freshwater marsh. Joining them in this slow-growing community are other marsh plants such as rushes, and wildflowers such as common monkeyflower and Pacific cinquefoil. Marshes are usually rich in bird life, providing food, nesting areas, and protective cover. To make way for development, many marshes have been drained and filled, or have had their water diverted elsewhere, causing a decline in this community. Lake Ilsanjo at Annadel State Park has examples of freshwater-marsh plants.

Labrador tea, a member of the heath family, grows 2 to 7 feet tall in wet, boggy areas.

Backshores of Sandy Beaches

Just back from the high-tide line begins this shoreline community, consisting mostly of wind-resistant and salt-tolerant plants. Among these are various beach grasses, including European beach grass, which was introduced to stabilize dunes, and low-growing succulents such as sand verbena, searocket, and iceplant, another dune stabilizer. The most common shrubs here are yellow bush lupine and coyote brush. You can find some of the above plants at Rodeo Lagoon in the Marin Headlands.

Coastal Salt Marsh

Found at the edges of bays and estuaries, this community is made up of plants that can tolerate salt in varying degrees. At the lowest level of the marsh, which is flooded twice daily by the tide, are various cord grasses (*Spartina*), some of which have come to our area from Humboldt Bay and the East Coast. Higher in the marsh are pickleweed and salt-marsh dodder, a parasitic plant that sends out orange threads to encircle its host. At a level reached only by the highest tides grow salt grass, alkali heath, and sea lavender, also called marsh rosemary. Decorating the marsh nearly year-round may be the yellow flowers of brass buttons and Pacific gumplant. Coastal salt marshes, like their freshwater cousins, are in decline, and each one lost deprives us of a highly productive ecosystem. San Francisco and San Pablo bays contain 90 per cent of California's salt-marsh acreage. Other bays and estuaries along the coast contain the rest. A fine salt marsh makes up part of the Rush Creek Open Space Preserve.

Plant Names

Because this is not a botanical text, I have used common names for plants rather than their scientific names. This creates a dilemma. Unlike birds (see below), plants have no "official" common names. The same plant may have two or more names, and the same name may apply to different plants. For example, a violet of the coast-redwood forest, *Viola ocellata*, appears in one plant guide as "two-eyed violet" and in another as "western heart's-ease." My solution was to pick a plant guide for the region I am writing about, and follow its choice of names. For the North Bay, I have settled on *Plants of the San Francisco Bay Region*, (see above) with a few modifications. Where it would not cause confusion to do so, I removed some hyphens, dropped some modifiers, such as "California" and "western," and renamed a few plants. Thus mule-ears becomes mule ears, western poison-oak becomes poison oak, and common Indian-paintbrush becomes paintbrush. Indian warrior, a parasitic plant found in association with members of the heath family such as madrone and manzanita, I renamed heath warrior. Hottentot fig, a common coastal ground cover, I call iceplant.

Animals

Mammals

Besides deer, rabbits, and squirrels, you probably won't see many other land mammals on your hikes in the North Bay, unless you time your visits near dawn or dusk. These are times when most mammals are active, and you may be rewarded with a fleeting glimpse of a coyote or a bobcat. Large mammals, such as black bear and mountain lion, are seldom seen. Other more common mammals in our area include gray fox, raccoon, skunk, opossum, and Sonoma chipmunk. A few mammals are of special concern. The endangered salt marsh harvest mouse is found only in salt marshes around San Francisco Bay. Tule elk, once nearly extinct, can be seen in Point Reyes National Seashore. Wild pigs are sometimes seen in North Bay parks, but should never be approached.

Marine mammals—whales, sea lions, and seals—can be seen from vantage points on the Marin and Sonoma coasts, especially Point Reyes. The best time of year to view migrating gray whales, which often travel close to shore, is from January to April. Sea lions, distinguished from true seals by the presence of external ears, are often seen hauled out on beaches or on offshore rocks. Harbor seals are commonly glimpsed as they float in quiet bays and harbors, their heads just poking up out of the water.

Birds

It is not hyperbole to call the North Bay one of the world's great birding areas. Its location on the western edge of the Pacific Flyway, combined with the presence of so many different habitats, from offshore islands to inland mountains, guarantees both a high species count and an enormous number—in the millions—of individual birds either resident, wintering, or passing through on migration. Point Reyes National Seashore, perhaps the area with the most variety of birds, has logged an impressive 440 different species, or just under half of all bird species found in North America north of Mexico. For the common names of birds, I rely on the American Ornithologists' Union's (AOU) checklist for birds of the continental US and Canada, 7th edition (1998). In this checklist, old friends such as our rufous-sided towhee and our scrub jay have new names—spotted towhee and western scrub-jay.

Season, location, weather, and even time of day—these together help determine which birds you are likely to see. In late summer, huge flocks of sooty shearwaters skim over the nearshore waters of the Pacific. Gulls, terns, cormorants, and brown pelicans enliven the coast as they soar and dive. Just inland from the coast, San Francisco and San Pablo bays together constitute the largest wetland complex in California and perhaps the largest wintering area in the US for shorebirds, a tribe that includes oystercatchers, avocets, stilts, plovers, willets, curlews, godwits, small sandpipers, dowitchers, and phalaropes. Also found in wetlands are wading birds such as herons and egrets.

You may spy loons, grebes, coots, ducks, geese, and swans floating on protected bays, harbors, lakes, and ponds. Raptors such as ospreys, red-tailed hawks, red-shouldered hawks, and American kestrels are found patrolling the skies above many North Bay parks. During fall migration,

Borders between woodlands and open fields are often good spots for birding.

many species of hawks and falcons soar over the Marin Headlands in order to gain altitude before crossing the Golden Gate. Among the most commonly seen land birds in the North Bay are acorn woodpeckers, western scrub-jays, spotted towhees, California quail, and turkey vultures. If you learn to "bird by ear," identifying species by their distinctive notes, calls, and songs, you will quickly expand your list, because many birds are frustratingly hard to spot, especially in dense foliage. Birding with a group also improves your odds of seeing and identifying a large number of species, including rarities.

Reptiles

A sudden scurrying in the leaves, which may take you by surprise, is probably nothing more than a western fence lizard, the North Bay's most commonly seen reptile. When threatened, these lizards may stand their ground and begin to do "push-ups," which perhaps strike terror in their foes. Also in our area is the California whiptail, a lizard with a tail as long as its body. Among the snakes in our area, only the gopher snake is common. Often mistaken for the present but seldom-seen western rattlesnake because of its appearance and behavior, a gopher snake has a slim head and a fat body, and kills its prey by constriction. Other snakes here include the rubber boa and the California whipsnake.

Human History

Players on the North Bay stage came from all over the globe. First on the scene were descendents of Stone Age people who crossed the Bering land bridge from what is now Siberia. In the area that was to become California, these native peoples divided themselves into tribes and tribelets based on geographic region, language, dialect, and cultural traditions. Living a relatively peaceful existence, the people subsisted by hunting animals and birds, fishing, and gathering shellfish, acorns, bulbs, and seeds. Before European colonization in the 18th century, it is estimated that 300,000 Indians lived in California.

There were three major tribes in the North Bay: Coast Miwok, Pomo, and Wappo. The Coast Miwok inhabited an area south of the Russian River from the coast to San Francisco Bay. The Pomo, whose baskets are considered among the finest ever woven, lived along the Russian River and northward. They were the southernmost tribe not brought into the Spanish missions. The Wappo were inland people living in what became Sonoma and Napa counties. It was Coast Miwok people who greeted Francis Drake when he landed somewhere on the Marin coast in 1579, 41 years before the Pilgrims landed at Provincetown, Massachusetts.

For almost the next 200 years, the world's greatest mariners missed the often fog-shrouded entrance to San Francisco Bay, leaving the native people here undisturbed. It was a Spanish overland expedition from Baja California, led by Gaspar de Portola, that in 1769 finally sighted San

Francisco Bay. Six years later, Juan Manuel de Ayala, in the ship *San Carlos*, became the first European to sail into the bay. In 1776, the Presidio of San Francisco was established at the entrance to the bay, and Mission San Francisco de Asis, today known as Mission Dolores, was located a few miles inland. To distinguish it from Baja California, the Spanish called the land from San Diego north Alta California.

The mission era in Alta California lasted from 1769 to 1834, when the Mexican government, freed from Spanish rule in 1821, began secularizing the missions. At their peak, around 1810, the missions controlled approximately 20,000 Indians, thousands of head of livestock, and millions of acres of land. Contact with Europeans forever altered the way native people lived. Many Indians resisted missionization, and tens of thousands died from diseases to which they had no resistance. Others accommodated themselves to the new ways. Once the missions were secularized, mission lands were converted to large ranchos and transferred to Mexican citizens living in the new province, who called themselves Californios. Cattle ranching and trading in hide and tallow were the main pursuits on the ranchos, whose owners in general enjoyed a prosperous and some say idyllic lifestyle. Those who labored on the ranchos were less fortunate. These included Indians released from the missions—some of them became vaqueros, or cowboys, but others lived in servitude.

During the 1840s, friction between Mexico and America, with its sights set westward, developed. Conflicts arose between the land-owning Californios and the new immigrants from America, many of whom occupied land illegally as squatters, found work as ranch hands, or hunted and trapped game. A debate ensued: would California remain a province of Mexico, or should it be annexed to the United States? On May 13, 1846, the war between US and Mexico began, and it would reshape the West. A little more than a month later, with the fighting many hundreds of miles away and not yet known about in northern California, the Bear Flag uprising in Sonoma created a bizarre North Bay drama whose motives are still argued about today.

Before dawn on June 14, a band of 30 or so armed settlers rode into Sonoma, site of an old mission and a small military post, seized the town, and arrested its most prominent citizen, General Mariano G. Vallejo, who had served as commandant general of Alta California but was now retired. Vallejo was a friend of the Americans and supported annexation, so he was understandably surprised and shocked by his arrest, but he nevertheless offered his captors a drink before they marched him off. The rebels proclaimed the Republic of California, created a flag showing a grizzly bear and a star, and raised it on the town's flag pole. Less than a month later, Commodore John Sloat, in response to the Bear Flag uprising, raised the US flag over Monterey, the capital of Alta California. Although skirmishes continued in southern California for some time, northern California had been seized with only a handful of casualties.

The Mexican War continued until 1848, when the Treaty of Guadalupe Hildago ended hostilities. After California became a state in 1850, Vallejo, despite his treatment during the uprising, donated land for a new capital, was a member of the state constitutional convention, served as a state senator, and was elected mayor of Sonoma.

The not-so-hidden hand behind the Bear Flag uprising belonged to John C. Frémont, an explorer, soldier, and political leader viewed by some as a hero but by many as an agitator and an ambitious opportunist. After the Bear Flag uprising, Frémont was made civil governor of California by Commodore Robert F. Stockton, commander of the Pacific squadron, who had relieved Sloat. Following a dispute between Stockton and General Stephen W. Kearny, leader of the Army of the West, Frémont was arrested, court-martialed, and convicted. His penalty remitted by President Polk, Frémont went on to become a US senator from California, the Republican presidential candidate in 1856, a Civil War commander with a troubled record, and governor of the Arizona Territory from 1878 to 1883. After the Mexican War, many California places, including a county, a canyon, and a pass, were named for Frémont, but as his reputation declined the names were changed. However, one of the names Frémont himself bestowed, the Golden Gate, endured.

Another development that shaped North Bay history was the arrival in April 1806 of the Russian ship *Juno*, commanded by Nikolai Resanov, in San Francisco Bay. Resanov had sailed south from Sitka, hoping to obtain relief supplies for the Alaskan colony there, which was facing starvation. Over the next few years, more Russian ships came south, hunting sea otters and fur seals, and searching for places to establish permanent settlements. Russian expansionism in the North Pacific was one of the factors that led Spain to seek control of Alta California. But with their forces stretched thin, there was little the Spanish could do to block the Russians. In March 1812, a handful of Russian settlers and about 80 native Alaskan hunters they had brought with them established a well armed and well guarded settlement, called Fort Ross, on the Sonoma coast north of the Russian River. Above the stockade flew the flag of the Russian-American Fur Company.

Capturing sea otters and fur seals for their valuable pelts was one of the Company's goals. For this they used native Alaskans paddling traditional bidarkas, or hunting kayaks. Depletion of the otters by 1820 forced the Russians to concentrate on agriculture and livestock, but their efforts produced little in the way of surplus for their comrades in Sitka. In 1839, an agreement with the Hudson Bay Company secured supplies from Oregon and Washington for the colony, and in 1841, the Russian-American Fur Company folded its settlement at Fort Ross, selling the livestock, arms, ammunition, and hardware to John Sutter, of Sutter's Fort in the Sacramento Valley. Many of the buildings were dismantled, and in 1873 the property was acquired by George W. Call, who established a 15,000-acre ranch. In 1903 the California Historical Landmarks Committee purchased the fort and a few acres of land, which were later turned over to the state. With more land added and buildings reconstructed or restored to their original condition, the area is now a 3,000-acre state historic park.

During the period of Mexican rule, land grants established large ranchos in the North Bay. General Vallejo himself wound up acquiring about 170,000 acres in the Sonoma District, which, after statehood, became Marin, Napa, Sonoma, and Solano counties. The combined effects of the Mexican War, the Gold Rush, and statehood shifted the balance of power in California. Many of the land grants were challenged, and many of the ranchos fell into American hands. A good example of this can be found in the Point Reyes area. As Dorothy L. Whitnah writes in *Point Reyes*, large land grants in the Olema Valley and elsewhere on the peninsula were issued in the 1830s, but by the time the dust had settled several decades later, three lawyers from Vermont ended up owning most of Point Reyes. They in turn began leasing the land for dairy farms that produced milk and butter prized for their quality.

Another agricultural product, wine, has brought great renown to the region. The Spanish missionaries grew their own grapes, the coarse Mission variety, and made wine for sacramental use, and the Russians at Fort Ross also planted grapes and made wine. The first commercial vine plantings in the North Bay took place in the 1860s, and wine making soon became an important business. The California wine industry actually began in southern California around Los Angeles, but soon shifted north and settled in Napa and Sonoma counties. The founder of Sonoma's Buena Vista Winery, Agoston Haraszthy, a colorful Hungarian, imported many varieties of grapes from Europe, prepared a report for the California legislature on wine making, and acted as a spokesman for the region's wine. General Vallejo too made wine in Sonoma, in friendly competition with his neighbor Haraszthy, and two of his daughters married two of Haraszthy's sons.

Wine in the Napa Valley got its start when George C. Yount planted Mission grapes on land granted to him by General Vallejo in 1836. The Gold Rush brought failed miners and other adventurers into the fertile valley during the 1850s. In 1858, Charles Krug, a German, apprenticed with Haraszthy and then opened his own Napa Valley winery. The 1880s and 1890s were boom years for the wine industry in Napa, and some of valley's remarkable buildings date from that era. Prohibition and the Depression took their toll on California's wine industry, but some names—Beringer, Beaulieu, Inglenook, Christian Brothers, Louis Martini, Mondavi—survived. In the years following World War II, growing prosperity and changing tastes led to a rebirth of the wine industry, with an emphasis on small, high-quality wineries. Today, Napa and Sonoma produce some of California's, and the world's, best wines.

Many of the North Bay parks and towns contain historic sites worth visiting. Olompali State Historic Park, north of Novato, and Point Reyes National Seashore are fine places to learn about the area's Native American history and its more recent ranching past. You can learn more about General Vallejo, one of early California's most interesting characters, by visiting his restored ranch at Petaluma Adobe State Historic Park and his Sonoma home, Lachryma Montis, "tear of the mountain." Sonoma State Historic Park, the Sonoma Mission, and the town's Plaza, with its Bear Flag monument, all help portray life during Mexican rule. Fort Ross, north of Jenner on the Sonoma coast, offers a fascinating look at the Russians who settled a forbidding outpost so far from home. The Marin Headlands and Angel Island State Park give you a chance to learn about the North Bay's military history. China Camp State Park and the Immigration Station on Angel Island detail the courage and resourcefulness of Chinese immigrants in the face of prejudice and outright violence. You can learn about the life of the North Bay's most famous author at Jack London State Historic Park. Many Napa and Sonoma wineries are open to the public.

USING THIS GUIDEBOOK

To earn its cover price, a hiking guidebook must do more than get you from Point A to Point B and back—a decent map can do that. Without being too cumbersome to carry, a good guidebook should help you select a route, find the trailhead, follow the trail, and learn something about the natural world you are passing through. Reading about a trail in advance should make you eager to hike it. And during your hike, the route description should provide helpful insights to make the trip more enjoyable. Taken as a whole, the book should convey the enthusiasm and spirit of adventure that went into its making. That is what I have set out to do.

In addition to describing routes and features of the terrain—bear left at the fork, enjoy the waterfall on your right—a guidebook is a reflection of its author. I have chosen which hikes in the North Bay to include and which to leave out. And within the route descriptions—besides vital information to keep you from getting lost—I have emphasized certain features and ignored others. When selecting a guidebook, know the author. In the interest of full disclosure, here are some of my preferences. I prefer loops to out-and-back routes. As a photographer, I enjoy finding vantage points with great views. I don't mind climbing a steep trail, but I am cautious coming down one. I'm crazy about variety and transitions. Water—the ocean, lakes, rivers, creeks, marshes—delights me. I love birds and wildflowers.

During the course of a year, I hiked every trail included in this book, and many more than once. My goal was to be accurate and thorough—

but in reality only a static world permits such certainty. The natural world, as we know, is ever-changing, so your experience on the trail will probably be different from mine. Many variables influence this, including season, weather, time of day, and acts of God and various federal, state, and local governments. I have tried to indicate this variability by the use of the word *may* in the text, as in "you may be accompanied by hummingbirds doing aerial displays." I certainly hope you are, but keep in mind that you may not be. For things that vary by season, such as blooming wildflowers, I have tried to be a specific as possible about when they occur, but this too, alas, is beyond my control.

Comments, corrections, and suggestions are certainly appreciated. Please send them to: Wilderness Press, 1200 Fifth Street, Berkeley, CA 94710. If your comments concern trail conditions, signage, or other park-related issues, please also send a copy of your letter to the appropriate government agency. A list of these is in Appendix C.

Favorite Hikes

Here are some of my favorite areas in the North Bay, places I'd return to and share with my friends. A few parks—Mt. Tamalpais, Point Reyes, the Sonoma Coast, Sugarloaf Ridge State Park—are so wonderful that I could not limit my choices, so I simply picked "All."

Park	Route	Highlights
China Camp State Park	Shoreline Trail	History
Marin County Open Space District	Burdell Mountain	Exercise, Flowers, Views
Marin County Open Space District	Ring Mountain	Exercise, Flowers, Views
Marin Municipal Water District	Pine Mountain	Exercise, Plants, Views
Mt. Tamalpais	All	Exercise, Plants, Views
Point Reyes National Seashore	All	Exercise, Plants, Views
Tomales Bay State Park	Pebble Beach	Beach, Plants
Bothe-Napa Valley State Park	Coyote Peak	Exercise, Plants
Robert Louis Stevenson State Park	Mt. St. Helena	Exercise, Plants, Views
Skyline Wilderness Park	Sugarloaf Mountain	Exercise, Flowers, Views
Armstrong Redwoods State Reserve	Nature Trail	Flowers, Plants, Redwoods
Sonoma Coast	All	Beach, Plants, Views
Sonoma County Regional Parks	Shiloh Ranch	Exercise, Plants
Sugarloaf Ridge State Park	All	Exercise, Flowers, Views

Selecting a Route

One of the great joys of hiking in the North Bay is that there are so many choices. Want to climb a mountain? No problem! Want to visit the coast? Sure! See towering redwoods? OK! Look at wildflowers? You bet! In fact, it's hard to go wrong. Whatever you want—exercise, scenery, nature study, or just a walk in the woods—you can probably find it in the pages of this book. Here are some things to consider when selecting a route. First, what time of year is it? Spring and fall are the best times to hike many of the trails described here, but there are year-round hikes too. In spring and summer, fog often shrouds the coast and areas near San Francisco and San Pablo bays, but certain places, like China Camp State Park and Mt. Tamalpais, may be fog-free. Away from the coast, summer temperatures may soar, so plan accordingly. Second, how far do you want to go? This depends on how fast you hike, how fit you are, and how rugged the terrain is. Third, what do you want to see along the way?

Each route description is preceded by a snapshot of what the hike entails. **Length** measures round-trip distance from what I designate as the trailhead, which is almost always adjacent to the parking area. **Time** is the estimated duration of the hike, including a few stops, based on an average hiking pace of 1.5 to 2 miles per hour. Bicyclists, equestrians, joggers, and hikers with a different pace will need to figure their own times. **Rating** indicates whether the route is Easy, Moderate, or Difficult. For this book, Easy means the route is mostly flat and can usually be completed in one hour or less. Moderate indicates a more challenging, hilly hike that will probably take two to four hours. I gave a Difficult rating to hikes more than 6 miles in length, and to those that involve an elevation gain of more than 1,000 feet.

Regulations tells you which agency or agencies have jurisdiction over the trails described (see the beginning of this Introduction for abbreviations used). I also indicate if a fee is required; whether or not dogs, bikes, and horses are allowed on the route as described; and if there are other special regulations of which you need to be aware. In **Highlights**, you can find out the type of route—loop, semi-loop, out-and-back, car shuttle—along with the names of the trails you'll use. You can also see at a glance the main attractions of the route, such as wildflowers or great views. **Directions** gets you to the parking area from the nearest major roadway. **Facilities** lists things like water, toilets, or a phone that may be near the trailhead. Finally, **Trailhead** tells you where to start your hike. In some parks you must walk from the parking area through a campground or other facility to find the trail. Nevertheless, for almost all the routes in this book, I designate the point at which you leave the parking area as the trailhead, and I measure round-trip mileage from that point.

Most of the hiking routes in the North Bay follow dirt roads and single-track trails. Within the route descriptions themselves, the subjective terms Gentle, Moderate, and Steep are used to indicate grade of ascent and descent. A gentle grade, if you are reasonably fit, is one that is almost imperceptible and requires no change of pace. A moderate uphill grade requires you to "shift down" a bit but should not interfere with regular breathing or conversation. Climbing steeply uphill forces you to concentrate your efforts, and is best done by maintaining a slow but measured pace coordinated with deep breathing. Moderate and steep downhill grades, especially over loose, rocky ground, require caution—a walking stick or trekking pole is invaluable here. Distances given in the route description are approximations, and always refer to the start of the hike. Thus "At about the 2-mile point, you step across Spike Buck Creek" means the creek is about 2 miles from the trailhead.

What to Wear
Boots

Lightweight, flexible, supportive, comfortable, durable—in the past you had to settle for only a few of these qualities when buying boots. Not any longer. Today's light hiking boots combine the weight, flexibility, and comfort of running shoes with the support and durability of heavier backpacking boots. A good pair of hiking boots will protect your feet and ankles, and provide essential traction on steep slopes. They will also help keep your feet dry in the event of a rain shower or a misstep while crossing a creek.

When buying boots, go to a reputable outdoor store with a variety of styles and sizes in stock. Wear the socks you are planning to wear hiking to try on boots (see below). A boot that fits properly will have plenty of toe room but will hold your foot snugly in place. Boots that are uncomfortable in the store, even slightly, will only get worse after hours on the trail. Above all, make sure the store will allow you to return the boots provided you do not wear them outdoors. That way, you can wear them around the house for several hours to make sure they fit.

Socks

Good socks can make the difference between happy feet and unhappy, blistered feet. Socks help cushion your feet and keep them dry by wicking moisture away from your skin. Most hikers wear two pairs of socks—a thin liner sock and a thicker outer sock. Wool and synthetics, often used in combination, are the best materials for socks. Cotton retains moisture and should not be an ingredient in hiking socks.

Other clothing

Unless you are trying to make a fashion statement—this is California, after all—clothing requirements for hiking in the North Bay are few. Comfort, and protection from sun, wind, poison oak, and ticks are the main requirements. Adjusting to changing conditions is the biggest challenge, and most people find the layer system works best, allowing you to doff and don as needed. For warm weather, I prefer thin pants and a long-sleeved sun-proof shirt. Light colors make it easier to see ticks on your clothing. If it is cool, I use heavier-weight pants and add a light-weight synthetic vest and a nylon windbreaker. A hat is an essential part of my wardrobe. I also carry a light pair of gloves and an insulating headband, and find these very effective if it gets cold. If you are hiking during the rainy season, avoid cotton clothing. Instead, rely on synthetics like Gore-Tex and Polartec to keep you warm and dry.

What to Take Along

Many of the trails in this book can be enjoyed almost empty-handed—the only required item being water. Dehydration is at best uncomfortable and debilitating, and at worst dangerous. Besides plenty of water, what else should you take? Certainly something to snack on, from an energy bar to a four-course picnic. Extra clothes, as mentioned above. Other items might be sunglasses, sunscreen, insect repellent, flashlight, knife, and basic first-aid supplies. Map and compass come in handy. I always use a trekking pole (and two when I'm backpacking.) Depending on your interests, you may want binoculars for birding, a hand lens for plant study, a camera for Kodak moments, and a pad for notes and sketches. Field guides are helpful but heavy—try leaving them in the car and perhaps making a sketch or taking a photograph instead. Please do not collect plant or flower specimens.

Trail Etiquette

Sharing the trail

Many of the trails in the North Bay are multi-use paths shared by hikers, equestrians, bicyclists, joggers, and dog-walkers. Each park has its own regulations, and it is your responsibility to know, understand, and obey them. Before selecting a particular route in this guidebook, check the **Regulations** section just above the route description. There you will

Equestrians on the San Andreas Fire Road.

find the agency having jurisdiction over the trails, along with specific restrictions concerning dogs, bikes, and horses on the route as described. If you see or hear horseback riders approaching, step off the trail to give them the right of way and remain motionless until they pass. Bicyclists should slow down and call out when approaching hikers, and dismount when near horses.

Protecting the environment

One of the tenets of environmentalism is that everything in nature is connected. Unfortunately, this interwoven web of life is sometimes hard to see and harder to understand. Hikers who stray from marked trails and cut switchbacks probably aren't thinking about threatened fish runs. But their actions cause erosion, which in turn allows fine silt to wash into our creeks during the rainy season. Excessive silt in these creeks spoils the spawning beds for threatened species such as coho salmon and steelhead trout. This is just one way in which thoughtless acts can have unintended consequences. In similar, if less dramatic ways, collecting plants and wildflowers, or leaving trash beside the trail, degrades the environment and spoils everyone's enjoyment of our parklands. Walking lightly on the land has its own rewards.

Preventing fires

Although lightning-caused wildfires play an important role in maintaining the health of certain ecosystems, fires caused by human carelessness often result in damage to parklands and property, and even loss of life. Illegal camp fires have caused major blazes at North Bay parks, including a 1993 fire at Salt Point State Park and the 1995 Vision Fire at Point Reyes. Each jurisdiction has its own regulations about camp fires, barbecues, and smoking: please obey them.

Controlling dogs

This is one of the most complex issues in the North Bay parks. Each jurisdiction has its own regulations. Dog lovers want to take their pets everywhere, but at the same time resist keeping them leashed and cleaning up their mess. Unleashed dogs chase and harass wildlife. They also frighten adults and children who don't enjoy being approached by an unfamiliar animal. Even those of us who love animals wonder why a dog owner would let his large, shaggy, wet pooch jump up and plant its muddy forepaws on our chest, all the while exclaiming from many yards away, "It's OK, he won't bite." And this on a state-park trail, where dogs are prohibited! If dog owners want their pets to be welcome in areas now closed to them, they need to control their animals.

The following is a summary of the various regulations governing dogs and other pets. In **state parks**, dogs are not permitted on hiking trails, but they are allowed in developed areas such as campgrounds and picnic areas on a 6-foot or shorter leash. In campgrounds at night, dogs must be in a vehicle or a tent. In the **Marin County Open Space District**, in the Deer Island, Ring Mountain, Rush Creek, and Santa Margarita Island preserves, and in all Wildlife Protection Areas, dogs must be on a 6-foot or shorter leash at all times. In all other preserves, on fire roads dogs may be unleashed but must be under voice control; on single-track trails they must be leashed. On **Marin Municipal Water District** trails, dogs must be on a 6-foot or shorter leash at all times. In the **Marin Headlands**, dogs are allowed on certain trails and prohibited on others. The visitor center has a free dog-trail map. Dogs are not allowed in **Muir Woods National Monument**.

In **Point Reyes National Seashore**, dogs are prohibited on trails and in campgrounds. They are permitted only on beaches that are not seal habitats or bird nesting areas—and then only on leash. In City of Napa parks, dogs are allowed in **Alston Park** but prohibited in **Westwood Hills Park**. In the **Napa River Ecological Reserve**, dogs are permitted on leash. In **Napa Valley Skyline Wilderness Park**, dogs are prohibited. In **Sonoma County Regional Parks**, dogs are allowed on the trails except in Shiloh Ranch Regional Park, where they are not allowed beyond the parking and picnic area.

In all areas where dogs and other pets are permitted, they must always be under the control of a responsible person. They should never be allowed to chase, harass, or attack people or wildlife. Owners should always clean up after their pets.

Safety on the Trail
Injury, illness

The North Bay parklands are generally benign places, but accidents do happen, and even a simple mishap like a twisted knee or a sprained ankle can render you immobile and in pain. Common-sense precautions can help prevent most accidents. First, pick a route that suits your ability, and don't let yourself become excessively fatigued, hungry, thirsty, cold, or hot. Second, use sturdy boots with traction soles, appropriate clothing, and perhaps a walking stick or trekking pole for added stability. Third, watch the trail while you are walking, and stop walking when you want to admire the scenery or take pictures.

Knowing CPR and first aid may help you feel more secure in the outdoors, and may also enable you to help someone in distress. One illness you may encounter on the trail is heat exhaustion, also called heat prostration. Its causes are physical exertion under hot, humid conditions, and dehydration. The victim may feel weak, have a rapid pulse, and experience headache, dizziness, and brief loss of consciousness. Get the victim out of the heat and give fluids, especially those with salt. Untreated, heat exhaustion can turn into heat stroke, a severe medical emergency.

Hikers check their position using a GPS device.

Getting lost

Seven different government agencies and one volunteer organization have jurisdiction over the trails described in this book. It is not surprising, then, that trail conditions and signage vary widely. And even on well-signed trails, you can still miss a junction, bear the wrong way at a fork, or wander off the main track to find a scenic vantage point or explore a field of flowers. If you become lost, don't panic. Try to return to your last known point: blundering ahead only gets you more lost. If you have a map and compass, use them to orient yourself with respect to known landmarks. An altimeter is extremely useful if you have a map with elevation contours. A Global Positioning System (GPS) receiver may help, but only if you have entered waypoints during your hike, and only if the receiver has a clear view of the GPS satellites overhead.

Poison oak

This common shrub, a member of the sumac family, produces an itchy rash in people allergic to its oil. Learn to identify poison oak's shiny green foliage—"leaves of three, let it be"—and avoid it. In fall the shrub's leaves turn yellow and red, adding a wonderful touch of color to the woods. In winter, you can identify the plant by its upward-reaching clusters of bare branches. Staying on the trail is the best way to avoid contact with poison oak, and wearing long pants and a long-sleeved shirt helps too. Anything that touches poison oak—clothing, pets—should be washed in soap and water.

Ticks

A tiny, almost invisible insect has been the cause of much woe among hikers and others who spend time outdoors. Western black-legged ticks carry a bacterium that causes Lyme disease, which can produce serious symptoms in people who have been bitten. These include flu-like aches and pains which, if left untreated, may progress to severe cardiac and neurological disorders. Often the tick bite produces a rash that over time clears from the center, producing a bull's-eye pattern. But in many cases there is no evidence of a bite at all. If caught in time, the disease can be treated with antibiotics. A recently approved preventive vaccine holds promise: talk to your doctor. Also encouraging, at least for West Coast hikers, are published reports saying that ticks which have fed on western fence lizards, their common hosts, do not transmit Lyme disease.

You can take several steps to protect against Lyme disease. Wear light-colored clothing, so ticks are easier to spot. Use long-sleeved pants with the legs tucked into your socks, and a long-sleeved shirt tucked into your pants. Spray your clothing with an insect repellent containing DEET before hiking. When you return home, shake out and brush all clothing, boots, and packs outdoors. Shower immediately after hiking, and check for ticks on your skin—there is evidence that ticks do not inject the bacterium until they have been attached for 24 hours. If you find one attached, use a tweezers to remove it by grasping the tick as close to your skin as possible and gently pulling straight out. Do not squeeze the tick while it is attached, as this may inject the bacterium. Wash the area and apply antiseptic, then call your doctor.

Rattlesnakes

Although present in the North Bay, western rattlesnakes are shy and seldom seen. Most snake bites are the result of a defensive reaction: a foot or hand has suddenly landed in the snake's territory. A rattlesnake often, but not always, gives a warning when it feels threatened. The sound, even if you have never before heard it, is instantly recognizable. Stand still until you have located the snake, and then back slowly away. Even if the snake strikes, it may fail to bite and inject venom. Clothing and boot material may absorb venom if the snake succeeds in biting—another reason to wear long pants and high-topped boots. Staying on the trail and not putting your hands or feet beyond your range of vision are other preventive measures. If you are bitten, seek medical attention as quickly and effortlessly as possible, to avoid spreading the venom.

Coyotes, Mountain Lions

Coyotes are common residents of the North Bay, feeding on small mammals, birds, and occasionally deer. They generally avoid contact with humans and are not often seen. Mountain lions, also called cougars or pumas, are rarely seen in our area. They hunt at night and feed mostly on deer. If you do encounter a mountain lion, experts advise standing your ground, making loud noises, waving your arms to appear larger, and fighting back if attacked. Above all, never run. Report all mountain lion sightings to park personnel.

Maps

Computers have revolutionized mapping. Anyone with a PC can obtain maps on CD-ROM or download them from the Internet. National Geographic Maps is producing computerized maps especially geared to hikers and other outdoor enthusiasts. The company's interactive mapping program, called TOPO!, allows you to view USGS maps, draw your own routes, measure distance traveled, plot elevation gain and loss, find features, and print your own customized maps. Another National Geographic product, TOPO! GPS USA, lets you transfer data between a TOPO! map and a GPS receiver. This allows you to load waypoints from a map into your GPS, so you can find them in the field, and also take waypoints stored in your GPS during a hike and plot them on a map. The maps for this book were created using a TOPO! CD that includes the San Francisco Bay Area, Wine Country, and Big Sur.

The quality and availability of printed maps for North Bay parks vary wildly. Some parks have maps available at visitor centers that are open every day. Others have visitor centers or entrance kiosks staffed only on weekends. Some maps are available in park vending machines, others only by mail. If you want to obtain a map for your hike, and are unable to print your own using TOPO!, your best bet is to call the appropriate agency and order one in advance. Appendix C has the addresses and phone numbers of the agencies responsible for all the North Bay parks covered in this book. When I refer to a map in a route description, it almost always means the map produced by the agency having jurisdiction over the trail being described.

Marin County hikers can choose from a variety of maps. The National Park Service (NPS) publishes a map for the Golden Gate National Recreation Area, which shows the Marin Headlands, Mt. Tamalpais, and Muir Woods. There are also NPS maps for Muir Woods and Point Reyes. NPS maps show trails and limited terrain details. The visitor centers at the Marin Headlands and Point Reyes have free trail maps, but these show little detail except for the trails. The Golden Gate National Parks Association publishes a somewhat more detailed map of Muir Woods, which also contains information about the human and natural history of the area.

The state parks in Marin County—Angel Island, China Camp, Mt. Tamalpais, Samuel P. Taylor, and Tomales Bay—all have good maps available. The Marin County Open Space District (MCOSD) publishes a set of four maps, which, although beautifully designed, convey very little information. The Marin Municipal Water District has a map for its lands on the north side of Mt. Tamalpais. The best Marin hiking map, which unfortunately covers only Mt. Tamalpais, the Marin Headlands, and Muir Woods, is *A Rambler's Guide to the Trails of Mt. Tamalpais and the Marin Headlands*, published by The Olmsted & Brothers Map Company.

In Napa County, the state parks—Bothe-Napa Valley, and Robert Louis Stevenson—are covered on a single map, which also shows Bale Grist Mill State Historic Park and many of the wineries in the upper Napa Valley. Maps for Alston and Westwood Hills parks may be obtained from the City of Napa Parks and Recreation Department. Skyline Wilderness Park has a free but very sketchy trail map available at the entrance kiosk.

In Sonoma County, the state parks—Annadel, Armstrong Redwoods/Austin Creek, Jack London, Salt Point, Sonoma Coast, Sugarloaf Ridge—all have good maps available. Sonoma County Regional Parks has trail maps for the parks included in this book—Crane Creek, Foothill, Helen Putnam, Shiloh Ranch, and Sonoma Valley. These are available only by mail.

The California State Automobile Association (CSAA) gives its members free maps. Two are useful for the routes in this guidebook: *San Francisco Bay Region*, taking in an area from Santa Rosa to San Jose, and from Point Reyes to Tracy; and *Mendocino and Sonoma Coast Region*, covering the coast from Bodega Bay to Westport, and inland to Clear Lake and Lake Berryessa.

Where to Get More Information

In addition to maps, other information about the North Bay may be found in books, pamphlets, and periodicals published by agencies and organizations listed in Appendix C.

◆ Marin County ◆

1	Angel Island State Park
	MT. LIVERMORE

Length: 4.5 miles

Time: 2 to 3 hours

Rating: Moderate

Regulations: CSP; fee for ferry service and park entrance; no dogs.

Highlights: Angel Island is a sentinel, guarding the entrance to San
                 Francisco Bay. This loop takes you around the island and
                 to its highest point, Mt. Caroline Livermore. The lower
                 part of the route is through oak-and-bay forest, but as you
                 ascend you pass through areas of chaparral and wild-
                 flower-filled meadows. The summit of Mt. Livermore is a
                 superb vantage point from which all the familiar land-
                 marks in the Bay Area are revealed. There is much historic
                 interest to the island as well, and the hike described below
                 can easily be combined with a tour of the island on foot,
                 by bicycle, or by tram. For camping and group picnicking
                 reservations, call (800) 444-7275.

Directions: Ferry service to Angel Island leaves from Tiburon, (415)
                 435-2131; San Francisco, (415) 773-1188; Oakland/
                 Alameda, (510) 522-3300; and Vallejo, (415) 773-1188.

Facilities: Visitor center, café, picnic tables, rest rooms, water, phone,
                 lockers, bike rental, tour tram.

Trailhead: Northeast side of ferry landing area, left of rest rooms and
                 telephone.

Angel Island, the largest island in San Francisco Bay, has played a role in
the area's history for thousands of years. Coast Miwok Indians used the
island as a fishing and hunting site. In August 1775, the first European to
enter the bay, Juan Manuel de Ayala, anchored his ship *San Carlos* in a
cove on the island's northwest side that now bears his name. Ayala's
pilot, Don Jose de Canizares, made the first maps of San Francisco Bay.
Before statehood, the island was a rancho, used for grazing cattle, and
afterwards it became the site of a rock quarry. The US military arrived
during the Civil War and maintained a presence on the island until the
early 1960s. During both world wars, Angel Island served as an embarka-
tion/debarkation point and also as prison for enemy aliens and prisoners
of war. Following World War II, the island was declared surplus proper-

(previous page) Wild iris adds color beside the trail in spring.

ty, and a campaign was started to make it a state park. The Marin Conservation League and the Angel Island Foundation played important roles in this effort. Mt. Caroline Livermore, the island's 781-foot high point, honors a leading Marin County conservationist who led the campaign. After acquiring bits and pieces of land, the State of California in 1963 finally got the whole island, except for two Coast Guard stations which remain active.

Until recently, one of the least-known aspects of Angel Island was its use as a detention center for immigrants, 97 percent of them Chinese. In fact, during its years of operation, 1910 to 1940, the Immigration Station on Angel Island was the point of entry for 175,000 Chinese who came to

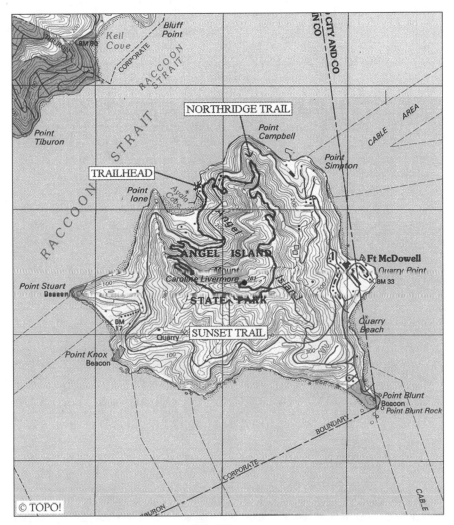

1. Mt. Livermore

the US. The detainees, who were held from two weeks to six months, faced tough questioning about their family and village background. It was not until the end of 1943, in the midst of World War II and with China as an ally of the US, that the Chinese Exclusion Act, adopted in 1882, was repealed. Thanks to the efforts of the late Paul Chow, a retired highway engineer who became head of the foundation to restore Angel Island, the Immigration Station on the island's northeast side is now a museum dedicated to educating the public about this sad episode in US history.

Leaving the trailhead, the North Ridge Trail, also signed for Perimeter Road, Immigration Station, Ft. McDowell, and Mt. Livermore, climbs steeply in the shade of coast live oak and Monterey pine. Along the sides of this hikers-only route, a dirt path, are toyon, French broom, and pride of Madeira, a large non-native shrub with spikes of purple flowers that is common in Marin County. Your ascent is aided by dozens of steps, supported by wooden slats, cut into the dirt path. Passing several picnic areas and the remains of a paved road, you soon reach Perimeter Road, the island's main paved thoroughfare. Here in a eucalyptus grove are more picnic tables and a rest bench. The state park has cleared many eucalyptuses and a lesser number of Monterey pines from the island in an effort to prevent their spread and encourage native plants. Stumps you may see beside the trail are evidence of this project.

Crossing the paved road, you turn right and in about 50 feet find the continuation of the North Ridge Trail, also signed for Mt. Livermore. A dramatic view extends west from here to Tiburon, the Marin Headlands,

Visitors enjoy picnic area on the lawn in front of the visitor center.

and Mt. Tamalpais. Now the grade eases to a gentle uphill as you alternate between forest and clearings full of wildflowers, including
California poppy, bluedicks, blue-eyed grass, morning glory, and wild
pea. As the trail curves around the north side of the island, you encounter
a densely overgrown area where California bay and hazelnut thrive amid
an understory of wild rose, blue blossom, hedgenettle, manroot, and
ferns. Carpets of forget-me-nots, abundant in the island's shady enclaves,
put on a fabulous spring and summer display of light blue flowers.

Suddenly the terrain opens, and you cross a sandy, rocky area dominated by manzanita. As the trail curves right, you walk along a ridgetop
through this manzanita barren and then re-enter dense forest, where
vines of blackberry and honeysuckle tangle with the trees and shrubs.
Just shy of the 1-mile point, you reach a dirt fire road which, like
Perimeter Road, circles the island. Here you turn left, and about 75 feet
ahead find the continuation of the North Ridge Trail on your right. Now
you pass stands of madrone and low clumps of gooseberry and snowberry growing beside the trail, still a dirt path. Weaving upward into the
trees here are huge woody vines of poison oak, reaching for sunlight.

Now circling the island's east side, the route makes a sharp switchback
right and climbs into a large grassy meadow, dotted with coyote brush
and decorated with wild iris, checkerbloom, and yarrow. The East Bay
hills are visible from here, framed by a stand of Monterey pines, many of
which are dying from the effects of the turpentine beetle, which is attack-
ing forests throughout the state. Leaving the meadow, you pass stands of
blue blossom, whose pale lavender flowers burst forth in spring. This
species of ceanothus, also called wild lilac, sometimes attains the size of
a small tree, as seen here. Now in a clearing you get your first view of Mt.
Livermore, not far away.

Downhill and left, near the shoreline at Quarry Point, is Fort
McDowell, a quarantine station dating from 1899 that was used to isolate
troops returning from the Spanish-American War and the Philippine
Insurrection. Reaching a T-junction with a paved road signed for Mt.
Livermore, you turn right and begin a steep climb, rewarded by fine
views of San Francisco, the Golden Gate Bridge, and the Pacific Ocean. As
you near the summit, you pass a hillside decorated with iceplant, poppy,
and lupine. The steep climb is broken by a single right-hand switchback,
and then you reach the top, where 360-degree views range from Mt. St.
Helena to Mt. Hamilton, and from Mt. Diablo to Mt. Tamalpais. There are
picnic tables here, and display panels that point out prominent geo-
graphical landmarks in the Bay Area. When you have finished enjoying
the views from this superb vantage point, retrace your steps to the junction with the North Ridge Trail.

About 50 feet downhill from the junction, you leave the paved road
and veer right to a dirt-and-gravel clearing with a toilet. Immediately
right is your route, the Sunset Trail, which traverses the south flank of Mt.

View northwest from the Sunset Trail across Racoon Strait to Tiburon, Richardson Bay, and Mt. Tam.

Livermore through a brushy area of coyote brush, cow parsnip, and poison oak. Camp Reynolds, a Civil War-era outpost on the island's southwestern edge, is visible downhill and left. This is one of the best places on the island for spring wildflowers, and the hillsides may be ablaze with poppies, narrow-leaf mule ears, blue-eyed grass, and scarlet pimpernel. After crossing a closed trail, your route curves right and, at about the 3-mile point, enters an oak-and-bay forest. When you reach the dirt fire road, you bear right and find the continuation of the Sunset Trail about 75 feet ahead and on your left.

Immediately the trail turns left and begins a series of switchbacks, where thoughtless visitors have made destructive short-cuts, despite a sign that reads FRAGILE AREA, STAY ON TRAIL. At a clearing, you have a beautiful view of Tiburon, Belvedere, and Raccoon Strait, named for a 19th century British warship that was repaired in Ayala Cove. Depending on the tide, the strait may be blue-green with water from the Pacific, or muddy brown with run-off from the Sacramento and San Joaquin rivers. Soon the island's natural sounds—birdsong, insects—may begin fade, especially on a busy weekend, beneath the buzz of human activity at Ayala Cove. As if to make up for that, you descend through a wooded area that is completely overrun with forget-me-nots, creating an almost surreal display. Passing just above a water tank and near a picnic area, you soon cross a small plank bridge over a watercourse and reach Perimeter Road.

Here a paved road from Ayala Cove rises to meet Perimeter Road. Crossing Perimeter Road, you follow the paved road down to Ayala Cove, through a corridor of eucalyptus. Before reaching the visitor center, you pass a bike trail, right, and another paved road, left. Continuing straight, you follow the paved road as it passes the visitor center and lawn, left, and then the Cove Café and bike rental stand, right, to the ferry loading dock. There are different waiting areas for each ferry, so be sure to get in the right one.

Purple-and-white Chinesehouses are lovely to see.

◆ China Camp State Park ◆

China Camp State Park takes its name from a Chinese fishing village that flourished here during the 1880s and 1890s, one of 26 on San Francisco Bay. The village was home to some 500 people and contained three general stores, a marine supply shop, and a barber shop. Its inhabitants were primarily immigrants from Canton province, drawn to California perhaps by the lure of Sierra gold. Chinese fishermen used boats and large nets, called bag nets, to catch shrimp. The shrimp were cooked and then spread to dry on the hillside behind the village. Once dry, they were crushed and winnowed, separating the lighter heads and shell from the meat. The dried shrimp meat was packed and shipped to China and to other Asian communities in the US. Passage in the early 1900s of a series of restrictive laws—the use of bag nets, fishing during peak season, and finally even possessing dried shrimp were all made illegal—shut down the Chinese shrimping industry, and the village soon suffered a precipious decline. A museum in China Camp Village, located just below the China Camp Point Picnic Area at the east end of the park, has a small but excellent display about the shrimping industry. The museum is open daily from 10 A.M. to 5 P.M. There is a concession stand in the village that sells food, cold drinks, and bait, and a nearby fishing pier. The stand and pier are open only on weekends and holidays.

Located on San Pablo Bay about three miles northeast of San Rafael, the park's 1514 acres contain a surprising diversity of habitat, from salt marsh to oak woodland and redwood groves. The land here has seen many uses, from subsistence hunting and gathering by Coast Miwok Indians to cattle grazing by Europeans and Americans. Sheltered from the prevailing west wind and the damp fog it brings to other parts of the North Bay, China Camp lies in a protected and relatively warm area, which is often fog-free. Plant species usually found on dry, sunny slopes, such as blue oak, black oak, and manzanita, thrive here. Wildlife includes deer, foxes, squirrels, and other small mammals, and many species of birds. Most of the park's trails are multi-use, open to hikers, bicyclists, and equestrians. Visitors to the park also enjoy sightseeing, picnicking, boating, swimming, fishing, and wind surfing. Dogs are not allowed on park trails or in non-developed areas, and must be on a 6-foot or shorter leash in picnic areas and campgrounds.

Overnight camping is available in the Back Ranch Meadows Walk-in Campground, located near North San Pedro Road at the west end of the park. There are 30 walk-in family campsites, each with picnic table, food locker, and fire ring. The campsites are located from 50 to 300 yards from the parking area. The Miwok Meadows Group Picnic Site is available for day use by reservation. Other picnic sites, with picnic tables, water, rest rooms, and barbecues, are scattered throughout the park along North San Pedro Road. There is a swimming beach in China Camp Village, with picnic tables, water, rest rooms, and an outdoor shower. The park headquarters and ranger station are located on an access road opposite the Bullhead Flat Picnic Area. Park maps may be purchased at the ranger station from a self-serve bin or at the museum.

CAMPING RESERVATIONS: (800) 444-7275

PICNIC SITE RESERVATIONS: (415) 456-0766

2 China Camp State Park
BAY VIEW LOOP

Length: 6 miles

Time: 3 to 4 hours

Rating: Moderate

Regulations: CSP; parking fee; no dogs.

Highlights: This loop, using the Bay View and Shoreline multi-use trails and the Ridge and Miwok fire trails, samples the wide variety of habitats that makes this wonderful park so attractive. From shady groves of coast redwood and California bay to sheltered enclaves where manzanita and madrone hold sway, this route starts and ends barely above sea level but climbs to 600 feet on its course between Back Ranch and Miwok meadows. The multi-use trails and fire trails of this park are enjoyed by bicyclists and equestrians as well as by hikers and joggers. This route can be combined with parts of the next one, "Shoreline Trail," to form a longer loop or a one-way trip using a car shuttle.

Directions: From Hwy. 101 northbound in San Rafael, take the N. San Pedro Rd. exit, which is also signed for the Marin County Civic Center and China Camp State Park. After exiting, bear right, following the lane marked EAST. After 0.3 mile you join N. San Pedro Rd. Once on it, go 2.9 miles to the Back Ranch Meadows Walk-in Campground entrance road, right. (Many people park along the shoulder of N. San Pedro Rd., near the entrance road, to avoid paying the day-use parking fee.) There is an entrance kiosk just off N.

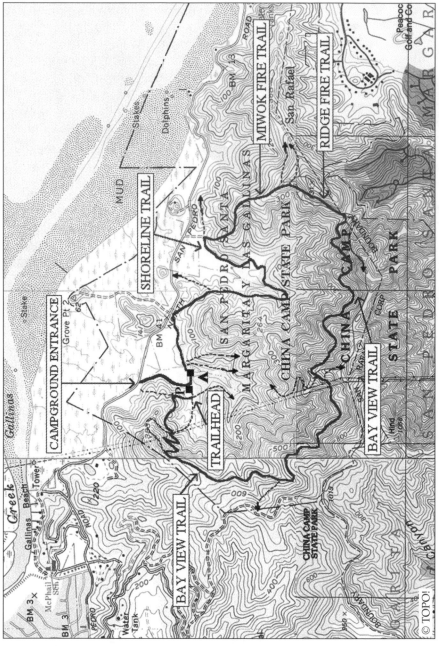

2. Bay View Loop

San Pedro Rd. If it is unattended, pay the parking fee at
the self-registration station in the day-use parking area,
which is 0.2 mile ahead on the right.

From Hwy. 101 southbound in San Rafael, take the N. San
Pedro Rd. exit, which is also signed for the Marin County
Civic Center and China Camp State Park. After 0.2 mile,
you come to a stop sign. Turn left, go 0.1 mile to a stop
light, and turn left again, onto N. San Pedro Rd. At 0.3
mile, the exit ramp from Hwy. 101 northbound joins on
your right. From here, follow the directions above.

Facilities: Picnic tables, toilet. There are rest rooms, water, phone,
and a campground host at the campground parking area,
about 0.1 mile ahead on the entrance road. Maps are sold
at the ranger station, 1.8 miles ahead on N. San Pedro Rd.
(The right-hand turn to the ranger station is poorly
marked.)

Trailhead: West side of day-use parking area.

From the west end of the parking area, just past the self-registration station and an information board, you pass through a gap in a split-rail
fence and come to a four-way junction marked with a trail post. Here the
Powerline Fire Trail goes straight, and the multi-use Shoreline Trail goes
both left and right. You turn right and walk through an open area dotted
with clumps of coyote brush and surrounded by coast live oak, California
bay, and thick stands of madrone. After about 100 feet, the route bends
right, passing a dirt-and-gravel road, left, and follows the split-rail fence.
Now turning left and crossing a wood bridge, the trail passes a seasonal
wetland full of sedges, pennyroyal, and Spanish broom.

Soon you enter a wonderful area dominated by manzanita and
madrone, both members of the heath (*Ericaceae*) family. Madrone, usually a tall tree, has orange bark and large, shiny green leaves. Manzanita,
often a small shrub but sometimes reaching 10 to 15 feet, has reddish bark
and short, pointed leaves that range from green to gray. You may also
notice toyon, a shrub that produces bright red berries in fall, growing
here. After a few hundred yards, you come to a T-junction. Here the
Shoreline Trail turns right and reaches the park's entrance kiosk in 0.2
mile. Your route, the multi-use Bay View Trail, turns left and makes a gentle ascent that alternates between open areas and stands of blue oak. Both
manzanita and blue oak are usually found on hot, dry terrain, often well
inland. Here they thrive in a relatively warm, fog-free zone, nestled
under the protective flanks of high ground to the west.

At about the 0.5-mile point, you reach another T-junction, this one
with the Powerline Fire Trail, a dirt road. A sign here directs you right
and uphill, and in 100 feet you come to a continuation of the Bay View

Hikers step off the multi-use Bay View Trail to let a biker pass.

Trail, going sharply left. Now you continue climbing on a well-graded trail, and after a sharp switchback to the right you begin to get a view through the trees of San Pablo Bay. Here you may find black oak, another species usually at home on dry, sunny slopes. The shade provided here by these tall, sturdy trees gives welcome relief on a warm day. More switchbacks bring you to a four-way junction, at about the 1-mile point. Here, the Powerline Fire Trail joins from the right, and your route, the Bay View Trail, turns sharply left. (The rough track going straight is an unofficial trail closed to bikes and horses.)

Following a split-rail fence, left, you soon pass a junction with a closed trail, right. Leaving the fence behind, you traverse just below the top of a north–south ridge, with a steep drop on your left. A nesting pair of golden eagles has been seen from time to time in this area. The ground here is carpeted with bay and oak leaves, which rustle loudly when disturbed by lizards or squirrels. A few coast redwoods grace a shady, cool ravine, left, and these trees, small for redwoods but tall nonetheless, challenge the bay trees in a race for the sun, sometimes provoking them to attempt untenable heights. When a bay finally falls, its descendants may sprout from the prone trunk. In addition to the tall trees, shrubs such as wild rose, creambush, mountain mahogany, hazelnut, and California sagebrush may be found here. Just past a picnic table, right, you get the first unobstructed view across San Pablo Bay to the East Bay shoreline and Point Pinole.

Using wooden bridges to cross several watercourses, the route wanders in deep shade through stands of redwoods. A frequent redwood companion, evergreen huckleberry, can be found nearby. Now on a gentle but rocky uphill grade, you soon reach a junction with a trail merging sharply from the right, signed TO BAY HILLS DRIVE. A few feet past this junction, you turn sharply left, cross a bridge over a watercourse, and enjoy a level walk that follows the folds of a hillside falling away left. More redwoods are clustered in a deep ravine just downhill. Under a set of power lines, the route descends, then levels and reaches a junction with the Back Ranch Fire Trail, which goes straight and also right. You continue straight, now on an eroded dirt road, descending past a power-line tower in a clearing, left, and then bending right and heading back into the trees. At a T-junction, you turn right onto the continuation of the Bay View Trail. (For a shorter loop, you can instead turn left and descend the Back Ranch Fire Trail to a four-way junction with the Shoreline Trail, turn left onto the Shoreline Trail, and follow it back to the day-use parking area.)

After slightly more than a mile of mostly level walking on a multi-use trail, you reach a junction in a clearing ringed with eucalyptus trees. There is a confusing welter of trails converging here, some of them unofficial. The Bay View Trail ends at a T-junction with the Ridge Fire Trail, a dirt road heading left and right. Across the clearing is an unofficial trail, blocked by a log barricade, from the end of Knight Drive, about 200 yards away. Sharply left is an unofficial trail to Miwok Meadows, closed to bikes and horses. Your route is the Ridge Fire Trail, the dirt road climbing left on a gentle grade.

For the first time on this hike, you begin to see landmarks to the northwest, including Big Rock Ridge, Burdell Mountain, and the north rim of San Pablo Bay. Once over a little rise, you begin to descend, only to climb again on a moderate grade to a T-junction with the Miwok Fire Trail, a dirt road. Here, at about the 4-mile point, you turn left and begin a moderate descent, passing in about 100 feet a junction with the Oak Ridge Trail, right. The road you are on has plenty of loose dirt and gravel, so be careful, especially where the grade steepens. Beside the road are stands of coast live oak, black oak, bay, and madrone, but the rest of the landscape is open and unbounded.

With a view of the marshlands bordering North San Pedro Road, you make a final steep descent over eroded ground and reach a gate, which you can pass around on either side. After about 75 feet you come to a four-way junction. Here you turn left onto a dirt road that provides access from North San Pedro Road to the group day-use area near Miwok Meadows. This is now the Shoreline Trail, which also heads right from the junction as a multi-use path. Out in the open now, you pass a marsh, right, full of pennyroyal, blackberry vines, teasels, sedges, and cattails. Soon the road divides. One branch goes straight, into the group day-use area, which has picnic tables and toilets. The other branch, your route, marked by a trail post for the Shoreline Trail, turns right into a large dirt parking area.

After about 150 feet, you reach the end of the parking area, where you turn left and find the continuation of the Shoreline Trail, marked by a trail post. After passing through a gap in a split-rail fence and crossing a short plank bridge, you turn right and begin a gentle uphill climb in the shade of tall, spindly bay trees. Finding a level course, the route crosses a wood bridge, swings right, and comes into the open. A grassy field, right, slopes down toward North San Pedro Road, and a wooded hillside rises left. At a junction, right, with the Bullet Hill Trail, you continue straight. Three hills—Turtle Back, Bullet Hill, and Chicken Coop Hill—rise from the salt marsh just north of North San Pedro Road. (The short trail around Turtle Back is described elsewhere in this book.)

Now the route gains elevation and bends left, running parallel to North San Pedro Road. Just south of Turtle Back, you veer away from the road and continue a level trek over mostly open ground, with woodland left and marshland right. Soon the route forks, and you bear right, toward the campground parking area. Once on pavement, go west across the parking area to the park entrance road, and follow it 100 yards to the day-use parking area.

Hikers on the Shoreline Trail near Miwok Meadows.

China Camp State Park
SHORELINE TRAIL

Length: 4.9 miles

Time: 2 to 3 hours

Rating: Moderate

Regulations: CSP; parking fee; no dogs.

Highlights: This semi-loop starts at China Camp Point and uses the Village, Shoreline, Oak Ridge, and Peacock Gap trails, and the Miwok Fire Trail, to explore the western part of this fine park. Except for a short but rigorous climb up the Miwok Fire Trail, most of the route is in the shade, making it pleasant on a warm day. Most of the park's signed and maintained trails are open to hikers, bicyclists, and equestrians. Be sure not to miss the visitor center, open daily 10 A.M. to 5 P.M., in the village just downhill from China Camp Point. This route can be combined with parts of the previous one, "Bay View Loop," to form a longer loop or a one-way trip using a car shuttle.

Directions: See the directions for "Bay View Loop." At the junction with the Back Ranch Meadows Walk-in Campground entrance road, continue east another 2.2 miles to the China Camp Village entrance, left, and a large paved parking area. If this parking area is full, continue downhill 0.1 mile into the village, where there are a large dirt parking area and a self-registration station.

Facilities: In upper parking area, rest rooms. In village, a visitor center with displays on the Chinese shrimp industry; picnic tables, rest rooms, water, phone; snack bar and fishing pier, open weekends only. Maps for sale from a coin-operated machine at the visitor center.

Trailhead: At northwest corner of upper parking area, just left of rest rooms.

From the upper parking area, even before setting off on the trail, you have fine views of San Pablo Bay, Point Pinole, the East Bay hills, and Mt. Diablo. After finding the trailhead for the Village Trail, just left of the rest rooms, you walk downhill on a gentle grade, beside tangles of blackberry vines and coyote brush, perhaps listening to the call of a California quail. After about 100 feet, you bear left at a fork marked by a trail post, where the Rat Rock Cove Trail heads right. Here, bush monkeyflower

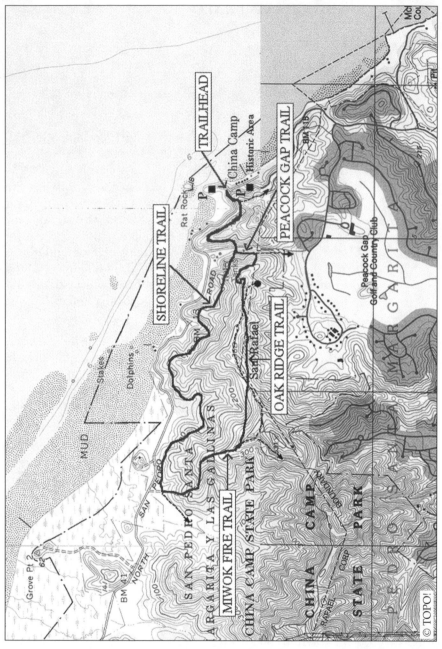

3. Shoreline Trail

puts on a showy display from spring through summer. The view right takes in a small cove with a beach and mud flats, San Pablo Bay, and in the distance beyond the Bay's northwest shore, Burdell Mountain.

Now passing through a weedy area, where honeysuckle vines cling to toyon bushes, you soon reach North San Pedro Road, which you cross. Finding the Village Trail on the other side of the road, you curve right and then make a switchback left, in the shade of coast live oak and California bay. After several hundred feet, a right-hand switchback puts you on a gentle uphill grade, and you enter an area where birds abound, including warblers, kinglets, chickadees, and towhees. The Village Trail soon merges with the Shoreline Trail, which goes straight and also sharply left. You continue straight.

Here the route levels and runs parallel to North San Pedro Road, which is downhill and right. Passing a rest bench, left, you walk by stands of madrone, black oak, and blue elderberry. As the route bends left, you have a view of the hills sloping down toward the Marin shoreline and Big Rock Ridge, the antenna-topped high ground that rises just north of Lucas Valley Road. Passing more rest benches, the trail finishes its leftward bend and descends to the park headquarters, where you will find a ranger station, picnic tables, and water. Maps are usually available from a self-serve bin at the ranger station. Just in front of the ranger station, you turn right, cross a paved road, a pick up the continuation of the Shoreline Trail, marked by a large sign.

Now the route climbs out of the headquarters area on a gentle grade via several switchbacks, then levels in the shade of bay and coast live oak.

Couple enjoys the historic area at China Camp.

Soon you reach a junction with the Peacock Gap Trail coming in sharply from the left. Here your route continues straight, and then begins to wind back and forth in a peaceful forest, ducking into gullies and bending around small promontories. Just past the 1-mile point, you emerge into an open field with a rest bench on your right. Now the route rounds the end of a ridge and begins a gentle descent, soon reaching level ground.

At the end of another promontory, the route bends left, passing a rest bench that invites you to sit for a moment and admire the fine view of San Pablo Bay. Near the head of a gully spanned by a bridge, you pass an unofficial trail going uphill and left. Then the route swings right, crosses the bridge, and jogs left. In this wooded area be alert for birds of prey such as Cooper's and sharp-shinned hawks. You may also see dark-eyed juncos flitting nervously about. Deer frequent this area, and you may be lucky enough to see a stately, plump buck with antlers. At the next gully, you cross another bridge, turn right, and begin to climb on a gentle grade. Breaking out of the trees near the 2-mile point, you have the best views yet, unobstructed, of San Pablo Bay.

Leaving the clearing and returning briefly to forest, you cross another bridge over a deep gully, and then, in a few paces, come into the open again. Descending now, through fields of tarweed—a yellow, daisy-like flower whose buds are sticky to the touch—you have a view across North San Pedro Road to Chicken Coop Hill. Don't be alarmed if the grassy hillsides nearby appear scorched. The park uses prescribed burns to remove non-native plants such as French broom and star thistle, and to stimulate native grasses and other native plants. The effects of this cleansing and

This cove was the site of a Chinese fishing village in the late 1880s.

rejuvenating process include an increase in forage for wildlife and a reduction in the amount of flammable material available to fuel a devastating wildfire.

Nearly at sea level, with a marsh sporting cattails just ahead, you reach a fork and bear left. The marshes on the south side of North San Pedro Road, infiltrated by salt water from San Pablo Bay flowing under the road through culverts, contain a blend of freshwater and coastal salt-marsh plants. Soon after the fork, you come to a four-way junction, where your route, the Miwok Fire Trail, a dirt road, rises steeply left. Also here is a dirt road that connects North San Pedro Road with the group day-use area. Turning left, in about 75 feet you reach a gate, which you can pass around on either side. Ahead is a steady 0.5-mile climb—the first part steep, the rest moderate and gentle—over eroded ground, with only patches of shade. Watch for bikes careening downhill!

Just shy of the 3-mile point, you arrive at a junction with the Oak Ridge Trail, left. Leaving the Miwok Fire Trail, you turn left and enter a cool, shady forest of coast live oak and bay, traversing a hillside that falls away left. Uphill and right is a eucalyptus forest on a ridge that slopes gradually down to meet your trail. You are heading east, roughly parallel to the Shoreline Trail, which is several hundred vertical feet below and left. Soon you merge with the McNears Fire Trail, coming sharply from the right, and in about 60 feet reach a fork. Here, at a low point on the ridge, the McNears Fire Trail veers left, but you bear right, still on the Oak Ridge Trail.

Now on the south side of the ridge, amid stands of young eucalyptus with blue-gray leaves, you begin to get views of Mt. Diablo, peeking through the trees. After a short distance, the vista expands, dramatically taking in San Francisco, Angel Island, the Bay Bridge, and the Richmond–San Rafael Bridge. Descending on a gentle grade and leaving the eucalyptus behind, you can look south, through gaps in stands of coast live oak, to the Marin Headlands, perhaps just spying one of the towers of the Golden Gate Bridge. Turkey vultures and red-tailed hawks may be seen from this vantage point.

At a junction marked by a trail post, you cross the McNears Fire Trail again and continue straight, still on the Oak Ridge Trail. With a split-rail fence on your left, follow the trail as it jogs right, then left. In about 100 yards you begin a gentle descent of a north-facing slope in dense forest, aided by several widely spaced switchbacks. Soon you begin to see the park headquarters through the trees, and, after passing briefly through a clearing, you come to a junction and the end of the Oak Ridge Trail. Here, you continue straight, now on the Peacock Gap Trail, which also goes sharply right. At the next junction, you return to the Shoreline Trail; now turn right and retrace your steps to the parking area.

4

China Camp State Park
TURTLE BACK NATURE TRAIL

Length: 0.75 mile

Time: 1 hour or less

Rating: Easy

Regulations: CSP; no bikes, no horses, no dogs.

Highlights: This hike, following the Turtle Back Nature Trail and the shoulder of N. San Pedro Rd., is deceptive. Although short and easy, it provides a close-up look at a wide variety of plant species, along with wonderful views across San Pablo Bay.

Directions: See the directions for "Bay View Loop" on pages 35–37. At the junction with the Back Ranch Meadows Walk-in Campground entrance road, continue east another 0.1 mile and park on the road shoulder, well off the pavement.

Facilities: None

Trailhead: North side of road.

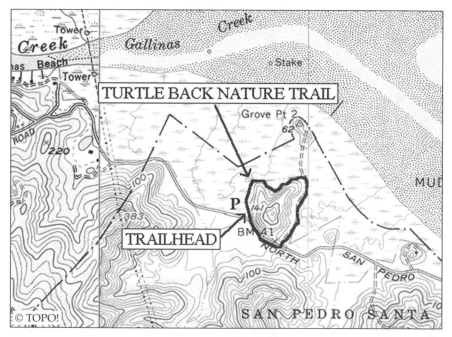

4. Turtle Back Nature Trail

This short loop, circling a hill called Turtle Back, stays just above the level of a large coastal salt marsh at the edge of San Pablo Bay. Certain species of birds, fish, and other animals depend for their survival on salt marshes, once common around San Francisco Bay but now much reduced by development. Plants that can tolerate salt in varying degrees, including pickleweed and salt grass, characterize a salt marsh, which is flooded twice daily by high tides. In drier areas of the marsh, you may notice Pacific gumplant, a rangy plant with yellow daisy-like flowers and sticky buds that blooms well into the fall.

As you follow the single-track trail that leaves the road shoulder near a large valley oak, you may notice two other oak species—blue and black—that are usually found in higher elevations on warm, dry hillsides. Also here are coast live oak, California bay, toyon, and manzanita, a chaparral plant. China Camp State Park occupies an area protected by several high ridges from the cool, damp coastal fog that often pours over other parts of Marin County. This creates a micro-climate that allows a wide variety of plants to live side by side.

Rounding the north end of Turtle Back, the trail rises slightly, and you can see tidal creeks running through the marsh and out toward San Pablo Bay. Turning away from the Bay, you may be surprised to find a dense forest, including some fine madrone and a understory of ferns, blanketing the north slope of Turtle Back. Here a steep path climbs right, but you continue straight on the main trail. When you reach a split-rail fence, pause for a moment if the day is clear to admire the fine view of San Pablo Bay, the East Bay hills, and, in the distance, Mt. Diablo.

Madrone shows distinctive urn-shaped flowers of the heath family.

Now your trail widens to a dirt road, and you pass a junction with another dirt road, left, that goes to Jake's Island, a hump rising from the marsh. The road to Jake's Island is permanently closed for habitat restoration. Your route bends right, taking you around the east side of Turtle Back. A stand of sedges, reed-like wetland plants known by their triangular stems, rises from the marsh. Along the way back to North San Pedro Road, several interpretive signs describe the marsh plants and explain the value of salt marshes, which, in the San Francisco Bay Area, are home to several threatened and endangered species, including the clapper rail and the salt marsh harvest mouse.

Now making a gentle ascent, you pass a hillside, right, that is home to clumps of native grass, which has largely been replaced in the West by European imports such as wild oats and other exotic grasses. Unlike the imports, native grass lives for several years and benefits from periodic fires. This park uses prescribed burns as a way to encourage native plants and reduce fuel build-up. Soon the Turtle Back Nature Trail reaches North San Pedro Road. Now cross the road carefully, turn right, and walk along the road shoulder back to the trailhead.

◆ Marin County Open Space District ◆

Residents of Marin County take great pride in their open space, and with good reason. Since 1972, when county voters approved the formation and funding of the Marin County Open Space District (MCOSD), thousands of acres of land that might otherwise have been lost to development were acquired and protected. In fact, some of the open-space preserves, as they are called, are bordered by housing tracts, making them fine examples of why the District was sorely needed. Other preserves, away from the hustle and bustle of Highway 101 and the county's population centers, offer a more wilderness-like experience, although for the most part the lands are hardly pristine. As in other parklands in the Bay Area, outdoor enthusiasts in Marin parklands today roam over ground that may once have been used by Native Americans for hunting and gathering food, and later perhaps belonged to vast ranchos teeming with cattle. Many of the ranchos were later subdivided into cattle ranches, farms, and orchards. But native trees, shrubs, and wildflowers, including rarities, are abundant in the preserves, which also teem with birds during most of the year. There is much joy in finding Mother Nature alive and well amid urban and suburban sprawl.

The District has created four separate maps to cover its holdings. These are titled Northern Preserves, Western Preserves, Central Preserves, and Southern Preserves. There are enough trails within the District to fill an entire guidebook, and the decision of which to include here was somewhat arbitrary and based on my desire to give a sample from each area. In the Northern Preserves, centered around the city of Novato, I selected three routes: Burdell Mountain, Rush Creek, and Deer Island. In the Western Preserves, which border Sir Francis Drake Blvd. near the town of Woodacre, I describe two: Gary Giacomini and Roy's Redwoods. In the Central Preserves, which line Highway 101 north of San Rafael and Sir Francis Drake Blvd. near Fairfax, I selected one route, Santa Margarita Island. And in the Southern Preserves, which are scattered from Mill Valley to Tiburon, I chose Ring Mountain.

The preserves are free and open to the public year-round. Use is restricted to activities which have little or no impact on the natural environment. In the Deer Island, Ring Mountain, Rush Creek, and Santa Margarita Island preserves, and in all Wildlife Protection Areas, dogs must be on a 6-foot or shorter leash at all times. In all other preserves, on fire roads dogs may be unleashed but must be under voice control; on single-track trails they must be leashed. Bikes are allowed only on fire roads unless otherwise designated. Parking at many preserves is extremely limited, and there are generally no facilities.

MARIN COUNTY DEPT. OF PARKS, OPEN SPACE, AND CULTURAL SERVICES:
(415) 499-6387

MCOSD FIELD OPERATIONS: (415) 499-6405

| 5 | Marin County Open Space District
BURDELL MOUNTAIN |

Length: 6 miles

Time: 3 to 4 hours

Rating: Difficult

Regulations: MCOSD; no bikes on single-track trails.

Highlights: This loop, using the San Andreas, Middle Burdell, Cobblestone, San Carlos, and Big Tank fire roads, and the Michako Trail, explores the open grasslands, groves, and high ground of Burdell Mountain, a bulky ridge that rises to 1558 feet and dominates the northeast corner of Marin County. The mountain's southern flank is designated the Mt. Burdell Open Space Preserve, and in spring its grassy slopes and oak woodlands come alive with carpets of wildflowers and a chorus of birdsong. This trip earns its "difficult" rating because of the elevation gain, more than 1,000 feet.

Directions: From Hwy. 101 in Novato, take the Atherton Ave./San Marin Dr. exit. Go west 2.2 miles on San Marin Dr., turn right onto San Andreas Dr., and go 0.6 mile to where the road makes a sweeping bend to the left. Park on the shoulder and observe the NO PARKING signs.

Facilities: None

Trailhead: At the foot of the San Andreas Fire Road, just northeast of the parking area.

At the foot of the San Andreas Fire Road, which is gated and locked, you head east on a dirt path, and, in about 50 feet pass through a gate and then make a sharp left-hand bend. After 100 feet or so, you merge with the San Andreas Fire Road, which climbs on a gentle grade. About 75 feet ahead, you pass the Big Tank Fire Road, signed as the Big Tank Fire Trail, which you will use on your return. Your route here is part of the Bay Area Ridge Trail, and it is popular with local residents, their horses, and their dogs. This is a lovely wooded area of coast live oak, California bay, and blue elderberry.

Soon you pass a single-track trail heading left through an opening in a barbed-wire fence. The area behind the fence, also part of the Mt. Burdell Open Space Preserve, is designated a Sensitive Wildlife Area, where dogs are prohibited. Now climbing on a moderate grade, you pass another trail taking off left and uphill, signed TO LITTLE TANK FIRE ROAD. (Neither this trail, nor the previous one, nor the Little Tank Fire Road appears on the MCOSD map.) About 75 feet farther, you pass through an opening in a fence, and then come to an area decorated in spring with exquisite displays of Chinesehouses, delicate whorls of purple-and-white flowers. Also here, the California buckeye's gorgeous upturned spikes of cream-colored flowers may vie for your attention. Passing a cement wall, right, you come to a clearing that affords a view of Burdell Mountain's summit ridge and the communication tower perched just below it. The middle ground of this beautiful scene is composed of rolling hills studded with oaks. The foreground, in spring, may be carpeted yellow with California buttercup and smooth owl's-clover.

At about the 0.4-mile point, you pass the junction, left, with the Dwarf Oak Trail (labeled incorrectly as the Dawn Oak Trail on the MCOSD map). During and just after the rainy season, the open ground surrounding the junction is a marshy area, home to red-winged blackbirds, west-

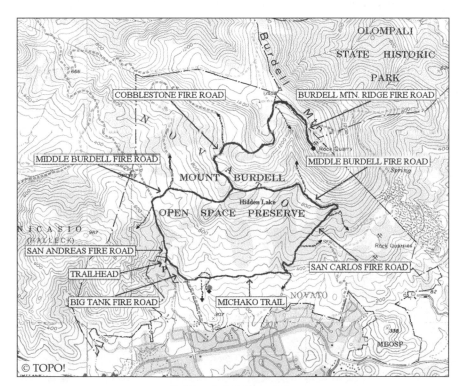

5. Burdell Mountain

ern bluebirds, and a wildflower called Douglas meadowfoam, sporting five yellow petals tipped with white. A few hundred feet farther, you pass two trails, right, not shown on the map: one is a dirt road that heads east and eventually merges with the Middle Burdell Fire Road; the other is a path heading southeast.

As you continue walking on a gentle downhill course, you are surrounded by open, grassy fields, and rising, rolling hills. The main ridge of Burdell Mountain trends east–west, and is topped with many rounded summits. The mountain was named for Galen Burdell, one of the first dentists in San Francisco, who lived with his wife Mary just north of here, in what is now Olompali State Park. The couple received the land in 1863 as a wedding present from Mary's father, James Black, one of Marin County's largest landowners. A route in neighboring Olompali State Park is described elsewhere in this guide.

Soon the road reaches a low point, then bends left and begins to climb. Lupine, fiddleneck, and California poppies may be hidden in the tall grass, which also contains big patches of milk thistle and Italian thistle. In a shady grove of valley oak, a single-track trail departs uphill and right, but you continue straight. In about 50 feet, you come to a junction marked by a trail post. Here, the San Andreas Fire Road heads left, into a massive patch of thistle, and your route, the Middle Burdell Fire Road, also part of the Bay Area Ridge Trail, goes straight.

Now the road, still rising, makes a sweeping right turn and then bends left. You may enjoy watching the antics here of California ground squirrels as they scamper through the grass. At an unsigned fork you bear left,

Hiker uses the Cobblestone Fire Road to reach the top of Burdell Mountain.

and soon pass a junction, right, with a dirt road, the other branch of the fork. Now your route wanders back and forth as it gains elevation. At about the 1-mile point, in a grove of oak and buckeye, you leave the Bay Area Ridge Trail route as it takes the Deer Camp Fire Road, left, by continuing straight, still on the Middle Burdell Fire Road. You have a fine view from here south to Big Rock Ridge, the high ground rising between Novato and Lucas Valley, topped by two communication towers.

Soon a trail joins sharply from the right—one of two you passed earlier that left the San Andreas Fire Road near its junction with the Dwarf Oak Trail. Your route climbs moderately over rocky ground, bends north, and follows a barbed-wire fence and a stream bed, both right. Passing a single-track trail that goes through a gate in the fence, you reach level ground and a T-junction. Here, the Middle Burdell Fire Road turns right, and the Cobblestone Fire Road, the way to the top of Burdell Mountain, heads left. (If you do not wish to make the approximately 700-foot, 1-mile climb, turn right and pick up the directions below to complete the loop.)

Turning left, you begin climbing on a moderate grade, past grassy fields full of poppies and bluedicks. The route gets steeper and rockier, but you are rewarded by terrific views west toward Bolinas Ridge, and southeast to San Pablo Bay and the peninsula that holds China Camp State Park. As the grade eases somewhat, you pass through groves of coast live oak and bay, offering welcome shade on a warm day. At about the 2-mile point, you come to a fork. Here the Deer Camp Fire Road branches left, and the Cobblestone Fire Road veers right. Stay right, and as you gain elevation, the communication tower near the summit of Burdell Mountain comes into view. The upper slopes of the mountain host dramatic displays of wildflowers in spring, and this area may be full of wild irises.

Now the road turns north, trying to find the easiest way up Burdell Mountain. The climbing is moderate, with a few level areas to ease your efforts, and some groves of bay and coast live oak for shade. Your view extends south, across the housing developments of Novato, all the way to triple-peaked Mt. Tamalpais. Along the way, you will pass faint trails that diverge from the main route: ignore them. The communication tower, once a distant feature, is now to the left and just slightly uphill. There is higher ground ahead, but the true summit of Burdell Mountain (1558') is just beyond the preserve boundary, unreachable on private land.

Nearing the end of the climb, you come to a junction with the Old Quarry Trail, right, and, almost immediately, a T-junction with the Burdell Mountain Ridge Fire Road, a paved road. The preserve's high point lies just ahead, across the road and at the end of a faint single-track trail that heads north and uphill through the grass, which is dotted blue with larkspur. A rock wall, reminiscent of New England but actually built by Chinese laborers who worked in a nearby quarry, marks the preserve boundary. The quarry, which produced rocks used for cobblestone streets, is about 0.25 mile southeast on the Burdell Mountain Ridge Fire Road. A rough path heads left from the road, through trees and brush, to the quarry.

After exploring Burdell Mountain's high ground, retrace your steps to the junction of the Cobblestone and Middle Burdell fire roads. As you continue straight, now back on the Middle Burdell Fire Road, you pass Hidden Lake, a large vernal pool on your right, which may hold ducks, egrets, and other water-loving birds. Growing around the lake are at least 10 species of rare plants, including white water-buttercup, pale navarretia, and yellow linanthus. Your route now heads east over level ground, with open, grassy slopes sweeping uphill on your left. Dipping into and then out of a small wooded ravine, you soon come to a junction, left, with the Old Quarry Trail, which climbs steeply to join the Cobblestone Fire Road just a few feet from the Burdell Mountain Ridge Fire Road. Continue straight, and in about 25 feet you pass a rough trail heading left and straight up the side of a high grassy ridge.

Several hundred feet past these trails, the continuation of the Old Quarry Trail heads right, but you continue straight. Passing through a wooded area, you may be startled by a flock of band-tailed pigeons taking flight. These cousins of the urban pigeon are large, beautifully marked birds that favor forested areas, where they often gather in large flocks. When disturbed, they leave their perches singly at first, and then in increasingly larger groups until the whole flock has departed.

Soon you reach a junction and a watering trough for animals, where the Middle Burdell Fire Road continues straight, and your route, the San Carlos Fire Road, turns right. Descending gently for about 75 feet, you come to a gated fence. After passing through the gate, you enjoy a level walk in the shade of coast live oak, bay, and buckeye, but soon resume a gentle descent in the open. At about the 4.5-mile point, you pass the Old Quarry Trail, right, and, about 350 feet ahead, the Salt Lick Fire Road, left. Continuing straight and downhill on the San Carlos Fire Road, your route soon veers right, and then makes a sharp left-hand bend, putting you on a southeast course.

At a four-way junction, where the San Carlos Fire Road continues straight and a faint trace heads left, you turn right onto the Michako Trail, a single track that is closed to bikes. Still descending, you pass through an opening in a fence, cross a seasonal creek on rocks, and then find level ground. Just past the creek, a faint trail heads left, but you continue straight and soon begin a gentle climb. Fields of clover may be in bloom here, and, because you are walking west, their flowers are beautifully backlit on a sunny afternoon.

Now a trail joins sharply from the left, and then you cross another seasonal creek. In about 100 feet, the route forks and you bear left, soon crossing yet another creek, this one the site of a stone hut, once used to protect a freshwater spring. After another 150 feet or so, your route is joined by a trail, right, coming from the previous fork. The high ground of Burdell Mountain is to your right. Soon you come to a four-way junction, where the Big Tank Fire Road crosses the Michako Trail. Here you continue straight across a grassy field, and, in about 200 feet, come to a watercourse that, when flowing, has a series of delightful miniature waterfalls. Once across this watercourse, you soon reach the next junction, where the Michako Trail merges with the San Marin Fire Road, coming from the left. About 25 feet past this spot, you reach a junction with the Big Tank Fire Road, joining from the right. From here, you continue straight, now on the Big Tank Fire Road, heading west.

About 150 feet past this junction, the route forks, the main road bending left and descending, and a single-track heading right. Here you bear left, passing a few private homes and the Andreas Court Fire Road, left. Your route now swings right, climbs, and is soon joined by the single-track trail coming from the previous fork. Now on an easy descent, you pass a landslide area where the road may have disappeared. If so, follow a narrow path next to the embankment, where a creek flows under the roadbed through a culvert. About 100 feet ahead is the junction with the San Andreas Fire Road you passed at the start of this loop. Turn left here and retrace your steps to the parking area.

Hidden Lake, a vernal pool at the junction of the Middle Burdell and Cobblestone fire roads, is home to at least 10 species of rare plants.

6	Marin County Open Space District
	DEER ISLAND

Length: 1.8 miles

Time: 1 to 1.5 hours

Rating: Easy

Regulations: MCOSD; no bikes, dogs on leash.

Highlights: This short walk on the Deer Island Loop Trail visits open fields and oak-and-bay woodlands on its way around Deer Island, one of several low hills rising from the flatlands between Hwy. 101 and Hwy. 37. This hike in the Deer Island Open Space Preserve can easily be combined with a visit to the marshlands of the nearby Rush Creek Open Space Preserve, a few miles north, described on pages 73–77.

Directions: From Hwy. 101 in Novato, take the Atherton Ave./San Marin Dr. exit and follow Atherton Ave. east, staying right at its intersection with Bugiea Ln. After 1.8 miles, turn right onto Olive Ave., go 0.6 mile, and turn left onto Deer Island Ln. Go 0.2 mile to a fork and bear right. About 75 feet ahead on the right is a gravel parking area. Be careful not to block any driveways.

Facilities: None

Trailhead: Southwest corner of parking area.

After walking through a gap in a barbed-wire fence, you pass the return part of the Deer Island Loop Trail, left, and then head straight uphill for about 75 feet to a junction marked by a trail post. The center trail is the De Borba Trail, but you veer right and follow the Deer Island Loop Trail through an open, weedy field. Soon the route levels, and you pass a private home, right, and the remains of some weathered sheds and other structures. Deer Island, which you are circling counter-clockwise, was once a true island, separated from mainland Novato by streams, marshes, and other wetlands. The area was diked beginning in the 1860s, and now only seasonal wetlands remain. Groves of California bay and coast live oak provide you with occasional shade, but soon after crossing several small watercourses you are in the open again, in a field perhaps dotted orange with California poppies. In spring, the grassy fields here are almost unbelievably green.

A plank bridge takes you across another watercourse, and now you traverse a wide valley, with the high ground of Deer Island to your left.

Your trail merges with a dirt road coming in sharply from the right, and after passing a trail post signed for the Russell Antonio Trail, you reach a fork. Here the Russell Antonio Trail veers right, but your route, once again a single track, bears left and climbs on a gentle grade. To the right, a series of seasonal marshes, bisected by Novato Creek, extend all the way to Highway 101, and you have a fine view of Big Rock Ridge, with its two communication towers, commanding the high ground south of Novato. Ahead, to the south, you can see the forested ridge that forms the backbone of China Camp State Park.

As the trail continues its leftward curve around Deer Island, you pass more groves of coast live oak, some of the trees old and draped with folds of lace lichen, sometimes called Spanish moss. A few venerable valley oaks prosper here as well. Within the confines of these oak groves, the hustle and bustle of nearby Highway 101 fades away, and you may find yourself surrounded by birds or face to face with a startled deer. Now you make a rising traverse on the south side of Deer Island, with Highway 37 to your right, and Mt. Diablo rising in the distance to the southeast. Black oak finds a home on the island's sunny south slope. In the flats south and east of Deer Island are flood-control channels and set-tling ponds used for sewage treatment. At the head of a ravine, the route bends right, then left, and continues its gentle ascent. Soon you turn left again, and enter a forest dominated by bay trees. To the right is a line of eucalyptus, the young trees sporting blue-gray leaves, a color not found on any other familiar trees.

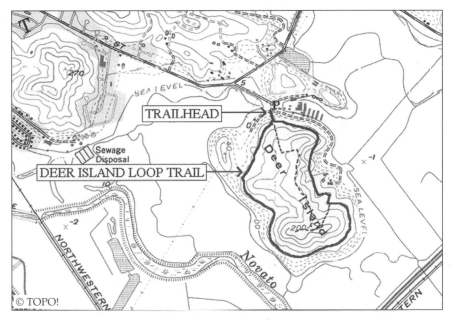

6. Deer Island

At about the 1-mile point, the route forks. Left is the De Borba Trail, but you continue straight, still on the Deer Island Loop Trail, enjoying a level, shady walk. California buckeye may be found here, and also a large fig tree. In places, patches of sunlight break up the shade, perhaps lighting up a flock of dark-eyed juncos. The oaks here attract acorn woodpeckers, who store their winter's supply of acorns in holes they drill in the tree trunks. The trail nears the head of a ravine, turns right to cross it, and then turns right again before resuming its leftward course. A large complex of storage sheds and an auto junkyard, right, signal your return to civilization. After crossing a watercourse, you emerge from dense forest and walk parallel to a paved road, separated from it by a barbed-wire fence. Soon you reach the junction with the start of the Deer Island Loop Trail; here you turn right, into the parking area.

Marin County Open Space District
GARY GIACOMINI TRAVERSE

Length:	5.1 miles
Time:	2 to 3 hours
Rating:	Moderate
Regulations:	MCOSD, MMWD; dogs on leash, no smoking. Fairfax–Bolinas Rd. to the Azalea Hill parking area may be closed because of high fire danger. To prevent stream damage caused by erosion, bikes and horses should not to use the trail in the Gary Giacomini Open Space Preserve during the rainy season.
Highlights:	This northwest-to-southeast traverse uses the Conifer Fire Road, San Geronimo Ridge Road, and Pine Mountain Road, along with an unnamed trail, to cross the Gary Giacomini Open Space Preserve, named for a Marin County supervisor, and adjacent lands of the Marin Municipal Water District. Climbing out of a shady redwood forest, the route, a favorite among mountain bikers, reaches high, chaparral-cloaked ground with superb views. Along the way you pass through an unusual forest of dwarf Sargent cypress, an evergreen restricted to serpentine soil. The traverse, a car-shuttle trip, may be combined with a climb of Pine Mountain, described on pages 91–94 to create a more rigorous 6.9-mile outing.
Directions:	This is a car shuttle trip, starting at the **Gary Giacomini** parking area in Woodacre, and ending at the **Azalea Hill**

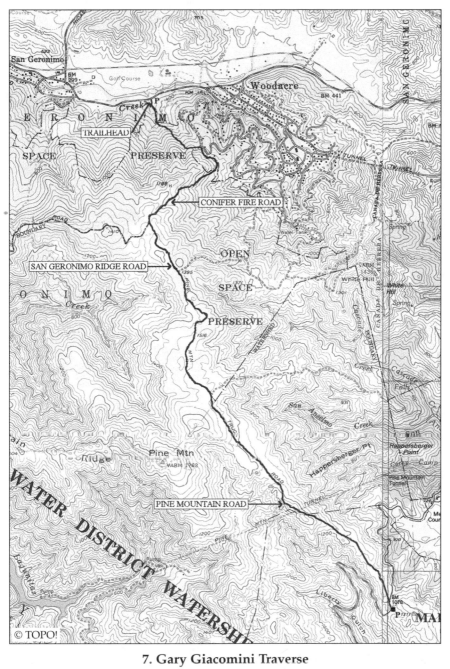

7. Gary Giacomini Traverse

parking area on Fairfax–Bolinas Rd. Drive first to the Azalea Hill parking area and leave a car there. Then drive to the Gary Giacomini parking area.

To reach the **Azalea Hill** parking area: From Hwy. 101 northbound, take the San Anselmo exit, also signed for San Quentin, Sir Francis Drake Blvd., and the Richmond Bridge. Stay in the left lane as you exit, toward San Anselmo, crossing over Hwy. 101. After 0.4 mile you join Sir Francis Drake Blvd., with traffic from Hwy. 101 southbound merging on your right. From here, it is 3.6 miles to a stop light at the intersection with Red Hill Ave. From the intersection, stay on Sir Francis Drake Blvd. as it goes straight and then immediately bends left.

At 5.5 miles from Hwy. 101, in Fairfax, turn left at a stop light onto Claus Dr., jog left onto Broadway and right onto Bolinas Rd., which is heavily used by bicyclists. After 0.4 mile, you pass an intersection with Cascade Dr., where you bear left. (Bolinas Rd. soon becomes Fairfax–Bolinas Rd.) At 1.5 miles, you pass Sky Oaks Rd., the turn-off, left, to Lake Lagunitas and Bon Tempe Lake. At 3.9 miles, turn left into a gravel parking area.

From Hwy. 101 southbound, take the Sir Francis Drake/Kentfield exit and follow the directions above.

To reach the **Gary Giacomini** parking area: Drive back to the intersection of Sir Francis Drake Blvd. and Claus Dr. in Fairfax. Turn left onto Sir Francis Drake Blvd., go 3.2 miles, and turn left onto San Geronimo Valley Dr. in Woodacre. At 1.4 miles you reach Redwood Canyon Dr., left. Because there is no legal parking here at the trailhead, continue on San Geronimo Valley Dr. for another 100 yards, passing Meadow View Ln., left, and park on the shoulder of San Geronimo Valley Dr. where it widens.

Facilities: None

Trailhead: On the west side of Redwood Canyon Dr., about 40 feet south of its intersection with San Geronimo Valley Dr.

The trailhead, marked by a wooden gate, is in a clearing ringed by coast live oak, California bay, white alder, and bigleaf maple. After walking south for several hundred feet through the clearing, you find an unnamed dirt road and enter a dense forest of coast redwoods, with a creek on your right. Large stumps along the way testify to the girth of the majestic old-growth trees before they were felled. Other members of the redwood forest are here, including tanbark oak, hazelnut, thimbleberry, wild ginger, and western sword fern. After ascending on a gentle grade for several hundred feet, you come to an unsigned junction, where a trail, right, crosses the creek via a bridge. You continue straight, listening perhaps to the repetitive cry of a red-shouldered hawk or the familiar note of a chestnut-backed chickadee.

Now the route begins to climb on a moderate grade, finding a course between the redwood forest, right, and a more open oak-and-bay woodland, left. The grade alternates between moderate and gentle as you continue uphill, and soon you have a deep ravine, right. The route bends right, crossing a creek that flows through a culvert and splashes into the ravine. Now, by means of some large bends in the trail, you gain elevation over rough and eroded ground. Sunlight filtering through the trees illuminates the leaves of bigleaf maples, which, in late summer and fall, turn yellow and orange.

As the trail makes a left-hand bend, you pass a narrow trail heading right and uphill. You route continues to bend left and then straightens. About 125 feet from the narrow trail, you come to a metal gate. Once around it, you continue about 75 feet to the intersection of Carson Road and Conifer Way. Here you turn right and walk uphill on Conifer Way, a mixture of dirt, gravel, and pavement. After about 150 feet, you reach a metal gate signed for the Gary Giacomini Open Space Preserve, behind which is your route, the Conifer Fire Road.

After passing an access road to a water tank, left, you begin a winding ascent, mostly moderate but in places steep, in the shade of Douglas fir, coast live oak, and bay. Leaving the trees behind, you emerge onto a grassy hillside that falls away left, and, where the route levels, reach a junction with a trail, right, that may be hard to see. The views here, at about the 1.5-mile point, are wonderful, taking in the open hills and forested ridges of Marin, the shimmering waters of San Pablo Bay, and, on the eastern horizon, Mt. Diablo. Now working your way southwest on the ascending dirt road, you pass through a notch between two hills, watched perhaps by a kestrel on patrol.

At a junction with a dirt road heading right, you continue straight, enjoying ever-improving views. After about 150 yards, you reach a junction with San Geronimo Ridge Road, going right and also straight. Here the Conifer Fire Road ends, and you continue straight, now on San Geronimo Ridge Road. The roads are unsigned, but there is a sign here for the Mt. Tamalpais Watershed, Marin Municipal Water District. The plant life now changes dramatically from grassland to chaparral, and you are surrounded by manzanita, chamise, chaparral pea, yerba santa, and spiny redberry. But the most unusual plant along this route is Sargent cypress, an evergreen tree confined to serpentine soil, here growing in a stunted form. This species of cypress has round, gray-brown cones, and gray bark that forms angled strips.

Behind you, to the north, are Mt. St. Helena, its tip barely visible, and Sonoma Mountain, a long ridge to its right. Now on a level course, you pass two dirt roads, about 100 feet apart, on the left. These merge in about 100 feet to form White's Hill Fire Road. Continuing straight, you may feel like you are on top of the world, as your gaze sweeps from left to right, taking in the remarkable scenery. Now the landscape turns rocky, with many outcrops and boulders. The route bends right, loses elevation slightly, and then begins to climb again, in places on a steep grade. In a shady enclave, left, you may see madrone and hazelnut, species usually found in more wooded areas. Once more in the clear, you come to a wonderful vantage point where the Bay Area's three tallest summits—Mt. Diablo, Mt. St. Helena, and Mt. Tamalpais—are on display.

Dropping to more sheltered ground, a relief on a windy day, you traverse a flat expanse filled with dwarf Sargent cypress trees, a unique biological treasure trove. From here, the three summits of Mt. Tamalpais range along the southeast skyline, and the mountain's rugged, steep northern flanks sweep dramatically down toward Lake Lagunitas. At about the 3-mile point, you pass the Cascade Canyon Fire Road, also known as Repack Road, left. Here another fine vantage point offers you views of San Pablo Bay, the East Bay Hills, and Mt. Diablo, which is framed between two Marin County high points—Bald Hill, rising north of Phoenix Lake, and the long ridge that forms the backbone of China Camp State Park.

Continuing your descent over gentle and then moderate ground, enjoying the views and a remarkable sense of isolation, you soon reach a junction with Pine Mountain Road, right. If you are going to climb Pine Mountain, named for a bishop-pine grove on its south side, turn right and follow the route description on pages 93–94. If not, continue straight on a rocky course, passing stands of cypress, manzanita, and chaparral pea, and clumps of spiny redberry. Pine Mountain (1762') is the summit to your right. When you reach a low point the vegetation changes, bringing back more familiar trees such as bay and coast live oak, and shrubs such as chamise, toyon, creambush, and yerba santa. Bolinas Ridge, a dark, forested rampart that extends northwest from Mt. Tamalpais to Tomales Bay, rises high on your right.

Now winning back some elevation, you pass Oat Hill Road, signed OATHILL, on the right. The grade soon eases, bringing you to a level spot where you can stop, rest, and enjoy the views. Between Pine Mountain and an unnamed hill to its northeast is The Saddle, a windy gap with no barriers between it and the Pacific Ocean. To the east, the green oasis of the Meadow Club's golf links is clearly visible, especially when the surrounding hills wear a coat of brown. Your route here runs through a corridor of madrone and chinquapin. On a moderate descent over loose, rocky ground, you can see ahead Azalea Hill, a bare hump due east of the parking area on Fairfax–Bolinas Road. Also visible is a finger of Alpine

Lake, at the mouth of Liberty Gulch, right. Rising behind the gulch is a ridge, heavily cloaked in trees and chaparral, topped by Liberty Peak and Dutchman's Rock.

The route, now on a rolling course, follows the top of a broad ridge, with grassy fields on either side. A few pines are present, but most of the vegetation—manzanita and an unusual shrubby oak called leather oak— is low and sprawling. With Fairfax–Bolinas Road in view downhill and left, the route meanders a bit, then makes a sweeping left-hand bend, and in about 150 feet reaches a metal gate. After stepping around the gate, you carefully cross Fairfax–Bolinas Road, turn right, and walk to the parking area.

Bikers heading southeast on Pine Mountain Road, with Mt. Tam on the skyline.

| 8 | Marin County Open Space District
RING MOUNTAIN |

Length: 3.25 miles

Time: 2 to 3 hours

Rating: Moderate

Regulations: MCOSD; no bikes, dogs on leash.

Highlights: Ring Mountain Open Space Preserve, surrounded by residential development near busy Corte Madera, perfectly
demonstrates the value of land conservation and protection. Its slopes are home to a wonderful array of trees,
shrubs, and wildflowers, some quite rare, and one, the
Tiburon Mariposa lily, found nowhere else in the world.
As a vantage point with great views, Ring Mountain's
summit rivals better-known Bay Area peaks. This route
uses the Loop and Phyllis Ellman trails, along with the
Taylor Ridge Fire Road, to explore the mountain's slopes
and summit.

Bold face numbers in the route description below refer to
numbered markers along the trail, which are keyed to
"Ring Mountain Self Guided Nature Trail," a brochure put
out by MCOSD in two editions, Spring and Fall.
Unfortunately, neither edition contains a map, and the
MCOSD Southern Preserves map is all but useless for
route-finding. Marker 1 is either missing or well hidden.

Directions: From Hwy. 101 in Corte Madera, take the Paradise
Dr./Tamalpais Dr. exit and go east on Tamalpais Dr., staying in the right lane, which becomes San Clemente Dr.
After 0.1 mile, San Clemente Dr. bends right; follow it and
go another 0.5 mile to a stop light at Paradise Dr. Turn left
onto Paradise Dr., go 0.9 mile, and park in a turn-out on
the right, near a gated dirt road.

Facilities: None

Trailhead: South side of Paradise Dr., at a gated dirt road.

From the trailhead, you head south on a dirt trail, with a seasonal creek
in a gully to your right. After about 100 feet, where a faint trail continues
straight, you turn right and cross a wooden bridge over the creek. This is
a weedy and overgrown area, full of sedges, teasel, fennel, and pennyroyal. About 50 feet from the bridge, as you are beginning to climb, you

pass an information board, left. The Ring Mountain Open Space Preserve honors two conservation activists. It was established by The Nature Conservancy in 1984 and dedicated to Patricia Bucko-Stormer by her friends and co-workers at the Conservancy. One of the main trails through the preserve is named for Phyllis Ellman, the organizer of a citizen's group that blocked a plan to put more than 1,000 homes atop Ring Mountain. Even so, development was allowed on the lower part of the mountain, and new homes are being built surprisingly close to the summit.

Continuing gently uphill on the Phyllis Ellman Trail, you pass familiar shrubs such as coyote brush, toyon, and poison oak, and tangles of blackberry vines. The low-lying area to your left is a seasonal freshwater marsh that captures water rushing down the mountain's north side during winter storms. Shortly after a leftward bend, the trail reaches a junction. Here your route, the Loop Trail goes straight, and the Phyllis Ellman Trail, which you will use on the descent, veers right. About 75 feet past the junction is marker **2** on the right. Because of soil differences, the moun-

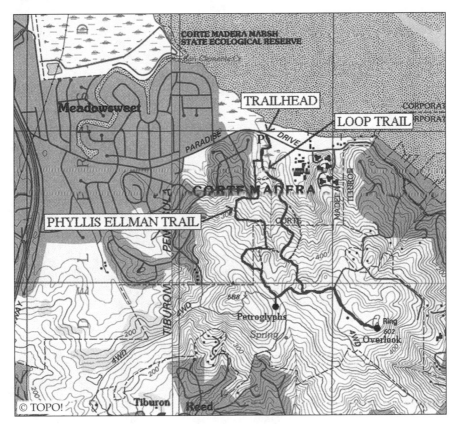

8. Ring Mountain

tain's upper and lower reaches host different types of vegetation. The lower reaches contain sandstone soil, perfect for a wide variety of plants, including wildflowers such as Ithuriel's spear, blue-eyed grass, false lupine, suncup, wild iris, and miniature lupine. The upper reaches contain serpentine soil, toxic to most plant species, but tolerated by a few, including the preserve's rarities.

A line of California bay and coast live oak, left, borders a seasonal stream that flows through a ravine and into the marsh, saturating it with water during the rainy season. Just before you reach the ravine, you pass a trail going right and steeply uphill. Your trail dips down to cross the ravine, and once across, turns sharply left, reaching in about 50 feet marker **3**, right. The large boulders seen from here are schists, composed of 12 to 15 different types of minerals—a relatively large number. (In comparison, Sierra granite contains only three to five different minerals.) The mineral composition of these schists differs from boulder to boulder on the mountain, making them of interest to geologists. The colored blotches on the boulders are lichens, composite plants containing both a fungus and an alga. The two work together: the fungus provides the structure and the alga carries on photosynthesis.

As you gain elevation on a moderate grade, be sure to stop often and admire the wonderful view north, which takes in Corte Madera, Larkspur, the Richmond–San Rafael Bridge, and San Pablo Bay. Out in the open, near a patch of bull thistle, you reach marker **4**. Plants, being fixed in one place, use a variety of strategies to disperse their seeds. For

View south from near Ring Mountain's summit takes in San Francisco, Alcatraz, and San Francisco Bay.

example, birds eat berries and then deposit the seeds after digestion. Other animals that depend on seeds for food often drop some during transport. The wind spreads the seeds of many plants, and bull thistle, with seeds attached to lightweight, fluffy hairs, is one of them. Just beyond marker **4**, at an unsigned junction, the trail forks. Here you stay right and climb over rocky ground, following the trail as it winds back and forth, and then makes a rising traverse across a hillside falling away right.

Nearing the seasonal creek, the route is now shaded by fragrant bay and coast live oak. At marker **5**, take a moment to study a leaf of a coast live oak—dark green, turned under at its edges, and spiny. To survive, plants must develop defenses against being eaten by insects, birds, and other animals. These defenses may involve toxic chemical agents, like tannins, and physical barriers, like spines. Oaks are well defended, but their seeds, acorns, are eagerly consumed by mammals and birds. At the T-junction just ahead, you turn left, and continue climbing, perhaps with turkey vultures circling overhead. The view north from here takes in the Corte Madera marshlands, one of the last remaining salt marshes close to San Francisco, and a great birding area. Also on display, to the northeast, is San Pablo Strait, the narrow water lane between Point San Pedro and Point San Pablo that joins San Francisco and San Pablo bays. To the west, Mt. Tamalpais is just visible above the intervening hills.

Soon you reach a junction, where the trail that forked left just beyond marker **4** rejoins your route. Ahead on the right is marker **6**, which refers to birds found in the preserve, including raptors and songbirds, and also to the large rock formation, described as "a gigantic Indian warrior" standing guard on the hill to your left. Your route now makes a gentle climb across an open hillside, heading for an obvious watercourse. The description for marker **7** explains the source of Ring Mountain's creeks and wet areas—rainwater that cannot penetrate deeply into the rocky soil on the mountain's upper reaches, and instead emerges as seeps and springs. Growing here are moisture-loving plants such as giant chain fern, rushes, and wax myrtle, a shrub related to New England's bayberry. Turning left, you cross a wet area via two plank bridges, and then climb a set of wooden steps that take you out of the watercourse.

As you work your way uphill on a moderate grade, you pass a large rock boulder and then a path beaten down in the grass, both left. At an unsigned T-junction you turn right, soon reaching a fork, where you bear left and continue climbing. About 100 feet past the fork is marker **8**. The grove of coast live oak, right, which you can visit on a short path, contains several huge trees, their trunks and limbs twisted and gnarled. Oaks may seem invincible, but practices such as land clearing, firewood cutting, and over-grazing are threatening California's oak woodlands. Restoration projects, combined with public awareness, may help reverse this trend.

Continuing straight on the main trail, you pass a four-way junction and then reach a junction marked by a blank trail post. Here a trail continues straight, but you turn right, into a grotto of bay trees strewn with rock boulders, where marker **9** awaits. This grotto is called a tree island, and like a real island it stands in marked contrast to its surroundings—a shady shelter for birds, small mammals, and insects in the midst of windswept, sun-baked fields. Within the grotto, the trail becomes indistinct, but keeping marker **9** on your left, you go about 30 feet past it, turn left, and continue uphill.

Leaving the grotto behind, you merge with the trail that went straight at the blank trail post. About 75 feet ahead, you pass a trail on the right, and your route bends left. To the west is a fine view of Mt. Tamalpais, with a foreground of open, boulder-strewn fields that dominate the upper reaches of Ring Mountain. On a windy day, exposed areas of the mountain, lacking vegetation and other forms of protection, get blasted. Soon you reach a fork marked by a trail post, one of the few on this route inscribed with useful information—an arrow pointing left. Turning left, you pass marker **10**, left, and continue winding your way uphill toward a grove of bay and coast live oak. According to the MCOSD brochure, spring wildflowers here include lupine, larkspur, and California poppy. When you reach the grove, another helpful arrow directs you to the right. As you emerge from the grove, a fabulous scene greets you—the San Francisco skyline, the Marin Headlands, Sausalito, Richardson Bay, and the towers of the Golden Gate Bridge. And as you walk downhill, passing marker **11**, right, the view improves, as Alcatraz and the Bay Bridge come into view. The description for marker **11** lists some of the drawbacks related to development, including habitat loss and extinction of species, and notes the abundance here of native grasses, often overwhelmed by non-native species in disturbed areas.

About 75 feet past marker **11**, you reach a four-way junction at the Taylor Ridge Fire Road, just past the 1-mile point. Ahead is a short path leading to a boulder sometimes used by rock climbers for practice. Turning left onto the fire road, you begin to gain elevation as you near the mountain's summit, a high point to the southeast. In the distance rise the East Bay hills and Mt. Diablo. Now the route levels, and you can see an outpost of residential development, downhill and left. At a **T**-junction with a paved road, you turn right, following it for about 150 yards and then bearing left onto a dirt-and-gravel road interrupted by stretches of broken pavement.

In the open fields near the summit, you may spot a western meadowlark or possibly a horned lark. Although unrelated, these two species share a preference for open terrain and some of the same field marks—black bib under the throat, white on the sides of the tail. The meadowlark, the larger of the two, usually travels in large flocks, and has a rich yellow breast. Horned larks are often seen singly or in pairs, and have distinctive black head feathers in the shape of two little horns. The summit of Ring Mountain (602') is located in a grove of trees just left of the road, which dead-ends in a broad, gravelly area. From here, a path heads south to a viewpoint. In addition to the fine views of San Francisco and Marin, a number of East Bay landmarks are visible, including UC Berkeley, the Richmond waterfront, Miller-Knox Regional Park, and the Port of Oakland. When you have had your fill of the scenery, retrace your steps to the junction of the Loop Trail and the Taylor Ridge Fire Road.

Continuing west on the fire road, you drop steeply over rough ground and then reach a junction where a road branches left. Here you go straight, and in about 75 feet come to a four-way junction marked by a trail post missing its number—it should be marker **12**. From this junction, the Phyllis Ellman Trail, your return route, goes right, and a trail to a rock inscribed with petroglyphs heads left. Before descending the Phyllis Ellman Trail, face south and look uphill and left: you should see a rock on a hillside, Turtle Rock, that looks like it had a turtle crawling up it. And if you want to examine the ancient petroglyphs—their exact age is unknown, but they resemble ones in the Sierra that are two to three thousand years old—head straight for about 100 feet and then veer right on a path to the rock. The deep semicircular carvings resemble deer prints, although their meaning to the Coast Miwok people who made them centuries ago is unknown.

Back at the four-way junction, you start down the Phyllis Ellman Trail, a single track heading northwest. In about 100 yards, you come to marker **13**, right, indicating the tree island ahead and right. Trees can grow on this site because the rock is fractured, allowing roots to penetrate until they find water. About 100 feet ahead, at a trail post, you turn onto a trail branching left, uphill. The trail gains a little elevation and then levels, taking you across a rocky hillside in the heart of the serpentine belt. In early fall, the air here may be fragrant with the smell of tarweed, a low-growing yellow flower. Now descending, you pick your way over rocky ground, passing a sign that says TRAIL on its downhill side, apparently for those walking the trail in reverse. A few paces beyond, on the left, is marker **14**, indicating rare plants, such as Marin dwarf flax, Tiburon paintbrush, serpentine reedgrass, and the Tiburon Mariposa lily, a late-May bloomer that grows nowhere else in the world.

Level for a while, the trail curves right, passes a grove of coast live oak, and then drops on a moderate grade. A line of vegetation, mostly wax myrtle, marks a watercourse on your right. At a junction where a trail merges from the right, you bear left and continue downhill. In about 100 yards, at the next junction, a sign with an arrow prompts you to turn right. Marker **15**, right, refers to soap plant, identified by its long, wavy leaves. The bulb of this widespread plant had several uses for Native Americans: it yields a cleansing substance when crushed; it contains toxins that stun fish; and, when detoxified by cooking, it can be eaten. Soap plant, which blooms from May through July, carries its flowers aloft on tall stalks, but these don't open until shade falls in the late afternoon.

Before you reach the next line of vegetation, marking the seasonal creek that flows into the marsh, you turn sharply left at a junction, where a path goes straight to the creek bed. After a leftward bend, the trail reaches a four-way junction just shy of a tree-lined ravine. Here you make a hard right and then work your way downhill on a moderate grade, aided in places by steps. The description for marker **16**, right, tells how plants use chemical inhibitors to prevent premature sprouting: only when enough rain falls will the inhibitors leach out, thereby allowing the seed to sprout at the right time. Nearing the seasonal creek again, your route bends left, winding downhill over rocky ground and passing a trail, right. A big thicket of blackberry vines, left, may be a good place to search for songbirds. Now swinging right, you reach a **T**-junction where the Loop Trail heads right. From here, about the 3-mile point, retrace your steps to the parking area.

Vistas from atop Ring Mountain are among the best in the North Bay

Marin County Open Space District
ROY'S REDWOODS

Length: 2 miles

Time: 1 to 2 hours

Rating: Easy

Regulations: MCOSD; no smoking, no bikes, dogs on leash.

Highlights: Although tiny, this open-space preserve, named for its 19th century owners, has a remarkable array of trees and shrubs, including old-growth coast redwoods. According to the MCOSD Western Preserves map, the previous owners of the property, which surrounds Nicasio Hill, just north of Sir Francis Drake Blvd., included Napoleon Bonaparte's nephew and Paul Revere's grandson.

Directions: See the directions for "Barnabe Mountain" on pages 151–153. At 10.7 miles from Hwy. 101, turn right onto Nicasio Valley Rd., go 0.5 mile, and park in one of the turn-outs on either side of the road.

Facilities: Toilets

Trailhead: On the southeast side of the road, where the turn-out narrows at its uphill end.

From the trailhead, you follow a path leading downhill to a gated dirt road. After walking around the gate, you pass a trail, right, leading to the toilets. The dirt road heads straight, past tangles of blackberry vines and poison oak, into the realm of the coast redwoods. The large meadow ahead is closed to horses—they must instead use the Roy's Redwoods Loop Trail, a track that branches toward a line of trees, left. Hikers should follow a wide path straight into the meadow, aiming for a cluster of tall redwoods on the meadow's far side. Just before reaching the trees, the path bends right, and soon you are in a shady grove, surrounded by giants. Where redwoods grow, other plants have a hard time competing. In this grove you will also find a few California bay trees and snowberry bushes. Continuing straight, the now-indistinct path dips briefly to cross a watercourse, and then begins to gain elevation on a gentle grade, soon emerging from the redwood grove.

Now on an open, grassy hillside, a moderate climb brings you to a junction with Roy's Redwoods Loop Trail, where you turn right and continue climbing. Stands of California buckeye, coast live oak, and bay offer temporary shade, but this part of the route is mostly open. After passing a trail that drops steeply right, your route bends left and soon finds an

almost level course. Just beyond a large grove of bay trees, fragrant on a
warm day, the trail swings right and begins a gentle ascent. At about the
0.5-mile point, you reach a four-way junction. Here a rough track climbs
uphill to a viewpoint, left, and your route, the Nature Trail turns right,
leaving Roy's Redwoods Loop Trail. The Nature Trail, closed to bikes and
horses, leads you through a weedy, overgrown patch and into dense forest. In this wild, jungle-like area, choked with berry vines and poison oak,
you will find redwood, Douglas fir, bay, hazelnut, western sword fern,
and wild rose.

Uphill and left is your goal, the top of Nicasio Hill (789'). Your climb is
aided by a few switchbacks, and soon you pass a trail, right, the end of
the loop you will follow clockwise around and over Nicasio Hill. Nearing
the summit, where more light filters through the forest canopy, the scene
brightens, and soon you come upon a fine stand of madrone, their green
leaves contrasting with their peeling orange bark. At the southeast edge
of the hill, the trail veers sharply right and continues to climb. When there
is no more high ground left to conquer, you have reached the summit,
surrounded by a wonderful little wilderness, but still within earshot of

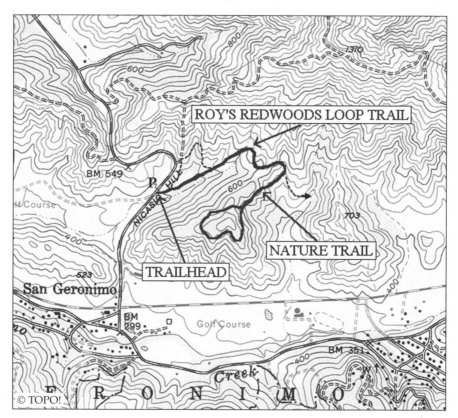

9. Roy's Redwoods

busy Sir Francis Drake Blvd. Now descending, the route continues its clockwise loop, dropping into the redwoods on the hill's northwest side. After a few sharp switchbacks, you reach a T-junction at about the 1-mile point, marking the end of the loop. From here, turn left and retrace your steps to the parking area.

10 Marin County Open Space District
RUSH CREEK

Length: 3.7 miles

Time: 2 to 3 hours

Rating: Easy

Regulations: MCOSD; dogs on leash, bikes only on fire roads.

Highlights: This semi-loop, using the Pinheiro Ridge and Rush Creek fire roads, and an unnamed trail, explores the Rush Creek Open Space Preserve, a fine example of coastal salt marsh and valley-and-foothill woodland adjacent to the Petaluma Marsh Wildlife Area. A pair of binoculars or a spotting scope will enhance your enjoyment of the many shorebirds, waders, and waterbirds found in the marsh. A visit here can easily be combined with a hike in the Deer Island Open Space Preserve, a few miles south, described on pages 56–58.

Directions: From Hwy. 101 in Novato, take the Atherton Ave./San Marin Dr. exit and go east 0.1 mile on Atherton Ave. Turn left onto Binford Rd. and go 0.1 mile to a turn-out on the right side of the road; park here.

Facilities: None

Trailhead: North end of the parking area.

From the north end of the parking area, you walk around the side of a wooden gate, pass a single-track trail veering right and uphill, and head northeast on a paved road which soon turns to dirt. On the MCOSD Northern Preserves map, this is called the Pinheiro Ridge Fire Road, although the route here is level and beside a marsh. Rush Creek, left, bordered by cattails, runs northeast through the marsh on its way to join Black John Slough just south of Gnoss Field, the Marin County airport. Above the din of traffic on nearby Hwy. 101, you begin to hear the sounds of birds—the "tu-tu-tu" of a greater yellowlegs in the marsh, the bright chatter of kinglets gathered on a shrub, or the clear whistle of a varied thrush hidden in a grove of trees. A hillside rises to the right of the trail, and on its slopes grow valley oak, California buckeye, madrone, California bay, and black oak. In spring, the right-hand embankment is carpeted with a luscious display of purple-and-white Chinesehouses.

Across the marsh to the northwest rises Burdell Mountain, a 1558-foot-high peak that dominates the landscape in this corner of Marin County. An expanse of shallow water, left, may hold ducks, shorebirds, herons, and egrets. Roadside plants here include coyote brush, toyon, snowberry, honeysuckle, and poison oak. Emerging from the shade, the road comes into an open area overgrown with star thistle, pennyroyal, and tarweed. When it is flooded by the tide, a low-lying area, left, provides perfect habitat for shorebirds, a tribe that includes oystercatchers, avocets, stilts, plovers, willets, curlews, godwits, small sandpipers, dowitchers, and phalaropes. Fall, winter, and spring are the best times of year to see shorebirds here: except for a few species, most breed outside the Bay Area. Among the common species seen around the Bay are American

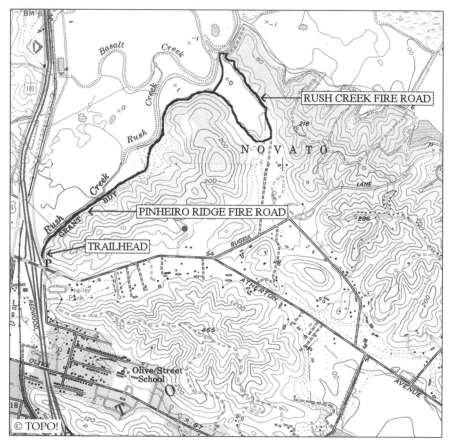

10. Rush Creek

avocet, black-necked stilt, killdeer, willet, long-billed curlew, marbled godwit, greater and lesser yellowlegs, western and least sandpipers, and short- and long-billed dowitchers.

Many casual birders fear they will never be able to sort out the various species of shorebirds. The marsh adjacent to Rush Creek is a particularly good place to study members of this tribe, because the birds are relatively close and accustomed to people. Also, without the presence of large flocks, which are found mostly on tidal mudflats, it is possible to concentrate on individuals of separate species and examine the differences between them. One of trickier identification problems is to distinguish between the two species of yellowlegs—greater and lesser. Both are large, upright sandpipers with long, black bills, and, as their name implies, bright yellow legs—the only common Bay-Area shorebirds so adorned. Greater yellowlegs is larger and stouter than its cousin. It has a longer, thicker bill, which may appear slightly upturned and two-toned—black overall but fading to dark gray near the bird's head. Seen beside the greater yellowlegs, a lesser yellowlegs appears dainty and delicate, with an all-black, needle-like bill and long, slender legs.

After you've had your fill of shorebirds, follow the road as it curves left, past open, gently sloping fields on the right. Flocks of goldfinches often stop to feed here on the seeds of thistle and canary grass. A belted kingfisher, giving its rattling call, may break from a perch in the trees to hunt over open water. Besides ducks and geese, the deeper water of the marshlands attracts American white pelicans, cousins of the brown pelicans that visit our coast during the summer. Unlike brown pelicans,

View from Pinheiro Ridge Fire Road takes in the marshes along Rush Creek and Burdell Mountain.

which are often seen cruising low over the surf or making spectacular dives for fish, white pelicans are an inland species, content to float lazily on still water, scooping up food with their bills. In a shady grove of coast live oak and bay, the road, here rocky and eroded, climbs gently, levels, and then descends, passing a trail taking off left and downhill, which you will use later on your return.

Swinging right, the road now parallels a brackish marsh extending south from the main marsh. Here grow some of the common salt-marsh plants, including spike grass, pickleweed, and orache, the latter two turning red in the fall. Here too are cattails, a freshwater species, indicating a lack of tidal influence in this part of the marsh. Plant distribution in a salt marsh is determined by the salinity of the water—plants that can tolerate high levels of salt, such as cord grass, grow at the lowest elevation and closest to the source of salt water. Freshwater creeks and streams draining into a marsh also affect its salinity and hence its plants.

Soon the road deteriorates to a rough track, which bends sharply left. At this bend the Pinheiro Fire Road continues right, but you follow the rough track as it crossess a wet and muddy area. After about 75 feet you reach a T-junction with the Rush Creek Fire Road. Right is a locked gate, but your route turns left. Now you are heading north on the east side of the brackish marsh, having made an almost 180-degree course change. The grassy hillsides, right, hold beautiful valley oaks, their trunks and limbs twisted with age. As you stride on level ground beside the marsh, you may put up flocks of ducks or startle a lone great blue heron. Just

Spring-blooming Chinesehouses lure photographer.

Shorebirds are often seen in the marshes along Rush Creek.

past the 2-mile point, you pass a single-track trail taking off right and steeply uphill. Then, in about 50 feet, you come to a fork, where you stay left. Just ahead, the route bends right and brings you to a junction, where you turn left onto a dirt road.

After 25 feet or so, you make another left-hand turn, this one taking you into the marsh on a narrow, raised trail. Your passing may be noticed by a marsh wren, a tiny brown bird well hidden in the marsh vegetation—if so, you won't escape its noisy scolding. From this vantage point, you may get to compare the Bay Area's two common egrets—great and snowy. As its name implies, the great egret is a large bird, one of our largest waders, smaller only than a great blue heron. It has a thick yellow bill and long black legs. The snowy egret, about the size of a large gull, has a slim black bill and black legs with golden feet. After taking a last look at the birds and plants of the marsh, continue on the trail, which takes you across the open end of the brackish marsh you circled earlier. Upon reaching the other side, the trail climbs steeply in the shade of bay trees to rejoin the Pinheiro Ridge Fire Road. Here you turn right and retrace your steps to the parking area.

11

Marin County Open Space District
SANTA MARGARITA ISLAND

Length: 0.5 mile

Time: Less than one hour

Rating: Easy

Regulations: MCOSD; no bikes, dogs on leash.

Highlights: This easy hike, using the Island Loop Trail and an unnamed trail, explores the shoreline of Santa Margarita Island and its forested uplands. This tiny gem, in a residential area on the outskirts of San Rafael, is a perfect example of why open space needs to be preserved. A visit to the Santa Margarita Open Space Preserve can easily be combined with a longer outing to China Camp State Park.

Directions: See the directions for "Bay View Loop" on pages 35 and 37. Once on N. San Pedro Rd., go 1.2 miles to Meadow Dr. and turn left. After 0.3 mile the road dead-ends at a gate; make a U-turn here and park on the right-hand road shoulder.

Facilities: None

Trailhead: At the gated end of Meadow Dr.

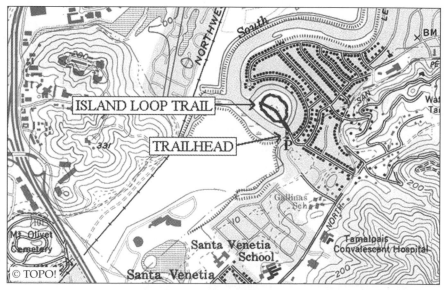

11. Santa Margarita Island

From the trailhead, you walk around the gate and cross a concrete bridge over the south fork of Las Gallinas Creek, which empties into San Pablo Bay. Santa Margarita Island, like so much of the surrounding land, might have been developed were it not for the protective mantle of the Marin County Open Space District. So instead of more suburban homes, we have a nine-acre preserve surrounded by coastal salt marsh, home to the endangered California clapper rail. The creek here is lined with homes, most with a dock and a boat. Planted palm trees give the residential areas an exotic touch, but on the island grow more representative species—valley oak, coast live oak, black oak, and California bay.

Once across the bridge you are on a dirt trail that soon splits to circle the island. Turning right, you pass a large jumble of rocks on the hillside rising left, and a number of paths leading to the water's edge, right. To look for clapper rail, plan your visit here for a higher-than-normal tide, when the bird's hiding places are flooded. Reluctant to fly, clapper rails are most often seen skulking in the marsh or swimming furtively across short stretches of open water. The rail's call, given usually at dusk and dawn, is a series of "kek-kek-kek" notes, almost like the barking of a small dog. Some of the common salt-marsh plants that make up the rail's habitat, including salt grass and Pacific gum plant, may be found here.

Continuing your counter-clockwise circuit, you soon arrive at the trail's northernmost point, where a path, right, leads to the very tip of the island. A wonderful view of Mt. Tamalpais, soaring above crowded San Rafael, greets you here. Your trail bends left and almost immediately

South Fork Gallinas Creek flows past tiny Santa Margarita Island.

reaches a junction. From here a rough track leads uphill and inland to the island's forested hilltop. The ascent is optional; you can complete the loop by simply following the main trail. But to explore further, turn left and begin climbing. After a steep, 100-yard ascent, you reach a flat open space studded with rock boulders. From here the trail bends right and continues across the hilltop, then descends gently to the south. Passing another rocky area and the fire-scarred trunk of a coast live oak, the route veers right and makes a steep plunge to a junction with the Island Loop Trail. Here you turn left, and in a few feet meet the trail's start. Now turn right and retrace your steps to the parking area.

Marin Headlands
GERBODE VALLEY

Length:	5.4 miles
Time:	3 to 4 hours
Rating:	Moderate
Regulations:	GGNRA; dogs allowed only on the Miwok Trail, and only to its junction with the Wolf Ridge Trail.
Highlights:	This scenic loop uses the Miwok and Bobcat trails to circle Gerbode Valley, an area slated in the 1960s for urban development but later protected as part of the Golden Gate National Recreation Area (GGNRA). The hills surrounding Gerbode Valley, part of the Marin Headlands, are vibrant in the spring with wildflowers, and alive with birdsong and avian acrobatics most of the year, but especially during the fall raptor migration. Views of San Francisco, Marin, and the Pacific Coast from the high points along this loop are superb.
Directions:	From Hwy. 101 northbound, just north of the Golden Gate Bridge, take the Alexander Ave. exit, go north 0.2 mile, and turn left onto Bunker Rd. After 0.1 mile you reach a one-direction-only tunnel where traffic is controlled by a stop light. After emerging from the 0.5-mile tunnel, go a total of 2.5 miles from Alexander Ave. Just past a horse stable, left, there is a parking turn-out on the right shoulder of Bunker Rd. Use caution when exiting your car. Additional parking is available at the Marin Headlands visitor center (see below), or in large gravel parking areas on the right side of Bunker Rd., at 2.8 and 2.9 miles from Alexander Ave.

From Hwy. 101 southbound, just south of the Waldo Tunnel, take the Sausalito Exit, which is also signed for the GGNRA. Bear right (despite the left-pointing GGNRA sign) and go 0.25 mile to Bunker Rd. Turn left, and follow the directions above.

Facilities: None at the parking area. The Marin Headlands visitor center—which has interpretive displays, books and maps for sale, helpful rangers, rest rooms, and water—is on Field Rd., which you can reach by going 0.2 mile past the first parking area on Bunker Rd. Turn left onto Field Rd. and go 0.1 to the visitor center.

Trailhead: On the north side of the parking area, at its mid-point.

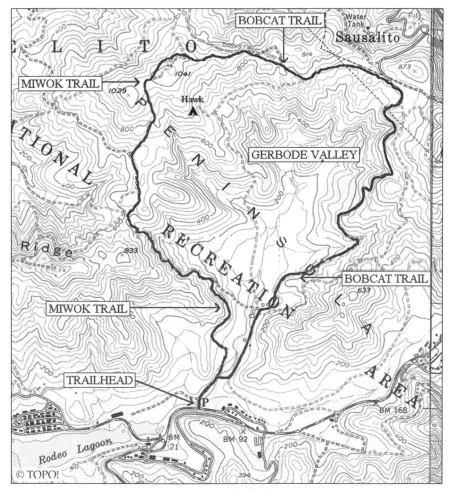

12. Gerbode Valley

You begin this scenic loop by walking north on a dirt-and-gravel path that is flanked by willows and tangles of blackberry vines. After about 100 feet, you reach a wood-plank bridge that crosses a creek. In another 75 feet or so you come to a T-junction with a dirt road. Just before the intersection is a trail post, left, telling you the trail ahead is open to hikers, equestrians, and bicyclists. There is also an information board, right, with a map and a description of how the fight to save Gerbode Valley, which you will circle on today's hike, helped inspire the legislation that in 1972 established the GGNRA.

Like its cousin to the north, Point Reyes National Seashore, the Marin Headlands was once the province of dairy ranches, supplying milk from the 1860s to the 1960s to an ever-growing San Francisco. One of the oldest of these dairies—run, as most were, by a Portuguese family—occupied the valley just north of here, sheltered from the Pacific's windy onslaughts by the barrier of Wolf Ridge to the west. In the mid-1960s, plans were afoot to create a self-contained city, called Marincello, complete with housing, high-rise buildings, shopping centers, and a hotel, in the valley and on the adjacent hills. Through the efforts of concerned citizens and The Nature Conservancy, the Marin Headlands escaped the fate that befell many other agricultural lands in the Bay Area and remained free from development. Plans for Marincello were cancelled, and the Headlands became part of the newly created GGNRA. The valley was named for Martha Gerbode, a San Francisco conservation activist who gave The Nature Conservancy the money to hold the land in trust until it was bought by the National Park Service.

At the T-junction you turn right onto the dirt-and-gravel road, the Miwok Trail. Bicyclists may use the Miwok and Bobcat trails to connect with the Bay Area Ridge Trail, which is farther east. On your left is a weedy area, with the hills of the Marin Headlands, dotted here and there with only a few clumps of shrubs and low trees, in the background. On your right is a low-lying marsh, formed by the creek that drains Gerbode Valley and empties into Rodeo Lagoon. The route here is level, bordered by wild radish, mustard, poison hemlock, coyote brush, and willows. After about 0.2 mile, you reach a junction. Here the Bobcat Trail goes right, and your route, the Miwok Trail, continues straight. Two kinds of non-native thistle are abundant along this stretch: Italian thistle, with small purple flowers, and milk thistle, with larger, bulbous flower heads and leaves that are veined with white. Two other weedy plants that resemble each other are abundant here—cow parsnip and poison hemlock. Cow parsnip has large, rounded heads of white flowers and broad, flat leaves. Poison hemlock has smaller clusters of white flowers, lacy leaves, and stalks with purple spots. Yarrow, which also has white flowers, is a much smaller, low-growing plant.

This is also a good place to look for red-winged blackbirds, which nest in marshy areas. These are very vocal birds, and fiercely protective of their nesting territory. Turkey vultures may be seen circling overhead, and in the fall the Marin Headlands is one of the best places on the West Coast to observe hawks and falcons in migration. These southward-bound raptors take advantage of rising air currents, called thermals, to gain elevation for their crossing of the Golden Gate.

Soon the Miwok Trail begins a relentless and unshaded climb toward the east end of Wolf Ridge. The hillside, right, falls steeply to Gerbode Valley. On the other side of the valley, you can see the Bobcat Trail, your return route. Today's loop takes you into some of the best wildflower terrain in the North Bay. Nearly 50 species are listed in the pamphlet "Frequently Seen Wildflowers of the Marin Headlands," available at the visitor center. In spring, especially after a wet winter, the hills are decorated with a dazzling display of California poppies, mule ears, paintbrush, Ithuriel's spear, yarrow, blow wives, and blue-eyed grass. Shrubs include bush monkeyflower, silver lupine, coffeeberry, and California sagebrush.

In only a few places does the grade ease from moderate to gentle, as the road bends back and forth to follow the shape of the hills. Accompanied perhaps by the melodious calls of mourning doves, wrentits, and song sparrows, you reach, at about the 1.25-mile point, a notch at the east end of Wolf Ridge. From this vantage point, you can look northwest to Mt. Tamalpais, and west, over a declivity in a neighboring ridge, to the Pacific Ocean. A few paces ahead is a junction with the Wolf Ridge Trail, left. This trail is for hikers only, and dogs must be leashed.

View north from the Marin Headlands near the junction of the Miwok and Bobcat trails.

Your route, the Miwok Trail, which from here on is closed to dogs, continues straight and uphill.

As you gain elevation, you begin to get views to the southeast, through notches in the Marin Headlands, of familiar San Francisco landmarks such as the Transamerica Building, Sutro Tower, Golden Gate Park, and, in the distance, San Bruno Mountain, topped with communication towers. These are tantalizing snippets of an ever-changing scene, rewarding your efforts so far. To the northwest, the three peaks of Mt. Tamalpais are visible, with the lookout tower on the east peak, the highest of the mountain's summits, just visible. Now the route descends on a gentle grade, giving you a chance to catch a glimpse of some of the trails that wind through the Tennessee Valley area immediately to the northwest.

After enjoying a brief respite from the climbing, you reach a four-way junction. From here, a single-track trail, not shown on the map, takes off uphill through the brush. Heading left and crossing a wooden bridge is the Old Springs Trail, open to hikers, horses, and bikes. Your route, the Miwok Trail, from here on closed to bikes, continues straight and begins to climb over severely eroded ground that alternates between moderate and steep. Beside the road grow yellow-flowering Bermuda buttercups, an alien that is actually from southern Africa. Its native cousin, redwood sorrel, sports white flowers and thrives in dense coastal forests.

As you make the arduous ascent, take time to admire the terrific views to the south: the surf-washed beach along San Francisco's Great Highway, and, rising above the often fog-cloaked coast, the highlands of the San Mateo coast. At one point, the north tower of the Golden Gate Bridge is just visible through a notch in the Headlands. In addition to the ever-present turkey vultures, you may see another large black bird, the common raven. These relatives of jays, crows, and magpies are able to make an astounding variety of sounds. And while Poe's "Nevermore" may not truly be part of their vocabulary, other weirdly human sounds certainly are. Ravens are also great aerial acrobats, and seem to enjoy chasing each other in frenzied pursuit.

As the route bends left, a new vista appears: Mt. Diablo, the Berkeley Hills, and the Bay Bridge, all seen through low points in the hills to the east. Your route is still a steep rocky track heading north. Look for purple owl's-clover, a paintbrush relative, beside the road here. Just past the 2-mile point, with Mt. Tamalpais and the north end of San Pablo Bay in view, you pass a faint trail through the grass to a viewpoint, left. You route bends right, and in a few hundred feet reaches a junction with a single-track trail, right, that climbs to a vantage point beside a fenced-in communication facility, used by the FAA to direct commercial aircraft. This facility appears on the Olmsted map as VORTAC, short for Very High Frequency Omni Range and Tactical Air Navigation Aid. Just left of this junction are a few large rocks, a convenient place to sit and rest.

If you stop here for a moment, you will enjoy 360-degree views that take in San Francisco, the Pacific coastline, Tennessee Valley, Mt. Tamalpais, Richardson Bay, and the Richmond–San Rafael Bridge. This is truly one of the great scenic spots in the Bay Area, and, if you are lucky, a bounding deer will complete the picture. After enjoying the scenery, you continue uphill on a gentle grade, following the road as it crests a rise, and then begin a moderate descent. The high point on the ridge dividing Tennessee and Gerbode valleys, a 1041-foot summit and home of VORTAC, is uphill and right. Your route levels and then makes a rising traverse across its north and east sides.

Just past the 2-mile point, you come to a four-way junction. Here, one dirt road crosses your route at right angles, and another takes off uphill and right, to the communication facility. At this junction, you turn left and begin walking downhill on a gentle grade. In about 50 feet, you come to another junction, with a road that joins from the left. There is a sign here, partially obliterated, that reads MIWOK TRAIL NORTH, which is open to hikers and horses but closed to bikes. On the Olmsted map this road is shown as a short stub heading north, and on the hand-out map from the visitor center, it is labeled as the Miwok Trail. Regardless of its true identity, you just continue downhill through an unattractive area that resembles a gravel pit.

Soon you reach a trail post signed for the Bobcat Trail, and about 30 feet farther, a junction, left, with the Marincello Trail, part of the Bay Area Ridge Trail. This trail is open to hikers, horses, and bikes. Here you may also spot your first tree since leaving Gerbode Valley, a coast live oak. Continuing straight on the Bobcat Trail, a dirt road that descends and then levels, you may be buffeted in this stretch by wind blowing unimpeded from the Pacific Ocean. Keep a sharp eye peeled for blacktail jackrabbits, distinguished from the more common brush rabbit by their large ears. After passing a steep dirt road that joins from the left, and an eroded dirt road, right, you come to a junction with the road to Hawk Camp, also right, one of the three walk-in campgrounds in the Headlands. Hawk Camp is the most primitive, with three sites that can each hold up to four people. There are picnic tables and a toilet, but no water. No fires are allowed, so if you want to cook, you need a camp stove. For reservations, call (415) 331-1540 between 9:30 A.M. and 4:30 P.M. You must pick up your permit at the visitor center during the above hours. Reservations may be made up to 90 days in advance.

Passing the road to Hawk Camp, your route continues downhill on a gentle and then moderate grade, reaching a low point directly under a set of power lines. From here the road follows a rolling course, passing under a second set of power lines. About 100 yards from this set, you pass a trail post, right, with the Bay Area Ridge Trail emblem, and then, in about 50 feet, you arrive at a junction. Here, hikers and equestrians on the Bay Area Ridge Trail turn left onto a route closed to bikes, but you continue straight on the Bobcat Trail, which is multi-use. Soon your route makes a sweeping right-hand bend and passes an unsigned hikers-only trail veering uphill and left. The Bobcat Trail now heads generally southwest, with some zigs and zags, as it descends to Gerbode Valley. At one point you pass a west-facing hillside covered with California sagebrush, coyote brush, and bush monkeyflower. Also growing beside the road are creambush, blue-blossom, hazelnut, blackberry vines, and a delightful assortment of wildflowers, some of which attract hummingbirds and butterflies. Here, if there is no fog, you will have views of Rodeo Lagoon and the Pacific Ocean. The descent is easy, thanks to a number of **S**-bends in the road. Among the trees planted in this area by the dairy ranchers who settled here are eucalyptus, acacia, and Monterey cypress.

When you finally reach Gerbode Valley, an open grassland with a shrub-bordered creek flowing through its center, you may notice an assortment of invasive, non-native plants, such as mustard, wild radish, thistle, and vetch—indications that this area, even though protected from development, has a long history of human disturbance to the natural landscape. After passing through a eucalyptus grove, you now enjoy a level walk parallel to the creek, which remains hidden from view by a screen of willow thickets. At about the 5-mile point, you pass the Rodeo Valley Trail, a dirt road heading uphill and left. And about 75 feet farther, a connector to that trail goes left, but your route bends right and continues its level course past a marshy area, right. Soon you cross the creek draining Gerbode Valley, which passes under the road through a culvert. In about 50 feet, you come to a T-junction with the Miwok Trail. Here you turn left and retrace your steps to the parking area.

13   Marin Headlands
RODEO LAGOON

Length: 1.8 miles

Time: 1 to 2 hours

Rating: Easy

Regulations: GGNRA; dogs on leash, no bikes.

Highlights: This easy circuit of Rodeo Lagoon, which may have been named for the Rodier family who settled nearby in the mid-1800s, or perhaps to reflect the area's ranching past, offers visitors a wonderful opportunity to explore several plant communities and to observe a diverse array of birds. Best birding is during fall, winter, and spring, when ducks and shorebirds are usually present. Gulls, herons, and egrets may be spotted year-round.

Directions: See the directions for "Gerbode Valley" on p. 80. Continue 0.2 mile past the parking area, turn left onto Field Rd., and go 0.1 mile to the Marin Headlands visitor center parking area, right.

Facilities: Visitor center with displays, books, maps, helpful staff; water, telephone, rest rooms.

Trailhead: West end of parking area.

After exploring the excellent visitor center, find the trailhead at the west end of the parking area. Here, just right of the rest rooms, you pass a sign for the Lagoon Trail, then walk around a gate and begin descending a dirt-and-gravel road, with Rodeo Lagoon on your right. Except during intense storms and periods of high run-off, the lagoon is landlocked, filled by the creek that drains Gerbode Valley. If high surf breaches the

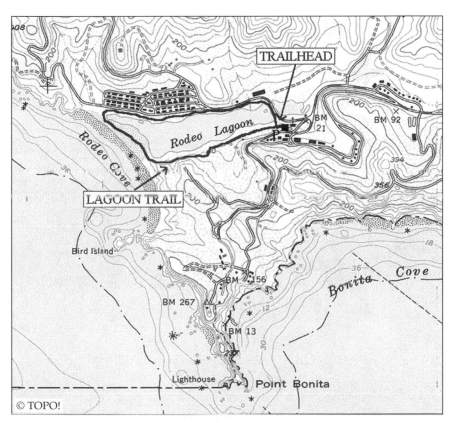

13. Rodeo Lagoon

narrow northwest corner of Rodeo Beach, usually during the winter, a channel to the Pacific is opened, and the rain-swollen lagoon finds an outlet. But once the storms abate, the wave action that caused the damage soon repairs it, depositing sand to fill the gap and sealing off the lagoon once more.

About 100 feet from the parking area, you pass the returning branch of the Lagoon Trail, right. The lagoon itself, a haven during fall, winter, and spring for waterfowl, wading birds, and shorebirds, is split into two unequal parts by the short causeway for Bunker Road. The larger part is bordered on the west by Rodeo Beach, and on the north by the low-slung army barracks that made up Fort Cronkhite. These barracks, called Mobilization Structures when they were built by the Army during the late 1930s, are now used by the National Park Service and its non-profit park partners for offices, studios, and classrooms. The smaller, eastern part of Rodeo Lagoon, shown on some maps as Rodeo Lake, is protected by a wall of vegetation and often contains a majority of the lagoon's waterfowl. Unlike the larger part of the lagoon, which contains brackish water, this part is 98 per cent fresh water. Rising north of the lagoon is Wolf Ridge, topped by Hill 88.

Continuing west toward the beach, you now enjoy an easy level walk, passing willow thickets, tangles of blackberry vines, and some stalwart eucalyptus and cypress trees. In one place, the road passes through a tunnel of vegetation, and this low-lying area, which may be muddy, has a wild, jungle-like feel. Soon you come into a more open area, the realm of hearty shrubs such as bush monkeyflower, California sagebrush, and

Fort Cronkhite and the waters of Rodeo Lagoon catch the late afternoon sun.

coyote brush, here battered by the wind into low-growing clumps. Now following the road as it bends left and rises, you begin to get fine views of the lagoon and the birds that call its waters home. Near the lagoon's west edge is the place to look for gulls, brown pelicans, and shorebirds. Diving ducks form flocks, usually separated by species, on the quieter, more protected east side.

Reaching a large, open area, the road swings sharply right and resumes its course toward the Pacific. From a vantage point about 60 feet above the lagoon, the wonderful scenery unfolding before you now has an audio track—the crashing of waves on Rodeo Beach. With a severe drop to your right, and a steep hillside rising left, you begin a descent toward the beach, passing a few stands of toyon and lupine. The ground cover here, as in many sandy areas along the California coast, is iceplant, a succulent in the seafig family, native to South Africa. Its leaves are triangular, fleshy, and stubby; its flowers can be yellow or pink. Rangers at the visitor center say it was planted here by the Army to stabilize the dunes.

At about the 0.6-mile point, you arrive at Rodeo Beach. The crest of the steep hillside on your left has dropped to meet the road in a little gully; it rises again toward the water's edge. Just south of Rodeo Beach is another fine stretch of shoreline, but it is isolated by high tide—be careful if you venture there. A sign here reminds you to keep dogs leashed, except from the crest of the dune, ahead, to the ocean, where they may be let off leash but must always be kept under voice control. This is an endangered-species habitat: dogs are never allowed to run at large, or to kill, injure, or molest wildlife.

The strand of beach at the edge of the lagoon, protected from the wind and waves of the open ocean, is a good place to find shorebirds, a tribe that includes oystercatchers, avocets, stilts, plovers, willets, curlews, godwits, small sandpipers, dowitchers, and phalaropes. The best times of year to look for shorebirds in the Bay Area are fall, winter, and spring; in summer, most go elsewhere to breed. Among the small sandpipers, three may often be found at the lagoon's edge. In order of size—small to large—these are least sandpiper, western sandpiper, and sanderling.

Least sandpipers are tiny brown birds with light-colored legs and a short, straight bill. Fearless, they will often ignore people as they probe at the margin of water and mud for food. Western sandpipers, dull gray in fall and winter, but graced with a rufous cap and shoulders in spring, have black legs and a longer bill that is slightly down-curved at its tip. Sanderlings too have black legs, but they are told apart from other sandpipers by their larger size and, out of the breeding season, by their pale gray color. Of the three, sanderlings are the most likely to venture to the outer beach, where you may see them running back and forth with the waves.

Driftwood thrown up on the beach, from whole logs to lumber scraps, illustrates well the power of the pounding surf. Turning northwest, you have your pick of routes—by the edge of the lagoon, along the crest of the beach, or near the Pacific's foam and froth. Growing on the sandy slope nearest the lagoon's edge are a variety of back-shore plants, most forming small clumps or low mats. One of the most common is horned searocket, with lobed, rubbery leaves, four-petaled lavender flowers, and pointed, rocket-shaped pods. Others here include beach primrose and sand verbena. Salt grass, a plant of coastal salt marshes, blankets patches of ground next to the lagoon. In the lagoon itself are sedges—triangular-stemmed, reed-like plants.

In addition to ducks, several species of waterbirds may be seen in the lagoon, including western grebes and double-crested cormorants. Both species ride low in the water and have long, slender necks held erect. Cormorants are all-black, whereas grebes sport a black-and-white coat. Each is an excellent diver and swimmer, hunting underwater for sushi. Cormorants are often seen flying singly or in flocks, and they also may be observed standing with outstretched wings, drying them in the sun. In spring, western grebes perform an elaborate mating ritual, which involves plucking bits of plant material from the lagoon bottom and then running across the water at high speed.

Eventually the beach narrows as you approach the spot where winter storms, high tides, and a rain-swollen lagoon conspire to make an outlet to the ocean. Here a long wooden bridge takes you across a narrow arm of the lagoon, where you may see egrets—great and snowy—or perhaps a great blue heron feeding in the shallows. Once across the bridge, you turn right, leaving behind a large, often busy parking area, which serves the beach, Fort Cronkhite, and the Coastal Trail, a route over Wolf Ridge that you may want to explore on another day. Now on a narrow path squeezed between Bunker Road, left, and the lagoon, right, you pass several interpretive panels describing the ever-changing landscape and a few of the more notable animals that live or visit here, including the endangered brown pelican and the tidewater goby, a small fish found here and perhaps nowhere else.

About 100 yards from the bridge, you pass a grassy field, right, with a few picnic tables. Some non-native plants are in evidence here, including olive trees and calla lilies. As you begin a slight climb, more familiar coastal scrub takes over—coyote brush, California sagebrush, blackberry, and fennel. At a high point, just right of a stop sign, you have a fine view downhill to the lagoon, and also ahead to a large cypress tree where egrets often roost. Now descending on a gentle grade, your trail soon veers right, passing a rest bench on the left. About 150 feet past the bench, you come to a cement causeway, where Bunker Road passes between the two lobes of the lagoon. From here you can see into the secluded east lobe, which may hold many more ducks and other waterbirds.

After crossing the causeway, you continue straight on a dirt-and-gravel path for about 250 feet. Then veering away from Bunker Road, you head downhill and right via a set of wooden steps, marked by a sign for the Lagoon Trail. Crossing a possibly wet and muddy area, you climb steeply, aided by more steps, until you reach the main dirt-and-gravel road you followed at the start of this route. Now you turn left and retrace your steps to the parking area.

14 Marin Municipal Water District
PINE MOUNTAIN

Length: 5 miles

Time: 2 to 3 hours

Rating: Moderate

Regulations: MMWD; dogs on leash. Fairfax–Bolinas Rd. to the Pine Mountain parking area may be closed because of high fire danger.

Highlights: This out-and-back route, using Pine Mountain Road and a short trail atop Pine Mountain to its summit, takes you to one of the best vantage points in the Bay Area, where your efforts on a clear day will be rewarded by fantastic views. Along the way, plant lovers will stay busy identifying a variety of trees and shrubs, some found only on the locally prevalent serpentine soil. This area is also a favorite with mountain bikers.

Directions: See the directions for "Gary Giacomini Traverse" on p. 60. Park at the Azalea Hill parking area.

Facilities: None

Trailhead: On the west side of Fairfax–Bolinas Rd., about 50 feet north of the parking area.

Rising directly east of the parking area is Azalea Hill, whose airspace may be occupied by circling turkey vultures and soaring red-tailed hawks. Your sights, however, are set on 1,762-foot Pine Mountain, several miles to the northwest. The name refers to a nearby grove of bishop pines—a coastal, two-needled species. After carefully crossing Fairfax–Bolinas Rd., you walk north about 50 feet from the parking area to a gated dirt road. This is Pine Mountain Road, which brings you, in about 2.5 miles, to within a hundred yards or so of the mountain's summit; a short, narrow trail covers the remaining ground. The terrain near the trailhead is open and provides fine views, especially east across San Pablo Bay. The surrounding fields are punctuated with groves of coast live oak and stands of toyon, coyote brush, and other shrubs.

Passing an information board and an old wooden sign, right, you follow the dirt road as it climbs, bends right, and then follows a rolling course atop a broad ridge. On your left is a deep canyon, Liberty Gulch, which descends to meet a finger of Alpine Lake. Behind you, to the south-

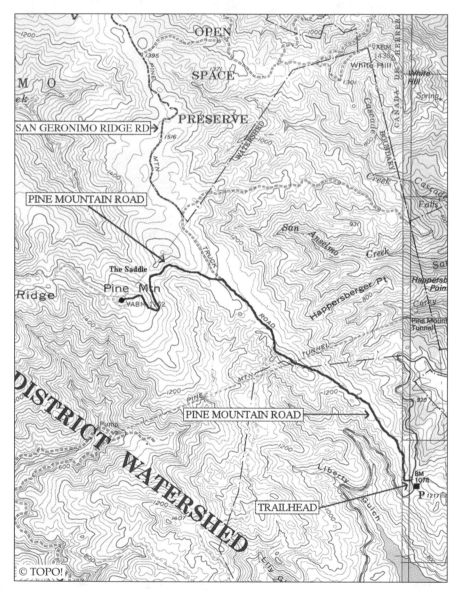

14. Pine Mountain

east, are visible two summits of Mt. Tamalpais—West and Middle peaks—but its highest rampart, East Peak, is hidden for now by Azalea Hill. The underlying rock in this area, serpentine, creates a soil that gives rise to a number of unusual plants. Among these are leather oak, a shrub, and Sargent cypress, an evergreen tree growing here in a stunted form. Leather oak grows in low clumps, its dull green, oval leaves curled under and often spiny. Sargent cypress, found farther up the road, has round, gray-brown cones, and angled strips of gray bark.

Other chaparral plants represented here include manzanita, spiny red-berry, and yerba santa. Now climbing on a moderate grade, distracted perhaps by a California quail, you can see across Liberty Gulch, left, to a ridge capped by Liberty Peak and Dutchman's Rock. Behind these high points is the even higher bulk of Bolinas Ridge, which runs northwest from Mt. Tamalpais to Tomales Bay. With just a little exertion, the views have improved dramatically, and now you have Mt. Diablo framed between two Marin County high points, Bald Hill and the long ridge that rises above China Camp State Park. The East Peak of Mt. Tamalpais finally appears from behind Azalea Hill.

To the east and far below is the Meadow Club, its golf links a lush green in contrast to the surrounding hills, which are often brown. North, in the distance, rises Big Rock Ridge, the divide between Lucas Valley and the City of Novato, topped by two communication towers. Now on rocky ground, you climb on a gentle and then moderate grade past a few pines and stands of manzanita, chinquapin, and chaparral pea. On your right is a dense thicket of oak—some of the trees are the dwarf form of interior live oak, and others are a hybrid variety, with light gray bark in strips and small, shallow-lobed leaves. The grade eases, and as you crest a high point, you can see The Saddle, a windy gap between Pine Mountain and an unnamed peak to its northeast.

Dropping slightly, you soon pass Oat Hill Road, signed as OATHILL, on your left. Now on a moderate descent, perhaps with a western scrub-jay or two for company, you may just be able to make out the summit of Mt. St. Helena, perched on the border of Sonoma, Napa, and Lake counties, to the north. Toyon and creambush, along with a tall ceanothus, grow beside the road. Gaining elevation once again, you begin to see a few Sargent cypress trees, the advance guard of a large forest that blankets a flat expanse to the north of Pine Mountain.

At about the 1.6-mile point, you reach a junction where Pine Mountain Road turns sharply left, and San Geronimo Ridge Road goes straight. Following Pine Mountain Road, now a rocky track, you begin a moderate ascent, with a deep valley on your left and a grassy hillside rising right. Chamise and bush monkeyflower thrive in this open terrain, devoid of shade. As you near The Saddle, flattened grasses downhill and left attest to the wind's power as it rushes through the gap. Briefly on level ground, you can look northwest from The Saddle to Barnabe

Mountain, a 1466-foot peak on the edge of Samuel P. Taylor State Park. (A route to Barnabe Mountain's summit is described elsewhere in this guide.)

From The Saddle, the road swings left and rises on a moderate grade, soon changing to steep. In contrast to the low, wind-resistant chaparral clinging to the slopes, a few trees—Douglas fir and California bay—stand tall and proud. The rough and rocky road eventually levels, and now you find a single-track trail, right, signed PINE MOUNTAIN SUMMIT. Turning right, you begin the final push to the summit, hemmed in on both sides by chaparral shrubs, among them chamise and silk tassel. Passing a large boulder sporting a metal spike, right, you continue for another 100 feet or so, to where a jumble of rocks forms the summit of Pine Mountain.

From here, the 360-degree panorama may keep you busy for a while, identifying such landmarks as Mt. Tamalpais, Mt. Diablo, the East Bay hills, San Pablo Bay, Big Rock Ridge, Bolinas Ridge, Tomales Bay, and Kent Lake. Without a doubt, this is one of the best vantage points in the Bay Area. After you've had your fill of the scenery, retrace your steps to the parking area.

Hiker uses hand lens to examine manzanita along Pine Mountain Road.

◆ Mt. Tamalpais ◆

More than any other natural feature in the North Bay, Mt. Tamalpais, or Mt. Tam as it is affectionately known, symbolizes outdoor recreation and the wisdom of protecting parklands that lie close to urban areas. Across its forested flanks and chaparral-clad highlands run more than 240 miles of trails, many of them multi-use, others reserved for hikers only. Three governmental agencies oversee recreational activities on the mountain—Mt. Tamalpais State Park (MTSP), the Marin Municipal Water District (MMWD), and the National Park Service (NPS). A fourth, the Marin County Open Space District, has preserves east and north of Mt. Tamalpais. The jurisdictional lines crisscross the mountain, and anything other than a short stroll is likely to take you from one agency's land to another's.

The agency with the most land is the MMWD, which controls an 18,000-acre swath reaching northwest from Panoramic Highway and the Mountain Theater all the way to Samuel P. Taylor State Park. This watershed includes the mountain's convoluted north side and its five lakes— Alpine, Bon Tempe, Kent, Lagunitas, and Phoenix. (Swimming is not permitted in any of the MMWD lakes.) The state park's 6,000 acres surround Muir Woods and follow Hwy. 1 northwest to Stinson Beach. The NPS administers Muir Woods National Monument, a small preserve of old-growth coast redwoods described elsewhere in this book. Dogs are not allowed on trails in the state park or in its undeveloped areas, or in Muir Woods. On MMWD lands, dogs must be leashed at all times. These regulations are strictly enforced. Equestrians and bicyclists should familiarize themselves with the regulations for each jurisdiction.

As San Francisco boomed after the California Gold Rush of 1849, its citizens looked around the Bay Area for recreational opportunities. Mt. Tamalpais was a logical choice, and by 1884 a wagon road had snaked its way to the mountain's summit. The Mill Valley and Mt. Tamalpais Scenic Railway was inaugurated in 1896, and by the following year passengers could enjoy the comforts of a newly built hotel and tavern near East Peak. The ride up the mountain from Mill Valley involved 281 curves, including the Double Bow Knot, where within 200 yards the track ran parallel to itself five times. This tortuous route earned the railroad its nickname— The Crookedest Railroad in the World. In 1907, a branch line opened to Muir Woods, and the railroad was renamed the Mt. Tamalpais and Muir Woods Railway. The popularity of automobiles and the construction of Ridgecrest Boulevard, along with a devastating 1929 fire, spelled doom for the railroad, which shut down in 1930.

The fight to protect Mt. Tamalpais, which began around the turn of the century, was of prime importance to Bay Area conservationists. Organizations such as the Sierra Club, the Tamalpais Conservation Club, the California Alpine Club, and the Marin Conservation League worked hard to educate the public, achieve legislation, and raise money. Individual benefactors contributed their time and resources as well. In 1905, William Kent, who had many holdings on Mt. Tamalpais, purchased 611 acres of old-growth redwoods on the mountain's south side, and then deeded them to the federal government to create Muir Woods National Monument. In 1912, the MMWD, created by Marin voters, took over land held by private water companies on the mountain's north side and opened them to recreational uses. Also in 1912, the Tamalpais Conservation Club was founded, with the goal of establishing a state park on Mt. Tamalpais. This arduous process took 18 years, but by 1930, enabling legislation had been passed, lands were purchased, and the park was open to the public. The Depression saw a flurry of activity in the park, as the Civilian Conservation Corps (CCC) worked on trails and built bridges and other structures, the most impressive of which is the Mountain Theater, described in "South Side Ramble" on p. 116. From the end of World War II through the 1970s, more lands were acquired and added to the state park.

The name Tamalpais is a combination of two Coast Miwok words: *tamal*, meaning west or west coast, or perhaps people of the west coast, and *pais*, meaning mountain. Because of the mountain's coastal location, hikers on its trails may experience a variety of conditions—sun, fog, heat, cold—and often all of them on a single day. Standing guard over the Golden Gate, the mountain's lower south- and west-facing slopes are exposed to wind and moisture sweeping in from the Pacific Ocean, creating microclimates that support redwood groves, oak-and-bay woodlands, grasslands, and bands of coastal scrub. The north side of Mt. Tamalpais, rugged and remote, is heavily forested with Douglas fir, coast redwood, and other species, but also has manzanita barrens and Sargent cypress groves. The mountain's upper reaches are blanketed with chaparral, a plant community consisting of hearty shrubs such as manzanita that are adapted to poor soils and periodic wildfires. The mountain itself, like the surrounding hills of Marin County, was formed from 100-million-year-old layers of ocean sediments, alternating with basalt lava and serpentine rock, which were folded and uplifted as earth-moving forces dragged some of the Pacific Ocean floor beneath the edge of North America.

In addition to its more than 240 miles of trails, Mt. Tamalpais also has day-use facilities and overnight campgrounds within the state park. There is a parking fee at three parking areas in the state park—Pantoll, Bootjack, and East Peak. There is free parking at Rock Spring, Upper Theater, Trojan Point, and along road shoulders. Pantoll Ranger Station, on Panoramic Highway at its junction with Pantoll Road, has maps and books for sale; there are rest rooms, picnic tables, and fire grates near the parking area. Call the ranger station or the Marin District Office to find out when the ranger station is open. Bootjack Picnic Area, on Panoramic Highway just east of the ranger station, has rest rooms, water, picnic tables, fire grates, and a group area that may be reserved by calling the ranger station.

East Peak, at the end of East Ridgecrest Boulevard, has rest rooms, picnic tables, water, and phone. A visitor center and a snack bar are usually open from 10 A.M. to 4 P.M. on weekends from late spring until early fall. Pantoll Campground, near the ranger station, has 16 walk-in sites available on a first-come, first-served basis. Steep Ravine Environmental Campground, one mile south of Stinson Beach, has ten rustic cabins and 6 walk-in campsites. Reservations for this very popular campground may be made from 10 days to 7 months in advance. Alice Eastwood Group Camp, off Panoramic Highway southwest of Mountain Home Inn, has two campsites for organized groups of from 10 to 75 people. For camping reservations, see below.

PANTOLL RANGER STATION (MTSP): (415) 388-2070

MARIN DISTRICT OFFICE (MTSP): (415) 893-1580

CAMPING RESERVATIONS: (800) 444-7275

MOUNTAIN PLAY ASSOCIATION: (415) 383-1100

MT. TAMALPAIS INTERPRETIVE ASSOCIATION: (415) 258-2410

SKY OAKS RANGER STATION (MMWD): (415) 945-1181

Mt. Tamalpais
HIGH MARSH LOOP

Length:	6.5 miles
Time:	4 to 5 hours
Rating:	Difficult
Regulations:	Parking, CSP; trails, MMWD; no bikes, no horses, no smoking, no swimming; dogs on leash.
Highlights:	This beautiful and strenuous loop, using the Cataract, High Marsh, Kent, Benstein, and Simmons trails, takes you past a scenic waterfall, beside a freshwater marsh, through areas of chaparral, and into groves of Sargent cypress and forests of Douglas fir and oak as it explores

the rugged canyons and ridges of MMWD lands above Alpine Lake on the north side of Mt. Tamalpais.

Directions: From Hwy. 101 northbound in Mill Valley, take the Hwy. 1/Mill Valley/Stinson Beach exit, which is also signed for Muir Woods and Mt. Tamalpais. After exiting, stay in the right lane as you go under Hwy. 101. You are now on Hwy. 1, Shoreline Highway. Go 1 mile, get in the left lane, and, at a stoplight, follow Shoreline Highway as it turns left.

Continue 2.7 miles to Panoramic Highway and turn right. After 0.8 mile, the road splits in three directions: hard left,

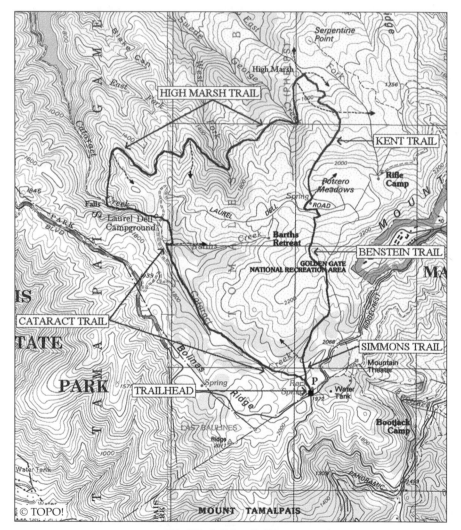

15. High Marsh Loop

Muir Woods Rd.; hard right, Sequoia Valley Rd.; gentle left, the continuation of Panoramic Highway to Stinson Beach and Mt. Tamalpais. Stay on Panoramic Highway. At 5.4 miles from Hwy. 1, you reach the Pantoll Campground and Ranger Station, left, and Pantoll Rd., right. Turn right, and go 1.4 miles to a T-junction with East Ridgecrest Blvd. and West Ridgecrest Blvd. Across the junction is a large paved parking area, shown on the Olmsted map as the Rock Spring Picnic Area. Park here.

From Hwy. 101 southbound in Mill Valley, take the Hwy. 1 North/Stinson Beach exit, which is also signed for Muir Woods and Mt. Tamalpais. After exiting, bear right, go 0.1 mile to a stop sign, and turn left. You are now on Hwy. 1, Shoreline Highway. Go 0.5 mile to a stoplight, turn left, and follow the directions above from the second paragraph.

Facilities: Toilets

Trailhead: North side of parking area, near its mid-point.

From the north side of the parking area, you head north on the Cataract Trail, a wide dirt-and-gravel path, passing a trail post and a faint trail heading right. The large, grassy meadow ahead and right is called Serpentine Swale, named for California's state rock, which is found on the upper reaches of Mt. Tamalpais and elsewhere throughout the state. Serpentine soil, rich in magnesium, makes life difficult for many plants, but some have adapted to it and others thrive in it. Later today, you will pass through a grove of Sargent cypress, a serpentine lover. Here, though, are more common trees such as coast live oak, canyon oak, and California bay.

The trail descends gently, and in about 100 yards you reach a fork. Here, the Simmons Trail, used later on the return part of this loop, bears right, but your route, the Cataract Trail, bends left. Trails in this heavily used area have been rerouted to control erosion and prevent damage to fragile meadows. About 200 feet past this fork, a faint trace heads straight, but you follow the Cataract Trail as it veers right. Now the route takes you gently downhill through a grove of Douglas fir and tanbark oak, and across a wood bridge over Cataract Creek, which drains Serpentine Swale and flows into Alpine Lake. Several hundred feet downstream from the bridge, you come to a jumble of big, moss-covered boulders. Although you may see a trail across the creek, left, stay on the creek's right side and follow the Cataract Trail through the boulders. Soon you reach a clearing and another wood bridge, this one over Ziesche Creek, named for Edward Ziesche, secretary of the Tamalpais

Club, a hiking group founded around 1880. In spring, this area is full of Douglas iris in bloom.

Now back in forest, you are serenaded by the lovely sound of rushing water from Cataract Creek, left. In a wet area, you may see giant chain ferns, their leaflets making a chevron pattern, growing up from the creek. Where the route once continued straight, it now turns left, descends a few wooden steps, and then crosses a bridge over Cataract Creek. Your course now swings northwest, with the creek on your right, passing through a beautiful area of ferns, boulders, and moss-covered trees which give the area a rain-forest feel. In this cool and shady dell, the downhill grade is so gentle that you are hardly aware of losing elevation. After briefly passing through a clearing, the trail leads you back into forest, with some fine examples of canyon oak, which has leaves whose tops are green, but whose undersides are either gray or gold. Just before you reach a large wood bridge over Cataract Creek, you pass a great tangle of evergreen huckleberry that hangs over the creek. Once across the creek, the trail rises slightly, taking you beside a rocky, moss-covered cliff, right. A wet area here is fertile ground for bigleaf maple and towering Douglas fir, reminiscent of forests in the Sierra.

Around the 1-mile point, you pass a trail, left, that crosses Cataract Creek via a large wood bridge and then joins Laurel Dell Road. You continue straight, keeping the creek, lined with bay and toyon, on your left. Sunlight filters through the trees, and if the air has a chill to it, walking here may remind you of an early-morning hike in the high mountains. Just as you emerge from forest, at the edge of a clearing, you reach a junction with the Mickey O'Brien Trail (O'BRIAN on the trail post), heading sharply right. O'Brien was president of the Tamalpais Conservation Club in the 1920s. Here the you turn right, as the Cataract and Mickey O'Brien trails join for a short distance. Then you follow the Cataract Trail as it branches left and crosses a bridge over a stream.

Skirting a large meadow, left, you soon reach Laurel Dell Road and the Laurel Dell Picnic Area. Here there are rest rooms, a watering trough, and a place to hitch horses. Crossing the road, you pass through the scenic picnic area, located at a bend in Cataract Creek. If you stay here for a few minutes, you will probably see and hear a variety of birds, including Steller's jay, identified by its black crested head and harsh call. Our two common jays—Steller's jay and western scrub-jay—are often called "blue jays," but this name is properly reserved for an Eastern species that is only rarely seen on the West Coast.

The Cataract Trail leaves the picnic area from its west side, with the creek on your left. A sign here warns of steep terrain ahead and urges hikers to stay on the trail—sound advice. This is a densely wooded area, full of California buckeye, madrone, and huckleberry, that becomes more and more gorge-like as you descend. During winter and spring, you will soon see a waterfall cascading down over the ledge of a rocky cliff, downhill and left. The hillside drops steeply here, so use caution: you will have a much better and safer view in a few minutes.

At a **T**-junction, the Cataract Trail turns left, and the High Marsh Trail goes right. Although you will be following the High Marsh Trail from here, you can get a fine view of the waterfall by turning left on the Cataract Trail and walking several hundred feet to a level area near the base of the falls. Now return to the **T**-junction and go north on the High Marsh Trail, a narrow single track perched on a steep hillside that falls away to Cataract Creek, left. Soon you reach a fork where the trail splits temporarily: follow the right-hand, uphill branch. The wooded area you are passing through holds a few huge canyon oaks, with multiple trunks and limbs that branch and spread above the trail. Woodpeckers have been active here, as evidenced by many small holes in the bark of the trees.

At the head of a narrow ravine, the trail turns left, breaks out of the trees, and traverses a steep, grassy hillside beautifully decorated in spring with California poppies, bluedicks, lupine, and mule ears. As you reach the end of a rounded ridge, the trail, which is trying to hold a contour, curves sharply right, taking you into a wooded area of canyon oak, Douglas fir, and tanbark oak. Here you may see a red-tailed hawk circling overhead, or hear its plaintive "kee-yeer" call. Soon a steep climb brings you to a junction with a short trail to Laurel Dell Road, uphill and right. Look nearby for madia, a yellow wildflower with three tiny lobes at the end of each petal, and hairy, lance-shaped leaves that emit a pleasant scent when rubbed.

Waterfall near the junction of the Cataract and High Marsh trails.

The route now alternates between wooded and open areas, and where there is little or no shade, chaparral shrubs such as manzanita, bush monkeyflower, chaparral pea, and chinquapin, a chestnut relative, have taken root. From one of these clearings, a superb view extends northeast to San Pablo Bay and beyond. Beyond this clearing, the trail descends in a narrow corridor through the shrubs, in some places via wooden steps. Soon you are back in a wonderful forest of Douglas fir, tanbark oak, bay, and California nutmeg. In wet areas nearby, look for fetid adder's-tongue, a wildflower with dark green, oval leaves that are spotted with purple. The flowers, held on long stems, are green with red veins.

The trail pursues a rolling course through the forest at it the follows ridges and indentations of the mountain's convoluted north side. Soon you pass a creek bed, which may be dry, and begin a steep climb, passing an unsigned trail heading uphill and right. Lining the trail here are thickets of dwarf interior live oak, a hearty tree found throughout Marin County, mostly in chaparral. Now breaking out of the forest, you climb over eroded and rocky ground through another area of chaparral, this time primarily chamise, buckbrush, yerba santa, and manzanita. When the manzanita has berries, you can see why it was given a name that, in Spanish, means "little apples." If you can see above the chaparral, there is a fine view to the northwest of Alpine Lake.

Descending over rough ground through a corridor of manzanita and chinquapin, you drop steeply into a ravine that holds a seasonal creek. Nearby you may find nutmeg, madrone, blue-blossom, and huckleberry. The trail fights to maintain a contour, but soon plunges steeply among rocks and small boulders to Swede George Creek, named for a mountain man who had a cabin in the area. If the creek is flowing, look uphill for a series of beautiful miniature waterfalls, with sunlight perhaps highlighting the water as it falls from pool to pool. Now you cross the creek on rocks and begin climbing, with Swede George Greek in a deep canyon on your left. After several hundred feet, your route bends slightly left and descends, passing an unsigned trail going right and uphill. About 100 yards from the unsigned trail, you reach an unsigned fork. Here, the Willow Trail descends left, but your route, the High Marsh Trail, climbs right on a moderate grade. (A sign here would be helpful!)

After topping a ridge, the trail descends and then reaches level ground and a T-junction. Here, the Cross County Boys Trail takes off uphill and right, and your route turns left. High Marsh, a seasonal wetland that may at times contain a lovely shallow pond, is visible through trees on your left. The route passes around the marsh's southeast edge and soon reaches, at about the 4-mile point, a four-way junction marked by a trail post. Here, the High Marsh Trail ends, the Kent Trail runs left-to-right, and the Azalea Meadow Trail continues straight. You turn right, onto the Kent Trail, and begin climbing over rocky ground, in places aided by wooden steps. As you gain elevation via nicely graded switchbacks, the hodge-podge of trees and shrubs gives way to a forest of Douglas fir.

Leaving the trees briefly, you pass through an area of chaparral, where blue-blossom may add color to the scene, and then return to a cool, shady forest. Now the trail, rocky and in places indistinct, runs parallel to a stream bed, which is downhill and left. Nearby you may see a showy wildflower, false lupine, with spikes of yellow pea-like flowers. Close examination shows its leaflets to be in groups of three, not the fan-like spread of four-to-many leaflets of the true lupines. After more climbing, the Cross Country Boys Trail, unsigned here, merges from the right, as does another fainter trail a few paces ahead. Out of the trees once again, you cross a manzanita barren, giving you a chance to enjoy a fine view north of Big Rock Ridge, topped by two communication towers, and, beyond it, Burdell Mountain. This barren is a good place to look for the California whipsnake—black with an orange stripe, slender-bodied, from 30 to 60 inches long. This snake, harmless to humans, is often found in chaparral, where it hunts lizards, insects, birds, and small mammals. Also here is the Oakland star tulip, with upright bowls of white, three-petaled flowers with lavender points between the petals. This wildflower, a ser-pentine lover, is on a watch list for plants of limited distribution.

Crossing a rocky rib, you now begin a moderate descent in a forest of Douglas fir, tanbark oak, and bay, soon finding a lovely stream, the head-waters of Swede George Creek, on your right. Reaching a trail post and a T-junction, you have Potrero Meadows in front of you, toilets to your left, and the Potrero Camp Picnic Area, with tables and fire grates, to your right. Turning right, you follow the trail as it crosses a bridge over the stream and leads, in about 75 feet, to the picnic area. Here you turn left and follow a dirt-and-gravel road steeply uphill and south about 100 yards to a T-junction with Laurel Dell Road.

Now you turn left onto a dirt road and descend gently for about 150 feet to a junction, right, with the Benstein Trail. Turn right and climb steeply on the Benstein Trail, a single track that is closed to bikes and horses. After about 100 feet, the route levels, bends left, and then makes a sharp switchback right, resuming a steep grade. Soon you are climbing almost entirely on serpentine, which can be slippery when wet, inter-spersed with dirt and gravel sections. The trees here, which appear stunt-ed and spindly, are Sargent cypress, lovers of serpentine soil. This won-derful tree, at home in the Coast Ranges of California, was named for Charles Sprague Sargent, who founded the Arnold Arboretum at Harvard and wrote 14 volumes on the trees of North America. The tree's bark, in strips, appears to spiral up its trunk. The small round cones, about an inch in diameter, are gray or dull brown.

At a fork in the route, you turn sharply right, head for open ground, and continue to climb. The trail soon bends left and, still climbing, leaves the cypress behind and enters a forest of tanbark oak and young Douglas fir. The moderate grade changes to steep as you near the top of a ridge, but once across it, the trail descends gently to a junction with Rock Spring–Lagunitas Road. Bear right as you merge with the road, and follow it slightly downhill to level ground, with the upper reaches of Ziesche Creek on your right. After about 100 yards, you come to a junction marked by a trail post. Here your route, the single track Benstein Trail, veers right, away from the road, and follows the creek. In spring, California buttercup and blue-eyed grass add color to the open hillsides. Crossing a serpentine ridge, you pass a trail heading right and downhill, through a meadow. Continue straight, through a possibly wet area, until you are back in a dense forest of Douglas fir, canyon oak, bay, and madrone. After stepping across a creek, you emerge from the forest into an open, grassy meadow, where the trail finds level ground.

Soon you reach a junction marked by a trail post. Here a trail to the Mountain Theater goes straight, but your route, the Benstein Trail, turns right and descends, in places on wooden steps. Seeing East Ridgecrest Boulevard across Serpentine Swale to your left means you are nearing the end of this loop. The trail stays in a wooded area along the edge of the swale, and after a few switchbacks reaches a T-junction with the Simmons Trail. A left turn here puts you on track for the Rock Spring Picnic Area and the trailhead you left hours ago. On your way to rejoin the Cataract Trail ahead, you step across the headwaters of Cataract Creek, flowing left to right through Serpentine Swale. About 100 feet from the creek, you reach the Cataract Trail. Here you bear left and retrace your steps to the parking area.

Mt. Tamalpais
MIDDLE PEAK LOOP

Length: 5 miles

Time: 2 to 3 hours

Rating: . Moderate

Regulations: Parking, CSP; trails, MMWD; parking fee; no bikes, no horses, no smoking; dogs on leash.

Highlights: This circuit of Middle Peak, using the Miller, International, Upper North Side, and North Side trails, and Old Railroad and Eldridge grades, explores a wonderful variety of terrain, from chaparral cloaking the mountain's upper reaches to redwood groves hidden on its northern side. Along the way, you have fine views of MMWD lands, including Bon Tempe Lake and Lake Lagunitas.

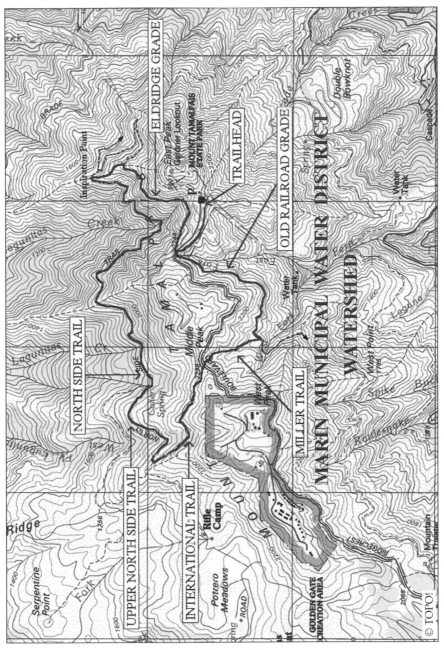

16. Middle Peak Loop

Directions: See the directions for "High Marsh Loop" on pages 98–99.
                    When you reach the T-junction with East Ridgecrest Blvd.
                    and West Ridgecrest Blvd., turn right and go 3 miles to the
                    East Peak parking area and a self-registration station, just
                    below East Peak.

Facilities: Rest rooms, picnic tables, water, phone; visitor center and
                    snack bar usually open 10 A.M. to 4 P.M. on weekends from
                    late spring until early fall.

Trailhead: East Peak parking area.

Even before you hit the trail, take a moment to admire the terrific views
from the parking area, which is perched just a few hundred feet below
and to the southwest of East Peak (2571'), highest of Mt. Tam's three summits. From here you can see San Francisco, Angel Island, the Bay Bridge,
the East Bay hills, the Marin Headlands, and the mountain's three summits—West Peak (2560'), with its prominent "golf ball" radar dome;
Middle Peak (2490'), with communication towers; and East Peak (2571'),
with a fire lookout. East Peak can be easily climbed via the well-graded
East Peak Trail, which starts off on a boardwalk just between the rest
rooms and the snack bar. You can also make a circuit of the peak by following the Verna Dunshee Trail, either to the left of the boardwalk or to
the right of the rest rooms.

Also here is a section of train track, from the days when the Mill Valley
and Mt. Tamalpais Scenic Railway brought visitors to the summit from
1896 to 1930. Ridgecrest Boulevard, now East Ridgecrest and West
Ridgecrest boulevards, was built in 1925 and hastened the demise of the
railway. Many of the hiking trails on Mt. Tamalpais were built during the
1920s and 30s by the Civilian Conservation Corps (CCC). One of the trails
used on today's loop, the Upper North Side Trail, was started in 1926 by
the Sierra Club and finished in 1937 by the CCC. Another part of the loop,
Eldridge Grade, is a road that dates from the 1880s.

From the west end of the parking area, you walk downhill on a narrow
paved road, closed to cars, that branches left from East Ridgecrest
Boulevard. Several hundred yards from the parking area, just as you join
East Ridgecrest Boulevard, you pass Eldridge Grade, a dirt road on your
right. About 100 feet farther, you turn left onto Old Railroad Grade, a dirt
road favored by mountain bikers. To your left is a sea of chaparral, typical of the vegetation that blankets the upper reaches of the mountain.
Chaparral plants—shrubs such as manzanita, chamise, buckbrush, and
toyon—are well adapted to poor soils and to the drought conditions that
often prevail in the Bay Area from May through October. Another plant
community, called coastal scrub or soft chaparral, is also represented
here. Among its members are California sagebrush and bush mon-

keyflower. In spring, the lacy new growth of the fragrant California sage-brush is the richest green imaginable.

Descending on a gentle grade, your view extends across the Marin Headlands to the Golden Gate. If its waters are fog-shrouded, it is easy to see why the entrance to San Francisco Bay eluded mariners in the 16th and 17th centuries. As you continue down the trail, you may be accompanied by hummingbirds doing aerial displays— flying skyward and then diving down on a collision course with the ground, only to pull up at the last minute. Other common birds in this area include turkey vultures, western scrub-jays, and wrentits, the latter more often heard than seen, giving a series of repeated, stuttering notes. Soon you reach a junction with the Tavern Pump Trail, heading left and steeply downhill. Now the road meanders, following the shape of the mountain's south side as it loses elevation. Silver lupine and bush poppy may add splashes of color to the scene. An outcrop of gray-green serpentine on the right side of the road tells you the next junction is near. When you reach the Miller Trail, turn right and begin a rocky uphill scramble, climbing moderately on a single track that crosses a zone of chaparral, mostly manzanita and chamise. Some varieties of manzanita flower as early as December, and others are still in bloom in May. This part of the route, exposed to sun and protected from the prevailing wind, may be hot. After a few steep sections, the trail arrives at East Ridgecrest Boulevard, which divides the north and south sides of the mountain.

After carefully crossing the paved road, find the International Trail heading northwest. Ahead and more than 1500 feet below lie Bon Tempe

The summit of Mt. Tam's East Peak is reached via a short trail from the parking area.

Lake and its smaller cousin, Lake Lagunitas, landmarks on Mt. Tam's north side. Now you descend through a dense corridor of Douglas fir, tanbark oak, California bay, and California nutmeg, with the trees gaining height as you get farther away from the ridgecrest. What an amazing contrast to the chaparral vegetation of just a few minutes ago! Several hundred feet from the road, you reach a junction marked by a trail post. Here the Colier Spring Trail, a shortcut to the North Side Trail, descends right, but your route continues straight, dropping in places to lose elevation, leveling in others.

Now crossing a rocky ravine, you soon reach a clearing ringed by large Sargent cypress trees, indicators of serpentine soil. Here, at about the 2-mile point, the International Trail ends at a T-junction with the Upper North Side Trail, and you turn right. If you are ready for a rest stop, one of the Sargent cypresses towering over the junction provides shade. Resuming your trek, follow the Upper North Side Trail, a single track, generally east into a dense forest of Douglas fir, some quite large. A ravine, left, holds the headwaters of Lagunitas Creek, West Fork, which flows into Lake Lagunitas. This is one of the best areas on Mt. Tam—a beautiful, remote forest with trails that are not heavily traveled.

At a bend in the trail, you step across several streams that merge downhill to form Lagunitas Creek, West Fork. The Douglas firs here are tall and robust, and this could easily be mistaken for a Sierra forest. The route holds a level grade now, heading northeast. Suddenly breaking out of the forest, you are confronted with a superb vista. Spread before you are Bon Tempe Lake, Lake Lagunitas, the towns of San Anselmo and

A lookout caps East Peak, highest of Mt. Tam's three summits.

Fairfax, San Pablo Bay, MMWD lands, and the coastal hills. Now the trail bends right and re-enters forest, where you begin to find some magical groves of coast redwoods and also a few beautiful madrone trees. The needles of the redwood, especially on young trees, resemble those of the California nutmeg, with one difference: the nutmeg's needles are tipped with sharp spines.

Redwoods, the world's tallest trees, block out more light than other trees, making a redwood forest a dark place. Only a few trees, among them bay and madrone, can compete with smaller redwoods for light. They do so by either growing tall themselves, to about 80 feet, or by bending toward an opening in the canopy, such as over a creek or a road. The madrones in this part of the forest are surprisingly tall. Soon you reach a junction at Colier Spring—named for John M. Colier, an early trail-builder, but signed COLLIER SPRING. Here, just before you reach a tributary of Lagunitas Creek, Middle Fork, the Lower North Side Trail joins sharply from the left, and the Colier Trail goes left and downhill. A few paces ahead, under a canopy of huge redwoods, several small streams merge to form the tributary, and two plank bridges are in place to take you across the wettest areas. A rest bench here invites you to linger at this lovely, secluded spot and listen to the magical sound of trickling water.

From the redwood grove you continue straight, now on the North Side Trail. Beyond the bridges, the route bends left and gains elevation on a gentle grade. Once past Lagunitas Creek, Middle Fork, which flows under the trail through a culvert, you make a moderate climb and then reach level ground. Here the forest, now mostly tanbark oak and madrone, is more open, with room for shrubs such as evergreen huckleberry to thrive. The trail, now just north of Middle Peak, winds back and forth, following the shape of the mountain. At about the 3-mile point, in an area of dwarf interior live oak and manzanita, the trail makes a sharp right-hand bend and arrives at a four-way junction. Here the Lagunitas Fire Trail crosses your route, and if you look uphill, you can see Middle Peak, topped by communication towers.

Continuing straight, you have at first an easy walk on mostly level ground, and then a rocky ascent across a hillside falling away steeply left. Now, where the trail starts to lose elevation, you pass a faint path heading uphill and right. About 150 feet farther, you reach Lagunitas Creek, East Fork, which flows under the trail through a culvert. Upstream from the trail, during winter and spring, you may see a lovely series of small waterfalls, flowing over moss-covered rocks. The route passes a seasonal creek, bends left, and soon reaches an open area where the view extends to Pilot Knob, which is just east of Lake Lagunitas, and Bon Tempe Lake. Use caution here: the trail is perched on the side of a cliff that drops steeply left. This is one of the most dramatic places on the mountain. You may even be able to look *down*, from this vantage point, on a turkey vulture in flight.

Soon, at about the 4-mile point, the trail reaches Inspiration Point, a clearing with a four-way junction marked by a trail post. Part of Eldridge Grade is visible straight ahead, and if you look south, sighting above a rough trail, right, you can see the lookout tower on the summit of East Peak. A faint trail also heads left. Turning right, you climb steeply over rocky ground, past a scrubby area of manzanita, live oak, coffeeberry, and Scotch broom. At a flat spot, you pass a trail heading left and uphill to a rock outcrop, and your route turns right, reaching in several hundred feet a T-junction with Eldridge Grade, a dirt road.

Here you turn right and follow the road southwest, with the summit of East Peak slightly left and only a few hundred feet above. Eldridge Grade, here on a gentle uphill course, is a popular biking route. As you come out of a wooded area, with perhaps welcome shade, you get a fine view of Middle Peak. And where the road bends left, you can look north and northwest over now-familiar ground to Bon Tempe Lake and the surrounding hills. The route skirts the west side of East Peak, swings right, and soon makes a moderate climb over rough ground to a gate. Just past the gate is East Ridgecrest Boulevard. Here you go around the gate, turn left, and retrace your steps to the parking area.

17 Mt. Tamalpais
SOUTH SIDE RAMBLE

Length:	7.1 miles
Time:	4 to 5 hours
Rating:	Difficult
Regulations:	Parking, CSP; trails CSP, MMWD; no bikes, no dogs, no smoking.
Highlights:	This semi-loop route, using the Hogback, Matt Davis, Nora, Rock Spring, and Bootjack trails, starts across Panoramic Highway from Mountain Home and takes you past two other Mt. Tamalpais landmarks, West Point Inn and Mountain Theater. Along the way, you will explore the mountain's south side, which alternates between forest, with some attractive stands of coast redwoods, and chaparral. Although the fire roads on this side of the mountain are popular with mountain bikers, this route stays mostly on single-track trails, which are closed to bikes. Gaining most of its elevation in the shade, this route is suitable for warm weather.

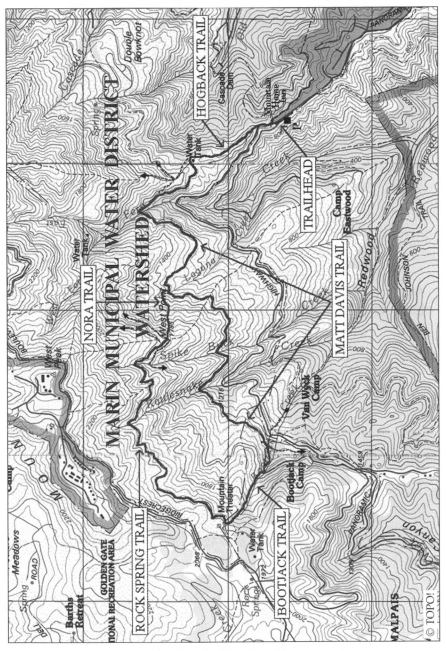

17. South Side Ramble

Directions: See the directions for "High Marsh Loop" on pages 98–99.
Once on Panoramic Highway, go 2.6 miles—passing the
turn-off to Muir Woods—to a parking area, left, just opposite the Mountain Home Inn. If this is full, as it may be on
nice weekends after 9 or 10 A.M., there is an overflow parking area 0.1 mile back (southeast) on Panoramic Highway.

It is also possible to park along the start of Gravity Car
Grade, just north of the main parking area, but this dirt
road is often deeply rutted and may damage your car. To
find Gravity Car Grade, continue northwest on Panoramic
Highway about 60 feet past the entrance to the main parking area. Turn right, go 75 feet, passing a private gravel
driveway, right. At a fork, bear right again, onto Gravity
Car Grade, a dirt road. (The left-hand fork is a fire-station
access road: do not block it!) Park along the side of the
road.

Facilities: Water, phone, toilets in parking area; food and lodging at
Mountain Home Inn, just across Panoramic Highway
from parking area.

Trailhead: North end of parking area.

From the north end of the main parking area, where the Trestle Trail
heads left and steeply downhill on wooden steps, carefully cross
Panoramic Highway, turn left, and continue north for about 60 feet to a
paved road that branches right. This is the access road to the
Throckmorton Ridge fire station. Follow this road uphill, veering left as
you pass first a private driveway and then the start of Gravity Car Grade,
a dirt road, both right. Gravity Car Grade is heavily used by mountain
bikers on their way up the south side of Mt. Tamalpais, and its first few
hundred yards are also used as an overflow parking area.

Continuing uphill toward the fire station on a gentle grade, you enter
MMWD lands, which are open from sunrise to sunset. When you reach
the station, you go around its left side and past a gate on a gravel road,
and then begin a moderate uphill climb on a dirt road, called the
Hogback Trail on the Olmsted map and the Throckmorton Trail on an
upcoming trail post. This area contains a preview of some of the trees and
shrubs commonly found on Mt. Tamalpais, including Douglas fir,
California bay, madrone, chamise, coyote brush, evergreen huckleberry,
bush poppy, and several varieties of manzanita. Also here is French
broom, an invasive alien that produces colorful yellow flowers but
crowds out native plants.

If you stop climbing for a moment and turn around, you'll be rewarded with a fine view of the Bay Area, including San Francisco, Sausalito,
Angel Island, the Pacific Ocean, and the San Mateo coastline. This is also

good habitat for hummingbirds—their wonderful aerial display involves a soaring climb and then a breathtaking dive. Passing a dirt-and-gravel road that joins from the left, you soon circle around the right side of a water tank and then, about 125 feet past the tank, reach a junction. Here the Hogback (Throckmorton) Trail continues steeply uphill, but your route, the single-track Matt Davis Trail, named for an early Mt. Tam trail builder and member of the Tamalpais Conservation Club, veers left and climbs a set of wooden steps.

After climbing the steps, you enter a brushy, overgrown area of trees and shrubs, dominated by the dwarf form of interior live oak, one of the most common chaparral species in Marin County. These thickets soon give way to a forest of mostly tanbark oak and madrone. Today's route will alternate between dense woods and chaparral for much of its course. Springtime brings a fine display of wildflowers to Mt. Tamalpais, and Douglas irises are especially plentiful along this loop. The trail now maintains a contour on the edge of a canyon that falls away left. After a wet winter, this canyon, which holds Fern Creek, may be filled with rushing water, its sound a pleasant accompaniment to your footfalls. Coast redwoods grow up from the canyon, and sword ferns sprout from its sloping hillsides—both species being indicators of moist soil.

Soon you reach an unsigned junction, right, with the Hoo-Koo-E Koo Trail. This odd name was bestowed by a member of the Tamalpais Conservation Club to honor an Indian tribe that was supposed to have lived nearby. Here you continue straight, and after about 150 feet reach a wood bridge that crosses Fern Creek. After crossing the bridge, you turn

Great views bring visitors to the West Point Inn.

left and begin a moderate climb that soon eases and then levels. Plants commonly associated with redwoods, including hazelnut and huckleberry, are beside the trail. Blue-blossom, one of the more than a dozen varieties of ceanothus found on the central California coast, is here too. In rocky areas, look for common paintbrush, whose orange flowers often attract hummingbirds. An area of chaparral gives you the chance to study plants such as chinquapin, manzanita, chaparral pea, and yerba santa. Gaining elevation again and crossing a few seasonal creeks which may dampen the trail, you can just barely see the buildings of West Point Inn through the trees uphill and left.

At about the 1.4-mile point, with Laguna Creek left and downhill, you come to a junction marked by a trail post, where the route forks. The Matt Davis Trail heads left across a bridge over the creek, but your route, the Nora Trail, goes straight and begins a relentless climb via switchbacks to West Point Inn. (Don't despair—the decimal point on the trail post here is often obscured by dirt, turning the 0.5-mile climb to the inn into 5 miles.) Soon the trail turns left, crosses Laguna Creek on a wooden bridge, and then turns right and resumes its uphill course, steep in places, through a forest of spindly redwoods. As you get farther from the creek, the redwoods give way to tanbark oak, toyon, huckleberry, and poison oak. Dark-eyed juncos—small black-headed birds with a pink bill and white along the side of the tail—may be flitting through the trees in noisy flocks.

A clearing with picnic tables and a water fountain signals your arrival at West Point Inn, a wonderful place to stop, rest, and enjoy the view. To reach the Inn, walk uphill past the picnic tables and water fountain, and, at the Inn's entranceway, climb on stone and then wooden steps to the deck. To the left of the entranceway is an information board showing some of the different ways people have ascended Mt. Tamalpais over the years, including horse and wagon, train, automobile, bicycle, and, of course, on foot. Rest rooms are on the Inn's east side; find them by walking through the covered deck area.

From the Inn's covered deck, you can see Mill Valley, Sausalito, San Francisco, the Pacific Ocean and coastline, the Bay Bridge, the Richmond–San Rafael Bridge, the Berkeley and Oakland hills, and Mt. Diablo. You also have a view, northwest, to East Peak, the highest of Mt. Tam's three summits, topped by a lookout tower.

The Inn itself is open all day on weekends, and during the afternoon Tuesdays through Fridays. It is closed Mondays. Drinks and snacks are available when the Inn is open. There are Sunday morning pancake breakfasts at the Inn, one each month from Mother's Day through October—a schedule is posted on an information board just as you come onto the deck. (Parking areas along Panoramic Highway may be full on these dates after about 8 A.M.) Rustic overnight accommodations at the Inn are available for $25 per person per night for adults, $12 for children under 18, free for children under 5. For reservations, call (415) 646-0702, Tuesday through Friday, 11 A.M. to 7 P.M.

Several roads converge at the Inn, making it an important hub for hikers and mountain bikers. Old Railroad Grade, which starts at the end of West Blithedale Avenue in Mill Valley and climbs to East Ridgecrest Boulevard, passes in front and around the west side of the Inn. Heading downhill and northwest from the Inn is Old Stage Road, which goes to Pantoll Campground and also gives access to the Bootjack Picnic Area. To resume hiking, you follow Old Railroad Grade uphill, around the west side of the Inn. About 125 feet from the Inn's entranceway, turn left onto Rock Spring Trail, a single track, and follow it on a level grade through a corridor of chaparral, the dominant form of vegetation on the mountain's upper reaches. At about the 2-mile point, you step across Spike Buck Creek, only a foot or so wide. A beautiful view unfolds to the left, taking in the Golden Gate, the Pacific coastline, and San Bruno Mountain. Now the trail begins to gain elevation over rocky, eroded ground, and you can see West Point Inn and, beyond it, landmarks such as Angel Island and Mt. Diablo.

Soon you reach a junction, right, with the Alice Eastwood Trail, named for a noted botanist who for 57 years was curator of botany at the California Academy of Sciences. The naming of Eastwood manzanita, a local species, and the designation of Camp Alice Eastwood were two other honors bestowed upon the woman whom author Dorothy L. Whitnah called "the patron saint" of Mt. Tamalpais. The unmaintained Eastwood Trail, which leads steeply uphill to East Ridgecrest Boulevard and joins with the Arturo Trail, is a rough but useful shortcut to the mountain's north side. Continuing straight on Rock Spring Trail, you walk on the edge of a steep drop-off, left, high above Old Stage Road. This is a fine, mostly level stretch of trail, with great views. After crossing Rattlesnake Creek on rocks, you follow the trail as it bends left and begins a gentle, then moderate, ascent. (Rattlesnakes are found on Mt. Tamalpais, and I have seen one in this area.)

The route soon crosses an outcrop of gray-green serpentine, then passes a seasonal stream, bends left, and enters a wooded area. Just as you emerge from the trees, you may notice a rock bearing a plaque with the inscription: TO JOHN M. COLIER, A LOVER OF NATURE. Colier, an eccentric Scot and one of the early Mt. Tam trail builders, has two features on the mountain's north side named for him, a spring and a trail. Now making a gentle descent over rough ground, the route crosses another stream, this one via a plank bridge, then veers left and resumes a level grade. You soon cross two more creeks, about 20 feet apart, on wooden bridges, and then follow the trail as it swings left and descends to a seasonal creek.

After a moderate climb, the trail turns right, passes a rest bench, left, and reaches a fork marked by a trail post. Here the Rock Spring Trail goes uphill and right, but you continue straight, passing two water fountains,

left, at the edge of the Mountain Theater, a large amphitheater with stone
seats. Dramatic productions have been given almost every summer since
1913 on Mt. Tamalpais, except during wartime. Most of the construction
on this impressive amphitheater, involving about 5000 massive stones
moved into position by cranes and derricks, was done during the 1930s
by the Civilian Conservation Corps. Just past the fountains, turn left and
walk down a series of stone steps, toward the stage area. Once at the level
of the stage, continue behind it. When you are directly behind the center
of the stage, you turn left and descend a few more steps and then walk
down a path that connects to the Bootjack Trail.

About 150 feet from the back of the stage, you reach a **T**-junction with
the Bootjack Trail. (Rest rooms are about 100 yards uphill and right.) Here
you turn left and follow the Bootjack Trail as it switchbacks downhill on
a moderate grade. This forested area, where little streams may be running
across the trail in places, contains spring wildflowers such as milkmaids
and hound's tongue. The streams gather to form the headwaters of
Redwood Creek, right, which eventually flows through the towering redwood groves of Muir Woods and then into the Pacific Ocean at Muir
Beach. Continuing downhill through a small ravine, you finally emerge
from the forest into a grassy area dotted with California poppies, blue-
eyed grass, and false lupine. A final descent on wooden steps brings you
to a **T**-junction, just past the 4-mile point, with Old Stage Road.

Here you turn right, walk about 40 feet to a paved road, and then turn
left. After 50 feet or so, you turn right onto the continuation of the

West Point is a favorite rest stop for hikers and bikers.

Bootjack Trail, a single track. Now, at first with the aid of a few wooden steps, you pursue a moderate downhill grade through forest, with the creek you have been following since just below the Mountain Theater on your right. You may hear the noise of cars on busy Panoramic Highway, ahead and downhill. Once in a while, their thrumming may be pierced by the sharp cry of a northern flicker.

A short descent puts you at the Bootjack Picnic Area, where trails sprout in all directions. From here, both the Bootjack Trail to Muir Woods and the Matt Davis Trail to the Pantoll Campground head right. Your route, the Matt Davis to Mountain Home, a single track, goes sharply left. Now heading northeast and alternating between sun and shade, the trail finds a rolling course over ridges and into gullies, one of which holds a stream that you cross via a wooden bridge. At the next watercourse, Rattlesnake Creek, where you turn right and cross a bridge, take a moment to enjoy your surroundings, as this is one of the loveliest places on the mountain. Upstream, if enough water is flowing, there is a series of miniature waterfalls. Downstream, the water cascades from pool to pool before rushing over a rocky jumble in dense forest.

When you reach open ground again, you have a view, right, of Panoramic Highway, and beyond, to the Pacific coastline and San Bruno Mountain. Now the route bends left, taking you into another indentation in the mountain's south side, this one holding Spike Buck Creek. This creek too has a bridge and some small waterfalls. Once across the bridge, the trail bends right and begins climbing toward a spur ridge. Here is a mixture of trees and shrubs, including madrone, manzanita, chamise, bush monkeyflower, and coffeeberry. When you begin to see the first stands of spindly redwoods, you know you are nearing Laguna Creek, familiar ground. The canyon that holds Laguna Creek is now on your right, and soon you cross a wooden bridge and arrive at a T-junction, where the Nora Trail heads left and uphill to the West Point Inn. Here you turn right and retrace your steps to the parking area.

◆ Muir Woods National Monument ◆

Coast redwoods (*Sequoia sempervirens*), found only on the California and Oregon coasts, are the world's tallest trees, in some places reaching more than 350 feet. Mature redwoods may live 400 to 500 years; the oldest known tree was more than 2,000 years old when it was cut. Fossil redwoods dating back to the Cretaceous period, the time of the dinosaurs, have been found. Before the arrival of Europeans, redwoods were plentiful, but logging in the 19th and 20th centuries reduced the vast old-growth forest to a few enclaves in federal, state, and private hands. In the building boom that followed California's Gold Rush, many of the Bay Area's redwood forests were logged, including one in the East Bay hills that contained more than 2,000 trees. The redwoods bordering Redwood Creek in Marin County were spared this onslaught mainly because it was too hard to get them to a mill.

As John Hart writes in *Muir Woods, Redwood Refuge*, the preservation of Redwood Creek's redwoods came about largely through the efforts of William Kent and his wife Elizabeth Thatcher Kent, who had large land-holdings on Mt. Tamalpais. As part of a plan to encourage tourism, Kent in 1903 created the Mount Tamalpais National Park Association at a meeting in Mill Valley. One of those in attendance was Gifford Pinchot, who later became secretary of agriculture under Theodore Roosevelt. At that time, Redwood Creek and adjacent lands were owned by the Tamalpais Land and Water Company, which offered to sell its holdings to Kent. It took him two years to decide, but in 1905 Kent agreed to buy the Company's 611 acres for $45,000. Kent had plans to create a private resort in the redwood grove and bring visitors in by railroad from Mill Valley.

Meanwhile, in 1907, a water company in Sausalito tried to get its hands on Redwood Creek to build a dam and a reservoir, using the legal process of condemnation. Fortunately, a new federal law, the Antiquities Act of 1906, granted the president the right to create National Monuments without a vote of Congress. Kent hung his hopes on this new law and enlisted the help of Pinchot to interest President Roosevelt in saving the redwoods. The plan worked, and in January 1908 the nation's seventh National Monument was created on 295 acres donated by Kent and his wife. The only condition they placed on the gift was that the Monument be named for John Muir, who replied: "This is the best tree-lover's monument that could possibly be found in all the forests of the world. You have done me great honor and I am proud of it." Kent later went on to serve in Congress from 1911 to 1918, introducing legislation to create the National Park Service, and he continued to press for parklands on Mt. Tamalpais.

The popularity of Muir Woods National Monument and its proximity to San Francisco almost led to its demise—the area was nearly loved to death. In 1907, a branch line of the Mill Valley and Mt. Tamalpais Scenic Railway began bringing visitors to Muir Woods, depositing them at the newly built Muir Woods Inn, located at the present-day site of Alice Eastwood Group Camp. From there, a road led down to the redwoods. The inn burned down in 1913; a second inn was built nearer the valley, but it 1929 it was consumed by a large wildfire. That year also saw the demise of the railway, mainly for economic reasons. Beginning in the 1920s, measures were taken to regulate the public's use of Muir Woods and to repair decades of damage. Cars and fires were banned, picnicking and overnight camping were eliminated, trails were narrowed and lined with low fences, bridges across Redwood Creek were removed, and native plants were reestablished. In 1978, Muir Woods came under the jurisdiction of the Golden Gate National Recreation Area, part of the National Park Service. It is a small but unique link in a chain of parklands stretching unbroken from the Golden Gate to the mouth of Tomales Bay.

MUIR WOODS NATIONAL MONUMENT: (415) 388-2595

Muir Woods National Monument
REDWOOD CREEK

Length: 1.9 miles

Time: 1 to 2 hours

Rating: Easy

Regulations: NPS; entrance fee; no picnicking, no smoking, no dogs, no bikes.

Highlights: Muir Woods, one of the last remaining stands of old-growth coast redwoods anywhere in the world, is a treasure not to be missed. This loop, using the paved Main Trail and the Hillside Trail, takes you among the giant redwoods on both sides of Redwood Creek, the monument's central watercourse, where you will also find other trees, shrubs, and wildflowers associated with a redwood forest. The parking areas and trails are usually crowded on weekends, especially during summer, so visit mid-week if you can. The Golden Gate National Parks Association publishes a fine map of Muir Woods, which contains descriptions of the flora and fauna, a history of the area, text for a self-guiding nature trail, and seven suggested hiking routes.

The map is on sale at the entrance station and in a vending machine about 0.25 mile up the Main Trail.

Directions: See the directions for "High Marsh Loop" on pages 98–99. At 0.8 mile on Panoramic Hwy., where the road splits in three directions, turn left onto Muir Woods Rd. After 1.6 miles, turn right, into main parking area for Muir Woods. If this area is full, there is another about 100 yards southeast on Muir Woods Rd.

Facilities: Visitor center with books, maps, helpful staff; cafe, gift shop, rest rooms, water, phone.

Trailhead: Northwest end of main parking area, just left of entrance. station and visitor center.

After perusing the books and maps at the visitor center, and paying a small entrance fee, you head northwest on a level, paved path, passing an information board with history of the park and of the redwood-conservation movement. This path is labeled the Main Trail on the Golden Gate

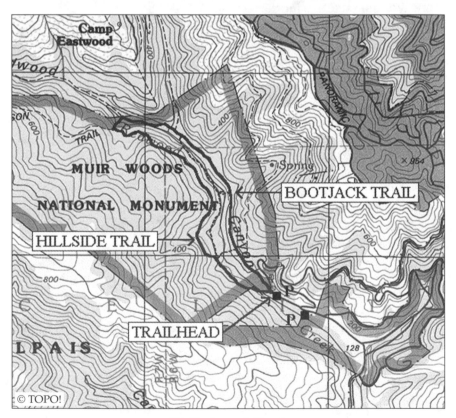

18. Redwood Creek

National Parks Association map, but it is also the continuation of the Bootjack Trail from Mt. Tamalpais State Park. About 100 feet from the trailhead, you pass a path, right, to the gift shop and the cafe, which are open 9 A.M. to 5 P.M. Redwood Creek, which gathers water from several tributaries cascading down the south side of Mt. Tamalpais, is on your left. Soon you begin to see some of the plants associated with a coast-redwood forest, including California bay, hazelnut, thimbleberry, western sword fern, and redwood sorrel. And when you reach Bridge 1, here are the venerable giants themselves, rising high overhead. Joining the redwoods are bigleaf maple, red alder, and a shrub called elk clover, sporting huge leaves and, in late summer, clusters of dark berries.

Leaving Bridge 1 behind, you stay on the east side of Redwood Creek. Rest benches here and there invite you to sit and contemplate the sights and sounds of this ancient forest, which, on weekends, may be full of visitors. On a quiet, fog-shrouded mornings, however, your only companions may be feathered ones. About 70 species of birds, including the secretive spotted owl, have been observed in Muir Woods. Be on the lookout for a blue bird with a black-crested head—the Steller's jay. This noisy forest denizen is common west of the Rockies but a real prize for East Coast birders, who must content themselves with its cousin, the blue jay. A junction with the Ocean View Trail, right, serves as a meeting place for ranger-led walks; times for these are posted near the entrance station. Continuing straight, you enter a realm dominated by redwoods, where clumps of western sword fern provide ground cover. Dense stands of redwoods create a shady environment suited to only certain other types of plants, and the thick carpet of needles and twigs deposited each winter, called duff, makes it hard for seeds to sprout.

When you reach Bridge 2, where a vending machine has maps for sale, look across the creek: there stand the monument's tallest tree—253 feet— and its most stout—13 feet in diameter. Stay on the east side of the creek for now; you'll visit the west side later. Beyond the bridge, the canyon holding Redwood Creek narrows, with steep hillsides rising both left and right. Here, tall bay trees fight with the redwoods for light, in places arching over the creek to find a break in the dense canopy. Tanbark oak, evergreen huckleberry, and trillium, three more redwood-forest denizens, are nearby.

Passing Bridge 3, left, you enter Cathedral Grove, where the path divides around this fantastic stand of trees. Here, on 19 May 1945, delegates who came to San Francisco to form the United Nations met to honor Franklin Roosevelt, who had just died. Some of the trees here show scars from fire; others have large, grotesque lumps called burls. Coast redwood, a species that first appeared some 250 million years ago, has developed, through evolution, strategies to withstand natural disasters. To withstand fire, a redwood tree relies on three main defenses: its thick bark provides insulation, its sap contains fire-resistant tannic acid, and its high

Tanbark oak is often found in redwood forests.

crown is beyond the reach of most flames. Damage or stress from other causes stimulates the growth of buds lying dormant within redwood root crowns or trunks. These buds eventually form burls, which can sprout into new limbs or entire new trees. A circle of redwoods around a dead ancestor, sometimes called a fairy ring or a family circle, is evidence of sprouting from burls.

Passing the Fern Creek Trail, right, you cross a stone bridge over Fern Creek, and then, in a couple of hundred feet, pass the Camp Eastwood Trail, right. Several hundred yards ahead, your path curves left, and a single-track trail, the Bootjack Trail, heads right, into Mt. Tamalpais State Park. After about 100 feet, you come to Bridge 4, which takes you across Redwood Creek. This bridge is a fine vantage point from which to admire the creek, the redwoods, and the play of light and shadow on the forest floor. Once across the bridge, now on a rocky trail, you begin a moderate ascent. A sign, at a T-junction ahead, marks the Ben Johnson Trail, right, and your route, the Hillside Trail, left. Turning left, you continue to climb, aided here by wooden steps.

Now the grade eases, and you follow a narrow trail, sliced from a steep hillside, into a ravine that holds a tributary of Redwood Creek. After crossing a plank bridge near a rest bench, the route swings sharply left, finds a short stretch of level ground, and then descends on a gentle grade. From this elevated perspective, you look down on massive redwood trunks, and, without too much neck strain, up at the towering canopy. In places, parts of the complex root system underlying a redwood-forest floor are exposed. These sprawling life-support networks are surprisingly shallow, only 10 to 12 feet underground, and may reach 100 feet out from each tree. Redwoods lack a main tap root, and instead stabilize themselves by interlocking their roots with those of other trees.

A steep drop, left, leads down to Redwood Creek, but your route stays well above it, in places squeezing between two or more giant trees. After wandering into another ravine, the trail runs parallel to the rushing waters of Redwood Creek, and you can see Cathedral Grove, downhill and left. Angled gently downward, the trail here is crisscrossed by roots, a hazard if you try to look at the scenery and walk at the same time. Now at creek-level, you come to a four-way junction and, just beyond it, Bridge 2. Here you turn right, staying on the west side of the creek and walking through Bohemian Grove, another stand of extraordinary trees, some of them fire-scarred. Fire is part of the natural cycle, and is often beneficial. The National Park Service now recognizes the importance of fire and since 1997 has conducted prescribed burns in Muir Woods.

Redwood Creek, close by on your left, has runs of coho salmon and steelhead trout, both listed as threatened species under federal law, during the rainy season. Channeled in the 1930s to prevent flooding, the creek is now being allowed to resume its winding course. This benefits the fish runs and also the streamside vegetation. When you reach a fallen tree, sawed to clear a path for the trail, take a minute to imagine yourself nearby on 6 April 1993, when this 419-year-old giant, its roots loosened by winter rains, came crashing down. Actually, the tree had begun to lean several centuries ago, but it responded by growing more wood on the supporting side. Thus its cross-section is an oval instead of a circle. At Bridge 1 the route crosses the creek and leads you to a T-junction. Here you turn right and retrace your steps to the parking area.

19. Muir Woods National Monument
TOURIST CLUB

Length: 5 miles

Time: 2 to 4 hours

Rating: Moderate

Regulations: NPS; CSP; entrance fee; no picnicking, no smoking, no dogs, no bikes.

Highlights: This loop, which uses the Main, Fern Creek, Lost, Ocean View, Panoramic, Redwood, Sun, and Dipsea trails, climbs high above Redwood Creek, visiting Mt. Tamalpais State Park and also the grounds of the Bavarian-style Tourist Club before plunging back to the redwood groves named for John Muir. Along the way you will walk beside giant

redwoods, enjoy views of the Pacific Ocean—or the fog
bank that shrouds it—and test your mettle on a stretch of
the famous foot-race route from Mill Valley to Stinson
Beach.

Directions: See the directions for "Redwood Creek" on p. 120.

Facilities: Visitor center with books, maps, helpful staff; cafe, gift
shop, rest rooms, water, phone.

Trailhead: Northwest end of main parking area, just left of entrance
station and visitor center.

Follow the route description for "Redwood Creek" on pages 120–122. to
the junction with the Fern Creek Trail. Here you turn right, leaving the
paved path, and get on a dirt trail. With Fern Creek on your left, you pass

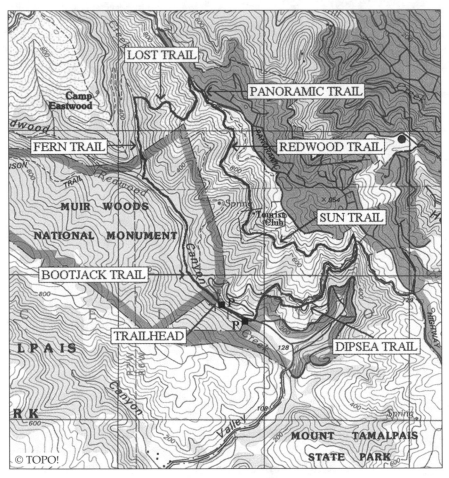

19. Tourist Club

a memorial plaque dedicated to Congressman William Kent, who, with his wife Elizabeth Thatcher Kent, purchased the large grove of redwoods bordering Redwood Creek in 1905 and then granted it to the federal government with the understanding that it be named after John Muir. Not far from the memorial, you enter Mt. Tamalpais State Park. After a short climb, the trail returns to the level of the creek, which runs along the bottom of a narrow canyon. The young redwoods here are so thin and spindly, it is hard to believe they will grow into magnificent giants like you see around you. Some of the redwoods have bark in vertical strips, but on others the bark strips form a spiral. And on some, the bark is contorted and twisted into fantastic bumps and burls.

Now a wooden bridge takes you across Fern Creek, and then the trail bends right, passing a set of steps leading down to the creek. A fire-hollowed tree, with room enough to stand inside, is on your left. The next bridge takes you back across Fern Creek, and a third, parallel to the creek, crosses a gully which holds a seasonal stream. Soon the trail makes a sharp right-hand switchback and begins to climb. After about 75 feet, you come to several more fire-gouged trees; just past them the route swings sharply left. At about the 1-mile point you reach a junction. Here, the Fern Creek Trail continues straight across a plank bridge nailed to the trunk of a fallen redwood. But your route, the Lost Trail, goes right, climbing a set of wooden steps, and then bends left, still climbing on a moderate grade. The trail, a single track, is cut into a steep hillside that falls dramatically left. More steps, along with a sharp right-hand switchback, aid your ascent.

Soon you are walking at the level of the redwood-forest canopy, and from this vantage point, you can measure the amazing height of these trees by see how far down into the canyon they go. A bridge takes you over a tributary of Fern Creek, and your climb continues, again aided by steps. A dramatic change in vegetation marks a transition out of the redwood forest, and nearby you find Douglas fir, canyon oak, and coffeeberry. The air here on a warm day may be fragrant with the smell of California-bay leaves. After following a winding course, the trail passes a small stand of redwoods and then, at a T-junction, meets the Ocean View Trail.

Here you turn left and continue climbing on a long, steady grade that changes from gentle to moderate. From above comes the sound of cars on Panoramic Highway. Thickets of French broom, an invasive non-native shrub with yellow flowers, border the trail. Now emerging from the forest, you can see two of the three summit on Mt. Tamalpais—West and Middle peaks. East Peak, the highest, is hidden from view. From the base of a large boulder, a rough path leads uphill and right, but your route curves left, then straightens and begins to climb. After a rising traverse across a steep, open hillside that falls away left, you come to a four-way junction. Here the Panoramic Trail crosses the Ocean View Trail, which continues uphill to Panoramic Highway. (A left turn here would take you, in about 0.3 mile, to a parking area just across Panoramic Highway from Mountain Home Inn. And from that parking area, there are routes leading to the top of Mt. Tamalpais—so a climb of the mountain starting from Muir Woods is something to consider for another day.)

Instead, you turn right onto the Panoramic Trail, which heads southeast just beneath Panoramic Highway. A breeze from the Pacific Ocean, visible from here when fog-free, is welcome on a warm day. California poppy, fennel, yerba santa, and Oregon grape are among the plants taking advantage of an open hillside. This is a lovely area, with fine views southwest to the dark forested canyon that holds Muir Woods, right, and north to Mt. Tamalpais. Coming around a bend, you pass a rough path, right, and a trail merging sharply from the left—both unsigned. The next junction, a fork, is signed: the Panoramic Trail goes left, but your route, the Redwood Trail, veers right and descends. After passing a wet area and negotiating a steep, rocky downhill pitch, you are back among the redwoods, although these trees are small compared to the giants beside Redwood Creek. But they are tall enough to challenge the bays in a race for sunlight. Also here are coast live oak, canyon oak, tanbark oak, poison oak, and evergreen huckleberry. And a short distance ahead, on open, southwest-facing slopes, you may find manzanita, chamise, bush poppy, and chaparral pea.

Leaving this botanical wonderland behind, you re-enter dense forest, crossing several creeks via wooden bridges. A sign marks the boundary of Mt. Tamalpais State Park, and you are now on land owned by the Tourist Club, which is just ahead, at about the 3-mile point. The Tourist Club is part of an international conservation organization, founded in 1895 in Vienna, that has approximately 600,000 members in the US and Europe. Immigrants from Germany and Austria in the early 1900s founded the club's Bay Area branch and bought several acres of land next to Muir Woods. The club's collection of colorful Bavarian-style buildings, set amid a Pacific-coastal forest, with a bandstand, a dance floor, and a few palm trees thrown in for good measure, is remarkable. The club is open year-round on weekends, and during the week if the care-taker is available. Hikers are welcome.

The Redwood Trail skirts the upper edge of the club's grounds and joins the dirt access road from Panoramic Highway just past a small shed. Bearing left onto the dirt road, after a couple of hundred feet you reach a junction with the Sun Trail, where you turn right. True to its name, this trail brings you out of the shade and into a clearing. The open terrain, with a steep drop to your right, offers great views of the ridges and ravines sloping down toward the Pacific Ocean. From here you can watch tendrils of fog creeping over the coastal hills and the marvelous interplay of sunlight and shadow on the surrounding landscape. Spring and summer visitors may enjoy colorful lupines and asters beside the trail. As you near Panoramic Highway and a nearby residential area, you may find exotic imports such as pampas grass and acacia.

Just shy of the 4-mile point, the Sun Trail ends at the Dipsea Trail, which goes straight and also sharply right. Stretching from Mill Valley to Stinson Beach, the Dipsea Trail is the route of a rugged foot race, held nearly every year since 1905. Here you turn right and descend over rocky ground, finally reaching Muir Woods Road via several sets of wooden steps. Beside the road is a small parking area in the shade of a redwood tree. A trail post directs you across the road to the continuation of the Dipsea Trail. After carefully crossing the road, you turn right, and in about 30 feet, find the trail, which descends over more wooden steps. A tributary of Redwood Creek may be flowing across the trail, shaded here by tall redwoods and bays. You continue to descend through this lovely, cool forest, now via a series of switchbacks, with a deep ravine on your left.

The winding trail soon leaves the forest and traverses an open hillside, just below Muir Woods Road, right. Downhill and left is a dirt road, Camino del Canyon, which will rise to meet you and join Muir Woods Road just ahead. After crossing Camino del Canyon, you find a sign

Bavarian-style Tourist Club is just west of Muir Woods.

pointing you to the Dipsea Trail, which drops steeply via wooden steps, and then finds a moderate grade down through a forest of Douglas fir. The Dipsea Trail is as famous for its knee-jarring descents as for its pulse-pounding uphills, and this part of the route shows you why. A sign here, STAY ON THE TRAIL, offers good advice—you have little choice over such steep and rugged ground.

After crossing a gully on a wooden bridge, you reach a clearing and a 100-foot stretch of pavement, which curves left and descends on a moderate grade. Now back on dirt, you pass a closed trail, left, and then swing sharply right, soon reaching pavement again. After about 150 feet, you arrive at Muir Woods Road, which you carefully cross. From here, at the entrance to the overflow parking area, you turn right and follow a dirt trail for about 100 yards to the main parking area.

20 Olompali State Historic Park
LOOP TRAIL

Length:	2.7 miles
Time:	1 to 2 hours
Rating:	Moderate
Regulations:	CSP: fees for parking and dogs; no bikes; no dogs on hiking trails, but dogs allowed on leash in park's picnic and historic areas.
Highlights:	Where else can you walk in the footsteps of Coast Miwok Indians, Jesuit seminarians, *and* the Grateful Dead rock band? This historic state park, whose colorful saga is described below, sits on the northeastern side of Burdell Mountain, a high ridge of rolling, grassy slopes graced with majestic oaks, and furrowed with deep, densely forested ravines. The Loop Trail, though short, gives you a fine introduction to the landscape, flora, and fauna of Marin County's northeast corner. The south side of Burdell Mountain, a Marin County open space preserve, can be explored by following the description for "Burdell Mountain" on pages 50-55. You can also make a traverse of Burdell Mountain from Olompali to the open space preserve on a trail opened in the Fall of 1999. For information about park programs call (415) 892-3383.
Directions:	From Hwy. 101 northbound, north of Novato, go 2.4 miles past the park entrance, which has no access from the northbound lane. At San Antonio Rd., carefully turn left,

across the southbound lane. Swing into a wide turn-out, where San Antonio Rd. joins Hwy. 101. Now merge into the southbound lane, go south on Hwy. 101 for 2.4 miles, and, at the signed entrance road, turn right. Go 0.2 mile to the parking area and a self-registration station.

From Hwy. 101 southbound, south of Petaluma, go 2.4 miles past San Antonio Rd, turn right at the signed entrance road, and go 0.2 mile to the parking area.

Facilities: Picnic tables and toilet next to parking area; more picnic tables in garden area; visitor center, water and toilet at the Burdell Frame House north of parking area.

Trailhead: West side of parking area.

This historic park, on the northeast side of Burdell Mountain, adjacent to San Antonio Creek and the Petaluma River, has a long and colorful past. The area, rich in game, shellfish, birds, and acorns, was inhabited by Coast Miwok Indians since about 6000 BC, and became a major trading center by 1300 AD. The name "Olompali" probably means "southern village" or "southern people." The arrival of Europeans in the 18th century brought Christianity, the mission system, and diseases to which the Indians had no resistance, spelling disaster for the Miwoks as a people. One who survived, Camilo Ynitia, a Christianized Miwok from

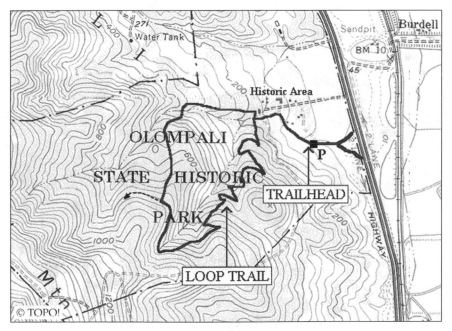

20. Loop Trail

Olompali, received in 1843 a land grant of almost 8,900 acres from the Mexican government.

During the Bear Flag uprising of 1846, rebel Americans fought Mexican troops on Ynitia's land, producing one the revolt's few casualties. Ynitia sold most of his land in 1852 to James Black, Marin's county assessor, who later amassed more large holdings in the county. In 1863, when Black's daughter Mary married Galen Burdell, one of San Francisco's first dentists, the couple received the ranch at Olompali as a wedding gift. The Burdells, and later their son, developed the property into a lavish estate, complete with a 26-room mansion and a Victorian garden. The mansion was destroyed by fire in 1969, but the Burdell Frame House, built in the 1870s, today serves as both ranger station and visitor center.

In the 1940s, after the Burdell family had sold the property, it passed to the University of San Francisco, which established a Jesuit retreat there. In the 1960s, the University tried to sell Olompali, but the various buyers always ran out of funds and defaulted. It was during this time that Olompali was used as the home of the Grateful Dead rock band and, later, as a hippie commune. During excavations in the 1970s, archaeologists discovered the historical importance of Olompali, and in 1977, the State of California and Marin County jointly acquired the property.

As you leave the parking area's west side, climbing an overgrown dirt road, you can see some of the park's historic buildings, right. It is cer-

Olompali's Heritage Day, the first Sunday in May, features nature walks, talks on the history of the area, Native American Dancing, and demonstrations of farming life.

tainly worth visiting the Burdell Frame House, the Victorian Garden, the Burdell Barns, and the remains of the Burdell Mansion. To find them, follow a trail from the north side of the parking area into the ranch complex. There are self-guiding interpretive panels throughout the ranch complex. One of the best times to learn more about the area and the people who lived here is on the park's annual Heritage Day, the first Sunday in May, from 10 A.M. to 4 P.M. Events include nature walks, discussions of the park's flora and fauna, talks on the history of the area, Native American dancing, and demonstrations of farming life.

With a split-rail fence on your left, you pass several venerable coast live oaks and valley oaks, and then, after the road makes a few jogs, you come to a T-junction in a grove of California bay. To the right is a 50-foot wooden bridge that crosses Olompali Creek; you will use this on the return part of the loop. To the left, a dirt road climbs parallel to a split-rail fence. Here you turn left and continue uphill on a gentle grade. If the winter has been a wet one, you may find yourself amid a fine display of spring wildflowers, including blue-eyed grass, winecup clarkia, and Ithuriel's spear. Other colorful bloomers here are bush monkeyflower, a shrub with yellow flowers and sticky leaves, and black locust, a nonnative tree that dangles beautiful clusters of creamy flowers.

Where the road bends sharply right, you have a fine view east over the marshy confluence of San Antonio Creek and the Petaluma River, and out across San Pablo Bay to Carquinez Strait and the Carquinez Bridge. Now in a forest of coast live oak, bay, and California buckeye, the route changes from dirt road to single-track trail and swings left. A ravine, right, holds a seasonal creek, and soon you pass into an area of blue oak and towering manzanita. A sharp switchback left continues the gentle ascent, and then the route bends right, passing a rest bench where you may want to sit for a moment and try identifying birds by their calls. Some of the common ones in this area are western scrub-jay, dark-eyed junco, western bluebird, and Anna's hummingbird.

The route continues its zigzag course uphill, alternating between gentle and moderate grades. The trail begins to get rough and rocky in places, but the walking is never difficult. Passing another rest bench, left, you encounter black oak—its leaves are shiny green, lobed, with pointed tips. If common paintbrush is blooming, stay a while and wait for a hummingbird to feed at its red flowers. Coming to the end of a gully, the route bends sharply right, taking you by a stand of large madrone trees. In this densely wooded area, which has a wild, jungle-like appearance, ferns and mosses grow on a rocky embankment beside the trail, along with shrubs such as snowberry and creambush, and wildflowers like California buttercup, bluedicks, and Chinesehouses.

Several more switchbacks put you at the head of a ravine that holds a seasonal creek. There is another rest bench here, inviting you to stop and enjoy the fragrance of bay leaves. Soon you come to a four-way junction,

Reconstructed Miwok village shows two different building styles—tule, left, and bark strips, right.

at about the 1.75-mile point. From here, a trail opened in the Fall of 1999 leads over Burdell Mountain to the Mount Burdell Open Space Preserve. Your route, the Loop Trail, goes right and begins to descend. This is a good area to compare hazelnut, a small tree often associated with coast redwoods, and creambush, a common shrub—both growing beside the trail. Each has soft, felt-like leaves. Hazelnut's leaves are larger and odorless, but the leaves of creambush, when you rub them lightly, have a wonderful apple-pie fragrance. Creambush, also called ocean spray, is named for its large clusters of white flowers which appear in late spring.

After the descent eases and you reach a flat spot in the midst of a dense forest, the trail make a 90-degree right turn and then continues on a gentle downhill grade. Nearing Olompali Creek, the grade steepens and the going becomes trickier as you skirt eroded patches and step over thick roots growing across the trail. Now a set of wooden steps brings you to a junction, where a wide dirt path merges from the left, and your route, now a dirt road, swings right. Olompali Creek is in a deep ravine, left, and the road, which may be muddy in places, heads downstream, soon passing a reservoir made by damming the creek.

Leaving a congested area of weeds and blackberry vines, you pass through an open, grassy area where buckeyes put on a beautiful display with their showy, candle-like flowers in late spring. Stately valley oaks are here too, and nearby is a reconstructed Coast Miwok village consisting of several typical houses, one made from tule, the other from bark.

After passing several picnic tables, the road swings left, crosses Olompali Creek, which flows through a culvert, and then veers back to the right. The Burdell Barns, part of the historic ranch complex, are just ahead. (You can visit the ranch complex by continuing straight at the trail post ahead.) When you reach a trail post, right, just in front of the first barn—one with a corrugated metal roof—you bear right, off the dirt road. Now a walk of perhaps 200 feet across a weedy field brings you to the 50-foot wooden bridge you saw at the start of this loop. Once across, you arrive at the junction you passed earlier with the path from the parking area; here you turn left and retrace your steps.

Golden globe lilies are delicate yellow flowers.

✦ Point Reyes National Seashore ✦

If the earth were a static place, residents of Santa Barbara would today be enjoying the nearby hiking trails and stunning ocean vistas of Point Reyes. But earth movements over millions of years have forced this chunk of land, whose rocks resemble those found in the Tehachapi Mountains of southern California, northward along the San Andreas fault at a rate of about 2 inches per year. Geologists call this chunk of land the Salinian Block, and estimate it has moved approximately 350 miles since it began its journey. Thus many of the bluffs and headlands along the central and northern California coast actually belong to southern California—let's hope they won't want them back someday! During the 1906 earthquake, the ground in the Olema Valley, where the San Andreas fault runs just east of Point Reyes, shifted by about 20 feet. You can see dramatic evidence of this slippage, in the form of a displaced fence, by walking the short Earthquake Trail, which starts from near the Bear Valley visitor center.

People visit Point Reyes for many reasons. Some come to walk on the beach and watch the surf crash against the shore. Others arrive to watch migrating whales, to search for rare birds, or to admire the peninsula's fine display of spring wildflowers. Hikers, equestrians, and bicyclists enjoy more than 140 miles of trails that crisscross Point Reyes National Seashore, an 85,000-acre preserve created in 1962 and administered by the National Park Service (NPS). It is the only national seashore on the West Coast. Within the Seashore lies Phillip Burton Wilderness Area, named to honor a San Francisco congressman who was a wilderness advocate. (Burton died in 1983.) Dogs are not allowed on the trails, and bicycles are prohibited in the Wilderness. Trailheads are scattered throughout the park. The most popular are Bear Valley, just south of the visitor center; Five Brooks, 3.5 miles south of Olema on Highway 1; Palomarin, at the end of Mesa Road, northwest of Bolinas; and Tomales Point, at the end of Pierce Point Road. Backcountry camping is available at four camps: Sky, Coast, Glen, and Wildcat. Each campground has toilets and water. Camping is by permit only, and reservations are strong suggested. Campsites can be reserved up to two months in advance, either by phone or in person at the Bear Valley visitor center (see below).

Point Reyes encompasses a wide variety of habitats, including shoreline, coastal salt marsh, coastal prairie, coastal scrub (soft chaparral), grassland, and forests of Douglas fir, bishop pine, oak, and California bay. The area has a ranching past dating back to the 1800s, and much of the coastal prairie has been, and still is, used to graze cows. The cattle and dairy ranches within the Seashore boundaries continue to operate under agreements with the NPS, and as you tour the peninsula please respect their privacy. Like other parklands in the North Bay, Point Reyes was saved from development just in the nick of time. Without the protection offered by the Seashore, logging and home building might have changed the peninsular forever. Starting from a nucleus of 53,000 acres, the Seashore has grown considerably, but instead of a developed park devoted to motorized forms of recreation, as may have been envisioned by planners in the 1960s, we have a still-rustic area with limited access, where travel by foot, bike, or horseback brings the most rewards.

The Point Reyes peninsular is at the heart of a historical dispute: did he or didn't he? The "he" in question is Sir Francis Drake, and the dispute is over exactly where on the California coast the intrepid mariner anchored his ship, the *Golden Hind*, in 1579. Greeted by Coast Miwok Indians as he landed in a protected but fog-bound harbor, Drake spent five weeks making repairs to his ship, and then continued west across the Pacific. Before leaving, Drake named the land around the harbor Nova Albion, or New England, and claimed it for Queen Elizabeth I by nailing a brass plate to a post. Drake's log disappeared after his return to England, and all other accounts of his voyage are second-hand. A vague sketch-map of Drake's anchorage was published in 1589, and over the years advocates for other landing sites, such as Bolinas Lagoon, Bodega Bay, and even San Francisco Bay, used the accounts and the map to support their claims.

In 1936, a picnicker near Point San Quentin found a brass plate like the one Drake had left behind. Did Drake land in San Francisco Bay? Soon another man claimed *he* found the plate at Drakes Bay, kept it in his car for three years, and then jettisoned it near Point San Quentin. The plate eventually landed in the Bancroft Library at UC Berkeley, and was subjected from time to time to metallurgical tests. The latest, in 1977, indicate it is probably a fake. Drake's name, like his landing site, has wandered over the map of coastal California, at times applied to San Francisco Bay and also to a port north of Point Reyes. The name Point Reyes, or *La Punta de Los Tres Reyes*, was conferred by Spanish explorer Don Sebastian Vizcaino on 6 January 1603, the day of the Feast of the Three Kings. (For a more complete discussion of the human and natural history of Point Reyes, see Dorothy L. Whitnah's fine book, *Point Reyes*, published by Wilderness Press.)

There are three visitor centers in the park. Bear Valley visitor center, on Bear Valley Road about 0.5 mile west of Olema, is the best place to begin your exploration of Point Reyes. Helpful staff are on hand to answer questions and make suggestions, even about where to buy a picnic lunch. There are engrossing exhibits about the natural and human history of the area, and a slide show is available upon request. Backcountry camping information, reservations, and permits are available here. Adjacent to the visitor center is a lovely oak-shaded picnic area. Near the Bear Valley visitor center are two exhibits and two short trails that may be of interest. Morgan Horse Ranch, with self-guiding exhibits, corrals, and demonstrations, is a working ranch for Morgan horses used by NPS rangers on backcountry patrol. The ranch is open daily from 9 A.M. to 4:30 P.M. Kule Loklo is a replica of a Coast Miwok Indian village, open daily sunrise to sunset. The Earthquake Trail, already mentioned, is a short paved loop along the San Andreas fault just east of the visitor center, open daily sunrise to sunset. The Woodpecker Trail is a short self-guiding nature trail.

The Lighthouse visitor center is at the end of Sir Francis Drake Boulevard, about 20 winding miles from Bear Valley. Here you will find exhibits on whales, wildflowers, birds, and maritime history—all at the base of a 308-step staircase. The Ken Patrick visitor center is on Drakes Beach, the turn-off to which is about 15 miles from Bear Valley on Sir Francis Drake Boulevard. Exhibits here focus on 16th-century maritime exploration, marine fossils, and marine environments. A 150-gallon saltwater aquarium here contains examples of marine life from Drakes Bay. Next to the visitor center is a café featuring home-style cooking. At the end of Pierce Point Road is Pierce Point Ranch, a renovated dairy ranch that was established in 1858. A short self-guiding trail winds past the ranch buildings, open daily sunrise to sunset.

BEAR VALLEY VISITOR CENTER: open Monday through Friday, 9 A.M. to 5 P.M.; weekends and holidays, 8 A.M. to 5 P.M. Closed December 25th.; (415) 663-1092

LIGHTHOUSE VISITOR CENTER: open Thursday through Sunday, 10 A.M. to 5 P.M. Closed December 25th.; (415) 669-1534

KEN PATRICK VISITOR CENTER: open weekends and holidays from 9 A.M. to 5 P.M. Closed December 25th.; (415) 669-1250

DRAKES BEACH CAFÉ: open Friday through Monday from 10 A.M. to 6 P.M.; (415) 669-1297

BACKCOUNTRY CAMPING RESERVATIONS AND PERMITS: in person at the Bear Valley visitor center during its hours of operation, or by phone Monday through Friday, 9 A.M. to 2 P.M.; (415) 663-8054

21 Point Reyes National Seashore
MT. WITTENBERG

Length:	5.1 miles
Time:	2 to 3 hours
Rating:	Moderate
Regulations:	NPS; no dogs, no bikes, no fires; camping by permit only.
Highlights:	Using the Bear Valley, Mt. Wittenberg, Sky, and Meadow trails, this athletic loop takes you up Inverness Ridge to the summit of Mt. Wittenberg, the highest point in Point Reyes National Seashore. No reason other than the joy of hiking is needed to try this route, but further inducements include a wonderful variety of plant and bird life, and great views. Be sure to check with rangers at the visitor center for the latest trail conditions and closures.
Directions:	From Hwy. 1 northbound in Olema, just north of the junction with Sir Francis Drake Blvd., turn left onto Bear Valley Road and go 0.5 mile to the visitor-center entrance road. Turn left and go 0.2 mile to a large paved parking

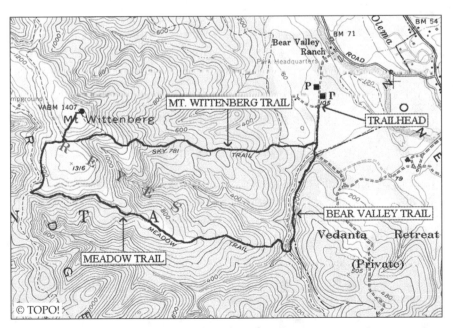

21. Mt. Wittenberg

area in front of the visitor center. If full, there is a dirt parking area ahead and left.

From Hwy. 1 southbound in Point Reyes Station, go 0.2 mile from the end of the town's main street to Sir Francis Drake Blvd. and turn right. Go 0.7 mile and turn left onto Bear Valley Rd. At 1.7 miles you reach the visitor-center entrance road; turn right and follow the directions above.

Facilities: Visitor center with displays, books, maps, helpful staff; picnic tables, rest rooms, telephone, water.

Trailhead: Bear Valley trailhead, at the end of the paved visitor-center entrance road, about 150 feet south of the paved parking area.

The Bear Valley trailhead is one of the busiest in Point Reyes National Seashore, giving visitors access to the heart of this wonderful area. Hikers, bikers, and equestrians share the main thoroughfare, a dirt road called the Bear Valley Trail, for most of its length; but bikes are not allowed past its junction with the Glen Trail, about 0.8 mile short of the coast, and horses are prohibited on weekends and holidays. After walking through a gap in a wooden fence that marks the trailhead, you pass the Rift Zone Trail, left, and the Woodpecker Trail, right. Acorn woodpeckers are common here—a good place to spot them is in the oak-shaded picnic area, just east of the visitor center. Look for a robin-sized bird, black with white wing patches, a white rump, and a red cap on its head. These busy birds collect fallen acorns and then stuff them one by one into holes they have drilled in the trunk of a tree. In addition to oaks, mostly coast live, the road is bordered here and there by stands of massive Douglas fir, California bay, and red elderberry. Many of the trees nearby are beautifully draped with lace lichen, sometimes called Spanish moss.

Coming over a low rise, you make a gentle descent into a more heavily wooded area, crossing a watercourse that goes under the trail through a culvert. When you reach the Mt. Wittenberg Trail, a single track, you turn right, walking under the outstretched limbs of a large, lichen-draped bay tree. The route begins to climb and soon enters a dense bay forest, with an understory of ferns and blackberry vines. The trail, now rough and rocky, widens and steepens, taking you uphill on a moderate grade. The forest here, with tanbark oak, hazelnut, evergreen huckleberry, and western sword fern, resembles a coast-redwood forest with one exception—no coast redwoods. The San Andreas fault defines the western limit of these trees in Marin County, perhaps because the granitic soil on the Point Reyes peninsula is unsuitable for them. Instead, there are tall Douglas firs that compete with the bays for light, in some cases forcing the thinner trees beyond their limit of stability. As a result, you may see collapsed bay trees lying prone on the ground, with new shoots reaching toward the sky.

Short level stretches relieve the otherwise constant climbing, and the variety of plants, including thimbleberry, gooseberry, California wild grape, and elk clover, provides ample reason to stop often and study your surroundings. After several switchbacks, at about the 1-mile point you come to a clearing filled with young Douglas firs. Beyond it, the route levels and takes you through a grassy meadow dotted with coyote brush and poison oak. Narrowing to single-track width, the trail leads uphill on a moderate grade and returns to dense forest. Here you may see flocks of dark-eyed juncos, hear the repeated "enk, enk, enk" call of a white-breasted nuthatch, or be raucously accosted by territorial Steller's jays.

After traversing a weedy clearing, you are back in forest, climbing on a steep grade. Now the trail makes a series of switchbacks to gain the crest of a ridge, along the way passing through another clearing filled with young Douglas firs. Before many years, these clearings may be indistinguishable from the mature forest that blankets Inverness Ridge. After a level section, and then a short downhill stretch, the trail resumes its uphill course, breaking out of the forest at last and crossing a open field, with Mt. Wittenberg rising to the right. The mountain is named for a rancher who once lived nearby, not for Hamlet's alma mater. At about the 2-mile point, you reach a junction, marked by a trail post, where a short trail to Mt. Wittenberg's summit, closed to horses, goes sharply right and uphill. Here too is the Z Ranch Trail, going right on a level

Bear Valley trailhead is the starting point for many hikes in Point Reyes National Seashore.

grade. Also from this junction, the continuation of the Mt. Wittenberg Trail veers slightly left.

To reach the summit of Mt. Wittenberg, at 1407 feet the highest point on Inverness Ridge, you turn sharply right and begin a moderate uphill climb, aided by a single right-hand switchback. After about 0.2 mile you arrive at the summit, where you have fine views of the Point Reyes peninsula, the Olema Valley, Mt. Tamalpais, and, on a clear day, other landmarks to the east, south, and southwest. The summit is a broad clearing bordered by an arc of trees that stretches from north to west, blocking views in those directions. After enjoying the summit, return to the junction and continue on the Mt. Wittenberg Trail, now descending on a gentle and then moderate grade, with a steep hillside falling away right. The view here extends west and southwest into the zone blackened by the October 1995 Vision Fire, where the once-dominant bishop-pine forest is slowly reestablishing itself. Beyond are Limantour Estero, Drakes Beach, and the great curving arm of the peninsula itself.

From the summit-spur junction, after a pleasant downhill ramble, the Mt. Wittenberg Trail ends, and you merge with the Sky Trail, which comes in sharply from the right. It was this trail, a dirt road, that finally blocked the fire's path after it had burned for three days and had charred more than 12,000 acres. About 50 feet past the junction, you leave the Sky Trail and turn left onto the Meadow Trail, a single track. At first running on a level course, the trail soon begins a descent that alternates between gentle and moderate, taking you down through the same Douglas fir forest you just visited on your way up from Bear Valley. At about the 3-mile point, the route suddenly breaks out of the trees and crosses a wide, grassy field, with a lovely view of Mt. Tamalpais straight ahead. For some reason this open expanse, the meadow that gives this trail its name, lacks the young Douglas fir trees that sprout in similar meadows along the Mt. Wittenberg Trail.

At the end of the meadow, the route returns to forest and begins a winding descent, often steep, over eroded, root-crossed ground. This area is home to some of the largest Douglas firs in the Bay Area, similar to ones found in the forests of the Pacific Northwest. The trail levels when it reaches a low divide, and then resumes its plunge off Inverness Ridge into Bear Valley. The sound of running water indicates a nearby creek, which you cross via a wooden bridge. Just ahead is a junction with the Bear Valley Trail, where you turn left. With the creek crossing back and forth under the trail through culverts, you walk downstream, alert for the cries of birds of prey, such as osprey, red-tailed hawk, and red-shouldered hawk, which are often heard before they are seen. Passing a rest bench, right, you soon arrive at the junction with the Mt. Wittenberg Trail. Continue straight to retrace your steps to the parking area.

<table>
<tr><td>22</td><td colspan="2">Point Reyes National Seashore
SKY TRAIL</td></tr>
</table>

Length: 10.5 miles

Time: 5 to 7 hours

Rating: Difficult

Regulations: NPS; no bikes, no dogs, no fires; camping by permit only.

Highlights: Long and strenuous, this is one of the premier hikes in the Point Reyes area, offering a grand tour of Inverness Ridge and Bear Valley, with the Pacific shoreline thrown in for good measure. Using the Bear Valley, Mt. Wittenberg, Sky, and Coast trails, this route gains elevation steeply at first, and then drifts slowly downhill as it approaches the Pacific. Your return is over mostly level ground. The route has something for everyone, including a wonderful array of plant and bird life, and fine views. Be sure to check with rangers at the visitor center for the latest trail conditions and closures.

Directions: See the directions for "Mt. Wittenberg" on pages 137–138.

Facilities: Visitor center with displays, books, maps, helpful staff; picnic tables, rest rooms, telephone, water.

Trailhead: Bear Valley trailhead, at the end of the paved visitor-center entrance road, about 150 feet south of the paved parking area.

Follow the route description for "Mt. Wittenberg" on pages 138–140. but, unless 10.5 miles isn't enough of a workout for you, omit the short excursion to the mountain's summit. When you reach the junction of the Sky and Meadow trails, at about the 2.4-mile point, stay on the Sky Trail, enjoying a rolling course through a wonderful Douglas-fir forest. Soon the route, a dirt road, begins to descend, alternating between gentle and moderate grades. As you tromp along the trail, you may scare up a covey of California quail, birds that run and hide to avoid predators, taking flight only as a last resort. From a small clearing, the Woodward Valley Trail heads right, but you continue straight, as you will at each upcoming intersection until the Sky Trail meets the Coast Trail near Kelham Beach, about 3 miles from here.

Now the route makes a moderate and then steep climb before reaching level ground on a track gouged out of a steep hillside that falls away left. Bordering the road are red elderberry, evergreen huckleberry, and western sword fern. At about the 3.4-mile point, you pass the Old Pine Trail,

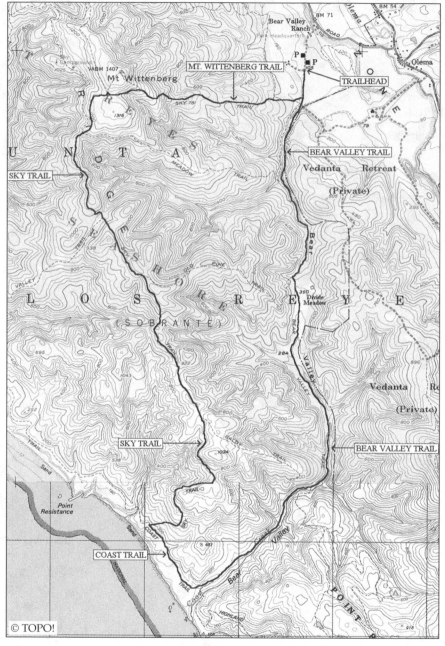

22. Sky Trail

left, which can be used to reach the Bear Valley Trail, your return route, as can the Baldy Trail, about 1.4 miles ahead. After cresting a low rise, you now enjoy a long, gentle downhill, with a ravine on your right in which you may see evidence of the 1995 Vision Fire, which stopped its eastward march at the Sky Trail. The route narrows and drops steeply into a gully, then climbs to higher ground where you may feel, for the first time today, a cooling ocean breeze.

Emerging from the forest, you negotiate a steep descent over rough ground near a weedy field, right, that may be decorated with California poppies. Passing the Baldy Trail, left, you enter the zone of coastal scrub, where shrubs such as California sagebrush, coyote brush, poison oak, bush monkeyflower, and silver lupine thrive. If the day has been hot, it may feel here, as you near the coast, like someone just turned on the air conditioning. Now you enter a corridor of Douglas fir, which also holds coffeeberry and honeysuckle, and, once out of the trees, begin a steep descent, serenaded by the crashing of surf against shore. Even with eyes shut and ears plugged, the scent of salt air would tell you the ocean is near. Here you may find wax myrtle, related to the bayberry found in New England, with long, lance-shaped leaves, and tiny hard berries attached to its branches.

After a 180-degree bend to the right, the route continues its now-perhaps-fog-shrouded descent, where the unmistakably human voices echoing in the mist may be only the cries of gulls. Turkey vultures glide in and out of view, and you may hear the call of a song sparrow or a spotted towhee. At about the 6-mile point, the Sky Trail merges with the Coast Trail, a dirt road, at a sharp angle. Here you continue nearly straight, now heading southeast on the Coast Trail, a few hundred feet above sea level. An easy 0.5-mile walk brings you to the turn-off for Arch Rock, right, a worthwhile detour on a sunny day, especially during spring wildflower season. Now the Coast Trail turns left, away from the coast, passing an exposed rock formation and also a large Monterey cypress, both left. The valley to your right holds Coast Creek, which flows south, then southwest, from Divide Meadow and empties into the Pacific near Arch Rock.

Soon you reach a junction where the Coast Trail bends sharply right and the

Lupine comes in many forms, including a woody shrub with purple flowers called silver lupine.

Bear Valley Trail, your route, goes straight. This pleasant dirt-and-gravel road is bordered by stands of Douglas fir, bay, red alder, and California buckeye. In moist places you may find common monkeyflower, sword fern, wood fern, and fivefinger fern. A beautiful stream tumbles down on your left, splashing over rocks and making little waterfalls, then flows under the road through a culvert. Climbing imperceptibly, you pass the Baldy Trail, left, and then reach a clearing where the Glen Trail takes off to the right. Because of wilderness-area regulations, bicyclists heading from the visitor center to the coast must park their bikes here and walk the rest of the way; a rack is provided for their use.

Continuing straight, and then following the road as it curves left, you pass willow thickets on your right, and what seem like acres of poison oak on your left. At Divide Meadow, there are rest rooms and a junction with the Old Pine Trail, both left. Dangling vines of California wild grape provide splashes of color in fall. The route makes a sweeping bend to the right and begins to descend. Beyond a rest bench, right, is another lovely creek, this one flowing north from Divide Meadow and meandering from one side of the trail to the other through culverts. Another rest bench signals a junction with the Meadow Trail, left, and now the roadsides are choked with elk clover, a weedy shrub with huge leaves and fantastic clusters of dark berries. Snags in the forest nearby make fine perches for birds of prey such as osprey and hawks. At the junction with the Mt. Wittenberg Trail, continue straight and retrace your steps to the parking area.

23 Point Reyes National Seashore
TOMALES POINT

Length: 9.4 miles

Time: 4 to 5 hours

Rating: Moderate

Regulations: NPS; no dogs, no camping.

Highlights: One of the premier hikes in the North Bay, this out-and-back trip over rolling terrain uses the Tomales Point Trail to reach Tomales Bluff, the northwest tip of Tomales Point. Starting from historic Pierce Point Ranch, the trail takes you through a tule-elk preserve, where these magnificent creatures are sometimes seen at close range. Exposed to the wind, this hike is best on a warm day.

Directions: From Hwy. 1 just south of Point Reyes Station, turn southwest onto Sir Francis Drake Blvd. and follow it for 6.5

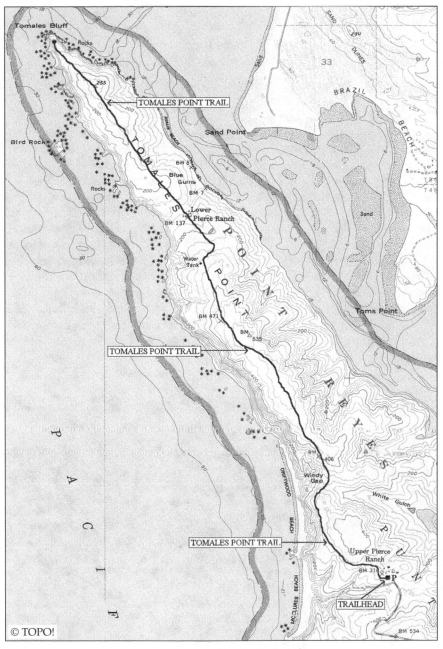

Tomales Bluff

Rocks

285

TOMALES POINT TRAIL

Sand Point

Bird Rock

BM 6

Blue
Gums

BM 7

Rocks

Lower
Pierce Ranch

BM 137

Water
Tank

BM 471

BM
535

TOMALES POINT TRAIL

Toms Point

TOMALES POINT TRAIL

Windy
Gap

406

White Gulch

TOMALES POINT TRAIL

Upper Pierce
Ranch

BM 31

P

TRAILHEAD

BM 534

© TOPO!

23. Tomales Point

miles to a fork, where you bear right onto Pierce Point Rd. At 9.2 miles from the fork, where Pierce Point Rd. bends sharply left toward McClures Beach, there is parking on the right for the Pierce Point Ranch and Tomales Point. If the parking area is full, park on the east side of Pierce Point Rd., just before the bend.

Facilities: None at the trailhead; rest rooms at McClures Beach.

Trailhead: West side of parking area.

Point Reyes was, and still is, a prime area for dairy ranching. On your way here, you passed three historic ranches on Pierce Point Road, and more are located on the road to the lighthouse. The ranch buildings adjacent to the parking area were part of a 2,200-acre spread purchased in 1858 by Solomon Pierce and later owned by his son Abram. The Pierce Ranch dairy, it is said, produced in a good year more butter than any other dairy in the area, most of it going to booming San Francisco. The ranch was sold by Abram's heirs to the McClure family, which ran it from 1929 to 1966. Now under NPS ownership, and on the National Register of Historic Places, Pierce Point Ranch is being restored and serves as a museum of ranching history. A path through the ranch complex leaves from the north side of the parking area.

To find the Tomales Point Trail, you leave the parking area's west side through a gap in the surrounding fence, passing an information board with a short history of the Point Reyes dairies. Other than a line of tall

Tule elk are often seen and heard from the trail to Tomales Point.

Monterey cypress and a few eucalyptus trees, the terrain is treeless—just rolling, grassy hills and fields. During spring and fall, groves of trees on otherwise barren stretches of Point Reyes act as "migrant traps," giving shelter to exhausted songbirds that may have been flying for many hours over open ocean. Savvy birders know to check these groves carefully, especially on foggy days when the wind is from the south or southwest. These conditions are often favorable for finding uncommon or even rare birds.

Rounding a large barn, right, the trail begins climbing on a gentle grade. A common coastal shrub, yellow bush lupine, may be displaying its buttery flowers nearby. If you hear eerie, high-pitched calling, don't be alarmed. You are in a tule elk preserve, and the male elk uses these weird vocalizations to assemble his harems of females and to announce his territorial intentions to competing males. During the fall rutting season, a male with a large harem is often challenged by a younger upstart, and will defend his turf by charging the outsider, locking antlers with him, and pushing him back across an unmarked, but very real, territorial limit. Even without a challenger present, a male may use his rack of antlers to uproot patches of grass and dirt and, with a toss of his head, throw them in the air. Throughout these displays, the females, for whom they are presumably intended, remain aloof and seemingly unimpressed.

Looking skyward, you may see turkey vultures, ravens, an occasional northern harrier on patrol, or a kestrel hovering in the breeze. On your left is the Pacific Ocean and wave-washed McClures Beach, several hundred feet below. During winter months, gray whales pass by on their journey from the Bering Sea to Baja and back. From August through October, huge flocks of sooty shearwaters, an ocean-going bird, skim above the near-shore swells. Tomales Point is a long finger of land jutting northwest and separating the outer reaches of Tomales Bay from the ocean. The name "Tomales" refers to a tribe of Indians called Tamal, which is Coast Miwok for "west" or "west coast," the same word that gave us Mt. Tamalpais. If you look south, you may be able to see the tip of Point Reyes, where the lighthouse is located. To the north lie Bodega Bay, Bodega Head, and the Sonoma County coast.

As the trail swings right, you have a great view of the steep, eroded cliffs that form the southwest rampart of Tomales Point. Low-lying California poppies border the trail, which now descends to a flat spot at the head of White Gulch, a valley heading down to Tomales Bay. This is a good place to glimpse tule elk, if you haven't already seen them. Now on a moderate and then steep uphill, you reach the top of a rocky bluff, a vantage point with views, on a clear day, of some North Bay landmarks, including the hulking outlines of Mt. St. Helena and Mt. Tamalpais. From this high point, at about the 2-mile point, the route begins to descend toward the site of Lower Pierce Ranch, devoid of buildings but marked by a grove of Monterey cypress and eucalyptus. Large rocks in the water ahead and left—the largest being Bird Rock—hold hundreds, perhaps thousands, of sea birds. Across Tomales Bay, near its outlet, is Dillon Beach, a popular recreation and camping spot.

Following the rough and rocky trail as it bends right, you pass a pond, right, that is a favorite elk hang-out. Hikers often gather here in large groups, conversing in hushed tones, to watch the elk. These beasts are used to people, and as long as you keep a safe distance, it is possible to observe them at your leisure. Males use the pond to bathe by splashing water over themselves with their antlers. Lounging females, if startled, rise and run, but their guardian and protector usually stays put until he can catch the intruder's scent and determine the level of threat. Once thought to be extinct, tule elk in California now number about 3,200 in 22 herds, thanks to active management by the Department of Fish and Game. On the Point Reyes peninsula, tule elk vanished around 1860, but were re-introduced in 1978 to Tomales Point. The elk herd here now has more than 500 members, and plans are underway to create a new refuge just east of Limantour Beach. Individuals from Tomales Point will be moved to Limantour to prevent overgrazing here.

After a final, steep descent to the ranch site, you cross a gully that may be seasonally wet, home to ferns, rushes, sedges, and tangles of blackberry vines. Beach pea decorates a slope just beyond the gully. Regaining lost elevation on a moderate grade, which eases as you near a high point, you may notice the stench of guano drifting over from Bird Rock, cloaked in white droppings. Lupine, coyote brush, and thistle offer perches beside

Tule elk graze and bathe in a pond just off Pierce Point Road just east of McClures Beach.

the trail for sparrows, gold finches, and an occasional monarch butterfly. At a signed junction, a faint trace veers left, but you continue straight, now climbing on soft sand. This soil seems to favor lupine above all else—it is everywhere, growing in large, shrubby clumps. On warm fall days, lupine seed pods open with a startling "pop!" When you reach a wide level spot where paths seem to lead in all directions, you continue straight, finding your way into a large, open, sandy area. These clearings, devoid of plants, resemble wind-scoured barrens that are called "blowouts" in New England.

Descending now over loose sand, you may hear the metallic clanging of the Tomales Bay entrance buoy. A gull gliding by on the wind is likely to be one of two species, ring-billed or western. A ring-billed gull is a crow-sized bird with a light gray mantle, black-tipped wings, yellow feet, and a black ring around its bill. A western gull is a larger bird with a dark mantle, pink feet, and a red spot on its bill. Brown pelicans, coastal birds that visit our area usually in summer, may be seen cruising low above the wave troughs. The trail takes you very close to the sheer cliffs fronting the Pacific, where a signed warning, TRAIL CLOSED, DANGEROUS CONDITIONS, should be heeded. The view does not improve beyond this point, but your risk of injury certainly does. When you've had your fill of this remote and wonderful place, called Tomales Bluff, retrace your steps to the parking area.

◆ Samuel P. Taylor State Park ◆

This secluded park is one link in an unbroken chain of public land that stretches from the Golden Gate to the mouth of Tomales Bay. Through it flow lovely Lagunitas Creek, also called Papermill Creek, and several of its tributaries, including Devil's Gulch Creek. Sir Francis Drake Boulevard, which parallels Lagunitas Creek, is the dividing line between two very different parts of the park. The southern part, at the foot of Bolinas Ridge, is dark and jungle-like, home to groves of coast redwood, mostly second-growth. The northern part consists of riparian vegetation, Douglas-fir forest, oak-and-bay woodlands, and grassland. Spring wildflowers put on a colorful show throughout the park.

Barnabe Mountain (1466'), about 1 mile northeast of the park entrance, is the park's highest point. Hikers, equestrians, and bicyclists can enjoy many miles of trails on the park's nearly 3000 acres. Lagunitas Creek has runs of steelhead trout and coho salmon, both listed as threatened species under federal law. The best time to view the migrating salmon is after the rains begin, usually in November and December. Steelhead migrate later, usually in February and March. The creek is also home to the tiny California freshwater shrimp, an endangered species.

The park's namesake, Samuel Penfield Taylor, sailed from Boston to San Francisco during the Gold Rush of 1849. Taylor made nearly $6,000 in the gold fields, and then returned to San Francisco, soon buying 100 acres of timberland along Arroyo San Geronimo, the present-day Lagunitas Creek. Instead of running a logging operation, Taylor built the West Coast's first paper mill, which used as raw materials rags, rope, burlap, and scrap paper from San Francisco and other towns. Many trees were cut, however, to build the mill and the housing for its workers. The mill, which opened in 1856, produced newsprint, fine paper for ballots and official documents, and paper bags.

In 1874, Taylor built a small hotel to accommodate visitors. That same year, the North Pacific Coast Railroad, a narrow-gauge line that eventually ran from Sausalito to Cazadero, north of the Russian River, began service through the Lagunitas Creek canyon. Seeing an opportunity, Taylor enlarged his hotel and added other amenities such as a dance pavilion, a rooming house, and tent cabins. By the 1880s, Taylorville, or Camp Taylor, as the resort was called, was one of Northern California's premier recreation spots, where vacationers could picnic, swim, ride horses, camp, row boats on the mill pond, and admire the hotel's rose garden and nearby wild azaleas. Taylor died in 1886 and is buried in a grave site between the Barnabe Trail and Deadman's Gulch. Sadly, the hotel burned in the early 1900s and was never rebuilt. Another fire in

1915 wiped out the entire settlement. The Marin Conservation League acquired the land in 1945 and gave it to the state, which opened the park a year later.

The park has 60 family campsites, open year-round. From April though October, reservations are required and may be made up to six months in advance. During the remainder of the year, campsites are available on a first-come, first-served basis. There are also several group campsites and a site for bicyclists and hikers. Devil's Gulch Horse Camp has three sites for overnight horse camping, and these may be reserved by calling the ranger station. There is a day-use picnic area near the park entrance, and also a reservable group picnic area called Redwood Grove. Dogs on leash are allowed in the park's campsites and on its dirt and paved roads, but not on its hiking trails.

RANGER STATION: (415) 488-9897

CAMPING RESERVATIONS: (800) 444-7275

GROUP PICNIC RESERVATIONS: (800) 444-7275

24

Samuel P. Taylor State Park
BARNABE MOUNTAIN

Length:	6.6 miles
Time:	3 to 4 hours
Rating:	Difficult
Regulations:	CSP; no dogs or bikes on single-track trails.
Highlights:	This loop, using Devils Gulch Creek, Bill's, Barnabe, and the Riding and Hiking trails, climbs gently through mixed forest, alive with birdsong and brightened by wildflowers, struggles steeply to high ground just below the summit of Barnabe Mountain (1466'), and then descends through open country with wonderful views of west Marin, Point Reyes and the Tomales Bay area. Near the end of the loop, before heading back into the forest, you can visit the grave site of Samuel P. Taylor (1827–1896), who established the West Coast's first paper mill on the banks of nearby Lagunitas Creek. (Barnabe Mountain is called Barnabe Peak on the state-park map.)
Directions:	From Hwy. 101 northbound, take the San Anselmo exit, also signed for San Quentin, Sir Francis Drake Blvd., and the Richmond Bridge. Stay in the left lane as you exit,

24. Barnabe Mountain

toward San Anselmo, crossing over Hwy. 101. After 0.4 mile you join Sir Francis Drake Blvd., with traffic from Hwy. 101 southbound merging on your right. From here, it is 3.6 miles to a stop light at the intersection with Red Hill Ave. Stay on Sir Francis Drake Blvd. as it first goes straight and then immediately bends left.

At 10.7 miles from Hwy. 101, you pass Nicasio Valley Rd., right, the turn-off to Roy's Redwoods Open Space Preserve. At 15.5 miles on Sir Francis Drake Blvd., you pass the main entrance to Samuel P. Taylor State Park. At 16.5 miles you reach a wide turn-out, left, at Devil's Gulch. Park here.

From Hwy. 101 southbound, take the Sir Francis Drake/Kentfield exit and follow the directions above.

Facilities: None at the trailhead. Water, phone, rest rooms, and picnic tables just inside the state park's main entrance.

Trailhead: Across Sir Francis Drake Blvd. from parking area.

After carefully crossing Sir Francis Drake Boulevard, you follow a paved road that heads northeast into a forest of bigleaf maple, California bay, blue elderberry, California buckeye, and white alder, with Devil's Gulch Creek downhill and right. The creek, when full, rushes and spills over large rock boulders, its steep banks home to shrubs such as hazelnut, coffeeberry, thimbleberry, and poison oak. In spring, the tiny blue flowers of forget-me-not, an import from Africa, greet you from the forest floor. After about 0.1 mile, you turn right onto unsigned Devil's Gulch Creek Trail, a single-track that descends toward the creek. Soon passing a set of wooden steps, left, that climb to a picnic area with toilets, you reach a four-way junction at the base of an enormous coast redwood. Here, Devil's Gulch Creek Trail continues straight, parallel to the creek, and a short trail heads left and uphill to Devil's Gulch Horse Camp. Your route turns right and crosses a long wooden bridge spanning the creek.

Once across, you arrive at a T-junction, drawn incorrectly on the state park map. Here the Riding and Hiking Trail to the Barnabe Trail, which you will use later on your descent, goes right. This trail is open to bikes and to dogs on leash. Your route, shown on the park map as "Bills' Trail," is closed to bikes and dogs. It heads left and begins a long, gentle climb. Red columbine and starflower may be blooming in great numbers after a wet winter. The bay trees here, struggling for light, arch over the creek, and their shade is welcome on a hot day. Soon the bays are joined by Douglas fir and coast live oak. A plank bridge takes you across a small ravine, and soon you begin to see eucalyptus leaves and strips of bark on the ground, and then the trees themselves, evidence of human intervention sometime in the past.

Another plank bridge takes you across a gully, where a beautiful tributary of Devil's Gulch Creek may be tumbling down toward a deep canyon, left. Soon you reach a junction with the Stairstep Falls Trail, left, a short trail to a vantage point where you can view the falls. From this junction, your route, Bill's Trail, turns right and uphill, its course etched out of a steep hillside that falls away left. On a sunny day, intense patches of light interrupt long stretches of shade, highlighting the rich green of fern fronds and hazelnut leaves growing beside the trail. Now, just past the 1-mile point, your ascent is aided by a series of sharp switchbacks, bringing you to a weedy area of poison hemlock, cow parsnip, Italian thistle, and tangled blackberry vines. A sunny, west-facing hillside is home to patches of blue nightshade.

The route soon levels and runs generally east, past stands of bigleaf maple, bay, Douglas fir, and California nutmeg, with its shiny, sharply pointed needles. More switchbacks help you gain elevation, and two wooden bridges, separated by a twisted stretch of trail, get you across a single deep ravine, around the 2.5-mile point. In maintaining a gentle grade, this trail covers lots of ground. Dark-eyed juncos and spotted towhees, both lovers of forest and dense cover, may be seen and heard here. Both species show white along the tail in flight, but the towhee is a larger, more dramatically patterned bird, colored black, white, and orange. The junco, classed with the sparrows, has a black head, buff sides, a white belly, and a pink bill. Juncos flit in noisy flocks from tree to tree.

California poppy, the state flower, colors North Bay grasslands in spring and summer.

Towhees are usually alone or in pairs, often scraping through fallen leaves for food.

Now sunny clearings interrupt the shady forest, as the trail, in places bordered by a split-rail fence, continues to zigzag its way uphill. In the clearings, grassy fields are dotted with California poppies, scarlet pimpernel, and wild geraniums. Finally leaving most of the trees behind, you reach a superb vantage point where the view extends west to the lands of Point Reyes National Seashore, and northwest to Tomales Bay. Now the trail forks: both arms lead, in about 40 feet, to the Barnabe Trail, a dirt road. Once

on the road, you can turn left to continue the ascent of Barnabe Mountain,
a climb of about 200 feet in 0.25 mile.
Or you can turn right to begin the
descent back to Sir Francis Drake
Boulevard.

If you choose to climb, you follow a
moderate and then steep course, with
the fire lookout on the summit of
Barnabe Mountain in view. Barnabe
Mountain honors a retired army mule,
formerly in the service of John C.
Frémont, that Taylor bought at the
Presidio in San Francisco. California
sagebrush, bush monkeyflower, and
silver lupine grace the roadsides. A
weedy, overgrown area contains coy-

*Paintbrush is a familiar red or orange
flower that comes in many varieties.*

ote brush, snowberry, and creambush. Even on a warm day, wind blowing uninterrupted from the Pacific Ocean can be chilling. Stunted bays
and Douglas firs are evidence of its power. At about the 4.25-mile point,
you reach a T-junction at the state park boundary, shown incorrectly on
the state-park map. From here, a dirt road goes left and uphill to the fire
lookout, and also right. Rising on the eastern horizon is Mt. Diablo; Mt.
Tamalpais is southeast, Kent Lake is south, and Big Rock Ridge, the high
divide between Lucas Valley and the City of Novato, is northeast.

When you have finished enjoying this wonderful vantage point, turn
and retrace your steps downhill to the junction with Bill's Trail. From
here, continue on the dirt road, descending over rocky ground that alternates between moderate and steep, with darting violet-green swallows
perhaps company. The terrain is open, and the grasslands beside the trail
may contain bluedicks, blue-eyed grass, common paintbrush, and bellar-
dia. After one steep drop, the road climbs over a rise and then resumes its
plunge. Soon you pass a junction, left, with the Riding and Hiking Trail
to the Madrone Picnic Area, and then reach a four-way junction. Here the
Barnabe Trail veers left and descends to Sir Francis Drake Blvd. A short
trail to the Samuel P. Taylor grave site, with a marker and a rest bench,
goes straight. And your route, the Riding and Hiking Trail to Devil's
Gulch, turns right.

Heading into a forest of now-familiar trees, you follow a rough, eroded road steeply downhill into Deadman's Gulch. Here a creek may be
pouring over a series of rock ledges, making little waterfalls, and then
flowing across the road. Now the road swings sharply right and climbs
to a junction. Leaving the road, signed here as the Barnabe Trail, you turn
left and follow another dirt road, perhaps scaring up a covey of California
quail. In about 75 feet, your route, now a single-track trail, veers left and

skirts the hillside. You are heading north, and the fire lookout on the summit of Barnabe Mountain is visible to the east.

Soon the route begins to descend, and then it merges with a dirt road coming downhill steeply from the right. This is the continuation of the dirt road, signed as the Barnabe Trail, that you left a short while ago. Bay and California nutmeg are joined here by canyon oak, and shrubs such as hazelnut, coffeeberry, creambush, and wild rose. Now with Devil's Gulch Creek downhill and left, you make a steep descent and soon reach the junction with Bill's Trail and the wooden bridge you passed at the start of this loop. Here you turn left, cross the bridge, turn left again, and retrace your steps to the parking area.

25

Samuel P. Taylor State Park
PIONEER TREE TRAIL

Length:	2.8 miles
Time:	1 to 2 hours
Rating:	Easy
Regulations:	CSP; parking fee; no dogs, no bikes.
Highlights:	This wonderful loop takes you into secluded Wildcat Canyon, home to some of the largest coast redwoods in the park, giants between 700 and 1000 years old. One of these, the Pioneer Tree, has been hollowed by fire, and you can actually stand inside its massive trunk. Along the way, you will also get acquainted with other members of the redwood forest community—plants and animals adapted to the cool, moist, shady environment.
Directions:	See the directions for "Barnabe Mountain" on pages 151 and 153. When you reach the state park's main entrance, at 15.5 miles on Sir Francis Drake Blvd., turn left and go 100 yards to the entrance kiosk. The main picnic area and day-use parking area are about 100 yards west of the kiosk. Park as far west as possible.
Facilities:	Visitor center, water, picnic tables, fire grates, rest rooms, phones.
Trailhead:	West end of day-use parking area.

Even before setting off to find the trail, you can enjoy some of the attractions of this lovely park. First, of course, are the towering coast redwoods, remnants of a great forest that once stretched along the fog-shrouded coast from central California to southern Oregon. Although most of the redwoods in the park are second-growth trees, their ancestors having been logged in the late 1800s to build San Francisco and other cities, today's hike takes you through some old-growth stands and brings you to the base of the Pioneer Tree, a fire-scarred giant that predates Columbus. Other members of this forest community, which you can find before leaving the picnic area, include tanbark oak, California bay, bigleaf maple, and hazelnut. Be on the lookout for poison oak as well.

From the west end of the day-use parking area, you follow a paved road west, with a rest room on your left. Soon the road forks, and you follow the left-hand branch, which immediately crosses a large cement bridge over Lagunitas Creek. A sign here reads CAMPGROUND AND RED-WOOD GROVE GROUP PICNIC AREA. After crossing the bridge, you come to a T-junction with another paved road. The campground is right, but your route heads left, bringing you, in about 100 yards, to a large paved parking area that serves the Redwood Grove Group Picnic Area. Lagunitas Creek, home to coho salmon and steelhead trout migrating from the

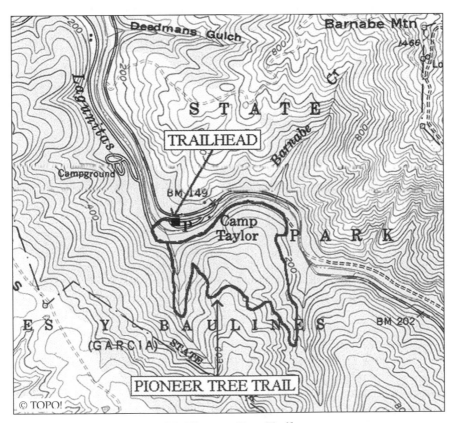

25. Pioneer Tree Trail

Pacific Ocean via Tomales Bay, is downhill and left. The salmon begin to arrive in November, and the steelhead run takes place in February and March. Both species of fish are listed as threatened under the federal Endangered Species Act. Also present in the creek are California fresh-water shrimp, listed as endangered under state and federal law.

About 100 feet past the parking area, the pavement ends, and you continue on a dirt road, part of the Cross Marin Trail, a route open to hikers, equestrians, and bicyclists. This is the roadbed of the narrow-gauge North Pacific Coast Railroad, which used to run from Sausalito to Cazadero, north of the Russian River. Another 100 feet brings you to a gate, and about 25 feet past the gate is the Pioneer Tree Trail, right. Turning onto it, a single track, you begin a gentle climb into Wildcat Canyon, a peaceful place of deep shade with a rain-forest feel. Several hundred feet from the trail's start, you cross a culvert that carries a tributary into the canyon's creek, left. Evergreen huckleberry and elk clover, a big-leaved, weedy shrub, form much of the understory here. The trail takes you past a rest bench, left, and then between two giant redwoods spaced so closely that you can touch them both at the same time. A fallen redwood spans the creek, left, and resembles a huge bridge. Redwoods lack deep tap roots, and instead rely on a shallow network of interlocking roots for stability. This makes them especially vulnerable to being toppled by high winds.

Soon a plank bridge takes you across the creek, where water splashes from one rocky pool to another and flows over and between downed redwood trunks and limbs. After a short, moderate climb, the route bends sharply left and finds a mostly level course. Here you may see California nutmeg, an evergreen that resembles a young redwood, but with sharply pointed needles. Ferns and mosses cover a hillside, right, while a pair of fire-scarred redwoods stand just to the left of the trail. Redwoods, like their Sierra cousins the giant sequoias, have thick, insulating bark to protect them from fire. Some of the trees here bear scars from fires as recent as 1945.

Just shy of the 1-mile point, a trail signed CLOSED joins sharply from the left. You continue straight, and then begin a moderate climb through a possibly muddy area. Soon you reach a rest bench and a junction, where another closed trail, this one a steep dirt road, descends left. Your route levels and bends right, bringing you to the head of a shallow draw, where a culvert diverts run-off under the trail. Just ahead, another closed trail climbs steeply right, but you veer sharply left, now in a forest of tall, thin bay trees. The closed trail you recently passed rejoins from the left, and you also pass a faint trace taking off uphill and right. As you continue straight, you return to the realm of the redwoods, here joined by Douglas fir.

Passing a dirt road on the right, you climb gently past stands of fire-scarred redwoods, noticing perhaps the difference between the redwood and Douglas-fir cones. Redwood cones are deeply cut spheres, less than 1 inch across, whereas Douglas-fir cones are tapered cylinders, several inches long. Protruding from between the Douglas-fir cone scales are three-pointed bracts, a field mark for this species. Where sunlight penetrates the dense forest canopy, you may find iris, wild rose, coffeeberry, and plenty of poison oak. After a possibly muddy area, the trail makes a sharp bend left. Here a signed trail, right, leads in about 25 feet to the Pioneer Tree.

This old-growth redwood, which has stood here for more than 500 years, was hollowed by fire, allowing you to stand inside its trunk—a wonderful experience, being wholly contained by a living thing. Surrounding the Pioneer Tree is a ring of smaller redwoods, youngsters gathered around their elder parent. This so-called fairy ring is an example of how redwoods reproduce by sprouting from the base of a felled or damaged ancestor. Just uphill from here is a rest bench, providing a vantage point from which you can better appreciate the massive proportions of the Pioneer Tree.

Back on the main trail, you enjoy a level walk and soon reach the head of a small ravine, where the route swings sharply left. Irving Creek is downhill and right, in the depths of a brushy canyon. Most of the redwoods have been temporarily left behind, replaced by coast live oaks. Blue-eyed grass and madia, a yellow, daisy-like flower, brighten the scene here in spring. Now a spur trail branches right and leads to a rock promontory, with fine views of Lagunitas Creek, Sir Francis Drake Boulevard, and Barnabe Mountain, whose summit you can visit by following the previous route description in this guidebook. If you take this short detour, be careful of the severe drop-off at the edge of the promontory.

Continuing on the main trail, you pass a tangle of blackberry vines and cross a possibly wet area, where water may be seeping from the hillside, left. Once again you find yourself among the redwoods, as the trail loses elevations via a series of switchbacks. Here the forest floor is carpeted with redwood sorrel, a plant with three heart-shaped leaves and pink, five-petaled flowers. Now a moderate

Sign on a stump at the west end of the parking area.

descent brings you to the end of the Pioneer Tree Trail and a junction with the Cross Marin Trail. You merge with it and continue straight. The Cross Marin Trail is paved here, but in about 60 feet reverts to a dirt road, running parallel to Lagunitas Creek. Big-leaf maple, a water-loving species, is prevalent here. You may also find blue-blossom, creambush, thimbleberry, and red columbine growing from the embankment, left. Passing a rest bench, right, you soon reach the junction with the Pioneer Tree Trail. From here, retrace your steps to the parking area.

Swimming hole on Lagunitas Creek, about 1 mile northwest of the Pioneer Tree Trail.

26 Tomales Bay State Park
PEBBLE BEACH

Length: 2.5 miles

Time: 1 to 2 hours

Rating: Easy

Regulations: CSP; no dogs, no bikes

Highlights: This easy loop, using the Jepson and Johnstone trails, takes you through a wonderful grove of rare bishop pines and then to Pebble Beach, a secluded cove on Tomales Bay with not a golf course in sight. The variety of plant life along the way is stunning, and it is no wonder the pine grove and one of the trails are named in honor of California's premier botanist, the late Willis Linn Jepson.

Directions: See the directions for "Tomales Point" on pages 144 and 146. After bearing right on Pierce Point Rd., go 1.2 miles to the state-park entrance road and turn right. At 0.7 mile you come to the entrance station, where you pay a day-use fee. If no ranger is on duty, pay at the self-registration station here. At 1.2 miles you pass the turn-off to Hearts Desire Beach. Continue another 0.1 mile to a fork, the start of a one-way loop leading to parking areas for the picnic grounds. Park in the upper area, along the left side of the road, before it makes a 180-degree bend to the left.

Facilities: Rest rooms, picnic tables, fire grates, water; maps for sale at park entrance station when ranger is on duty.

Trailhead: In the upper parking area, on the right side of the one-way loop, midway between its start and the 180-degree bend to the left.

Your route, a single-track trail climbing on a moderate grade, honors the late Willis Linn Jepson, a UC Botanist who wrote the definitive guide to California plants. This state park encloses a grove of rare bishop pines, which lies a short distance ahead. The grove is also named for Dr. Jepson. Bishop pine, restricted to coastal California and a few locations in Mexico, has thick, deeply furrowed gray bark, spiny cones that remain closed and attached to the tree for many years, and needles in bundles of two. As an adaptation to fire, the cones open and release their seeds after a blaze, allowing the forest to renew itself. An example of this can be seen nearby on Inverness Ridge in Point Reyes National Seashore, where a devastating wildfire in October 1995 charred more than 12,000 acres.

Although most of the adult trees were killed, surveys conducted in 1996 and 1997 found an "abundance of bishop pine seedlings" sprouting in the fire area.

In addition to bishop pines, the park has a rich abundance of other trees, including coast live oak, California bay, and madrone, along with common shrubs such hazelnut, coffeeberry, bush monkeyflower, several varieties of ceanothus, toyon, thimbleberry, and evergreen huckleberry, all of which may be seen along the first stretch of trail. A dense understory of ferns gives the area a jungle-like appearance. But it is the pines that hold center stage, their tall, stout trunks supporting wide crowns of needle-encircled limbs. A number of trees are lying prone on the forest floor—mute testimony perhaps to the power of the wind. The tree's common name, incidentally, was apparently taken from its place of discovery in 1835, near the mission of San Luis Obispo—a mission named for Saint Louis, Bishop of Toulouse.

26. Pebble Beach

Beyond several rest benches, the trail levels and passes through an area thick with poison oak, California wild grape, and salal. Where a fallen pine has been cut, you can see just how thick its bark is and how it is cracked into deep furrows. Soon you reach a junction where a branch of the Jepson Trail turns right to an overnight-parking area beside Pierce Point Rd. Here you continue straight, still on the main branch of the Jepson Trail, and in about 100 yards cross a paved road that winds downhill from a locked gate at the overnight-parking area, right, to a swath of private beach-front property on Tomales Bay. After crossing the road, you descend a few wooden steps and then enjoy a gentle downhill ramble through a weedy, overgrown area where asters may add color in the fall.

The Jepson Trail now ends at a **T** junction with the Johnstone Trail, a single track named for Bruce and Elsie Johnstone, who helped with efforts to create Tomales Bay State Park. Turning left, you follow a level course amid the by-now-familiar trees and shrubs, with tanbark oak and manzanita added for good measure. Certainly this park is a botanical paradise, and it is easy to see why so many local conservation groups made the area's protection a top priority. Just past the 1-mile point, you again cross the paved access road, and begin a winding downhill course. The large, oak-like trees beside the trail here are chinquapin, a chestnut relative, often found as a small shrub associated with manzanita and evergreen huckleberry. Chinquapin's dark green leaves are coated on their undersides with golden scales, making it easy to confuse with canyon oak. This golden coloration is alluded to in the scientific names of

Bush monkeyflower, a shrub, adds yellow color to chaparral from spring through summer.

both chinquapin (*Chrysolepis chrysophylla*) and canyon oak (*Quercus chrysolepis*)—"chrysolepis" is Greek for "golden scale."

Making several sharp switchbacks, the route descends to the floor of a small valley, a wet and muddy area that you cross via raised boardwalks. Joining the dense array of shrubs thriving in this moist and sheltered area is red alder, a tree that favors stream banks and other damp locations. Rising from the valley, and then descending gently, the route soon reaches a **T**-junction, where a short trail, right, takes you in a couple of hundred feet to Pebble Beach. Passing some toilets, left, you arrive at a sandy cove on Tomales Bay, a secluded spot enjoyed by swimmers, picnickers, sun-bathers, and boaters. At either end of the cove, a rugged coast-line drops steeply to meet the bay. Behind the beach is a little marsh with cattails and sedges. After visiting the beach, retrace your steps to the previous junction, and continue straight on the Johnstone Trail, climbing on a moderate grade. The bay, right, is well hidden by trees and shrubs.

Cresting a low rise, you follow a rolling course on a winding trail, passing a path to a viewpoint, right. Soon you come to a picnic area, with tables and fire grates. A large sign lists distances on the Johnstone Trail to various points, including Hearts Desire Beach, which is 0.2 mile ahead. Once past the sign, you leave the Johnstone Trail, bearing left through the picnic area until you reach the rest rooms and then, in about 100 feet, the lower parking area. From here turn left and follow the paved parking-area road to the upper parking area.

27 Tomales Bay State Park
SHELL BEACH

Length: 7 miles

Time: 3 to 4 hours

Rating: Difficult

Regulations: CSP; no dogs, no bikes

Highlights: This semi-loop trip, rated difficult because of its length, takes you on a grand tour of the park, passing through the Jepson Memorial Grove of rare bishop pines, and visiting two lovely beaches, Shell and Pebble. Along the way you will encounter the area's famous diversity of trees, shrubs, and other plant life, leaving no doubt about the wisdom of including this stretch of valuable beach-front property in our state park system.

Directions: See the directions for "Pebble Beach" on p. 161.

Facilities: Rest rooms, picnic tables, fire grates, water; maps for sale at park entrance station when ranger is on duty.

Trailhead: In the upper parking area, on the right side of the one-way loop, midway between its start and the 180-degree bend to the left.

Follow the route description for "Pebble Beach" on pages 161–163. When you reach the T-junction with the Johnstone Trail, a single track, turn right and traverse across a hillside dropping steeply left, past stands of tanbark oak, toyon, thimbleberry, and evergreen huckleberry. When their fruit ripens, huckleberry shrubs usually get picked clean, the lower branches by hikers, the upper ones by birds, including noisy Steller's jays, who will scold you for trying to poach their berries. The rain-forest feel here is accentuated by the presence of salal, a low-growing shrub found in coast-redwood forests and in coastal regions of the Pacific Northwest. In fact, many of the plants here are indicative of a redwood forest, but where are the towering giants themselves? The western limit of redwood distribution in Marin County is marked by the San Andreas fault, which runs through Tomales Bay. The granitic soils found west of the fault are apparently unsuitable for redwoods.

A moderate uphill climb takes you past a stand of manzanita and a few venerable coast live oaks, and back to the realm of the bishop pines. The cones of these magnificent pines are spherical and sharply barbed. Compared with redwood or Douglas fir, bishop pines create a canopy that is less dense, so the forest here seems brighter and more open. More

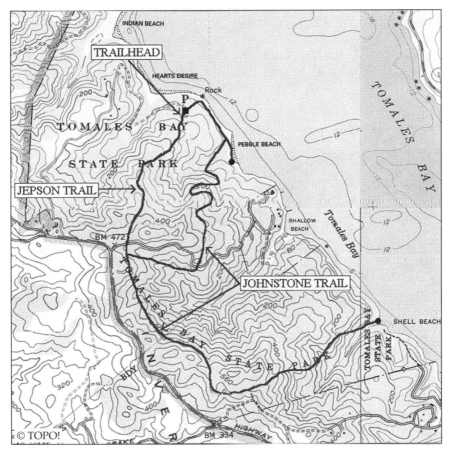

27. Shell Beach

light means more underbrush, and a nearby clearing holds coyote brush, creambush, and blackberry vines. Climbing near the crest of a ridge, the route make a leftward bend toward Tomales Bay, and pursues a rolling course. At about the 2-mile point, an unsigned trail heads right, but your route continues to veer left. Red elderberry, with its round clusters of white flowers, is common on the Point Reyes peninsula, and may be found here growing as a tall shrub or a small tree.

Now the route makes many gyrations in an attempt to find the path of least resistance down a ridge leading northeast toward the bay, which here and there comes into view through the trees. After a long descent, you may begin to hear the noise of people frolicking on Shell Beach. When you arrive at the beach, you may be startled, especially on a warm weekend day, to see the crowds swimming, picnicking, sunbathing, and boating. Rest assured, you haven't stumbled on a convention of extreme hikers—most of the beach-goers probably took the easy way in, from the end of Camino Del Mar, off Sir Francis Drake Blvd. You can find that trail, and the wooden steps that lead to it, across an inlet at the south end of the beach. There is a toilet at Shell Beach, but no other facilities. After enjoying the beach, retrace your steps to the junction of the Johnstone and Jepson Trails. From here, follow the route description for "Pebble Beach" on pages 163-164 back to the parking area.

Shell Beach is popular with bathers and boaters.

◆ Napa County ◆

28	Alston Park
	DRY CREEK TRAIL

Length: 1.4 miles

Time: 1 hour or less

Rating: Easy

Regulations: City of Napa Parks and Recreation Department.

Highlights: This short, easy loop, using the Dry Creek Trail and a paved service road, explores the north end of Alston Park, a City of Napa park. Formerly used for grazing cattle and growing fruit trees, this 157-acre enclave, sandwiched between housing developments and vineyards, is now enjoyed by hikers, equestrians, bicyclists, joggers, and dog walkers. Late winter and spring, when the grasses are refreshed and the flowers in bloom, are the best times to visit. The south end of the park, described in "Orchard Loop" on pages 171–173, can be easily reached from the trailhead below, or from a separate parking area about 0.5 mile southeast on Dry Creek Rd. The trails in Alston Park are unsigned, but a crude map showing the park's eight named trails is available from the City of Napa Parks and Recreation Department, 1100 West Street, (707) 257-9529.

Directions: From Hwy. 29 in Napa, turn west onto Redwood Rd, go 1 mile, and turn right onto Dry Creek Rd. Go 0.9 mile to a parking area, left.

Facilities: None

Trailhead: Southwest end of parking area, at a gate.

Several dirt trails and a paved service road leave from the parking area, which is surrounded by open, rolling hills. To find the Dry Creek Trail, you go through a gate on the right side of the paved road and turn right, ignoring a narrow dirt track running left and steeply uphill. Your route, a hard-packed dirt path, soon bends left and begins a moderate climb. Despite the residential setting, a vineyard, right, reminds you that this park is situated in California's premier wine-growing region. The grassy fields beside the trail, full of weeds and wildflowers, also hold young oaks planted by the City of Napa Parks and Recreation Department. Cattle grazing in years past took its toll here, and recovery is now underway. Passing an unsigned junction with the Jack Rabbit Trail, left, you

(previous page) Yellow Mariposa lilies are among the North Bay's most beautiful wildflowers.

continue straight on a level course. A few hundred feet past the junction you come to a short bridge across a seasonal creek. To the right is a larger seasonal watercourse, lined with oaks—valley and coast live—and an occasional madrone. This watercourse is referred to by some as Dry Creek, but the year-round Dry Creek shown on maps passes well north of here, on its way to join the Napa River near the junction of Oak Knoll Avenue and the Silverado Trail. On the park's western boundary flows Redwood Creek, another tributary of the Napa River.

Staying left at a fork, the trail soon drops into an eroded area beside the watercourse and works its way over rough ground, now rising on a gentle grade. A few fruit trees show you this was once an agricultural area, and the park's southern corner, until it was purchased in the 1970s by the City of Napa Parks and Recreation Department, held an orchard of fruit and nut trees. As you continue uphill, the watercourse, right, soon becomes merely a shallow, rocky depression. As your route makes a leftward bend, it is joined by a narrow trail coming from the right. Nearing the park's highest ground, you have the canyon holding Redwood Creek on your right.

Now passing a junction where a broad dirt path joins from the right, your route begins to descend on a gentle grade. Just ahead, at about the 0.75-mile point, is a single-track trail, closed to bikes, which takes off

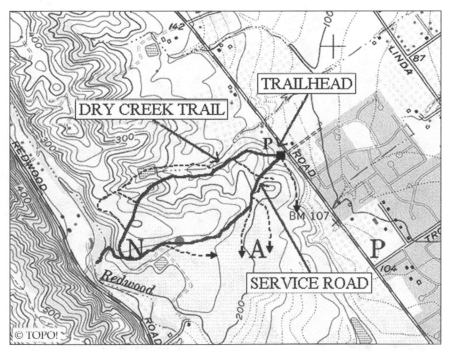

28. Dry Creek Trail

sharply right. If you want to explore the shady canyon bordering
Redwood Creek, turn right and follow the trail downhill, aided in places
by wooden steps, past stands of oak and California buckeye to a locked
gate marking the park boundary. When you have finished enjoying this
hidden corner of the park, retrace your steps to the main trail. From here,
the route curves left, passing through open, weedy fields, with a vineyard
on your right. Growing beside the trail are poison oak, coyote brush,
California poppies, fennel, and blackberry vines.

Topping a low rise, the trail now descends past a fork, where you bear
left. A picnic table, left, sits on a vantage point that commands a fine view
of the agricultural land and housing developments surrounding the City
of Napa. At a junction with the paved service road, you turn left and follow it downhill on a grade that alternates between gentle and moderate.
In about 125 feet, you come to another junction, where two dirt trails
branch right. One immediately bends left and climbs to a picnic table. The
other, called the Valley View Trail on the map, veers sharply right and
leads to the park's southern end. Continuing downhill on pavement, you
next pass a four-way junction where the Jack Rabbit Trail goes left and
steeply uphill, and an unnamed trail goes right. Just before reaching the
parking area, you pass a trail, right, called the Orchard Trail on the map,
which is another access route to the south end of the park. From here, the
parking area is only a few paces ahead.

California buckeye shows cream-colored flowers in spring.

29 Alston Park
ORCHARD LOOP

Length: 0.9 mile

Time: 1 hour or less

Rating: Easy

Regulations: City of Napa Parks and Recreation Department.

Highlights: This short, easy loop, using the Valley View and Prune Picker trails, circles an old orchard in the south end of Alston Park. Birders will especially enjoy searching here for songbirds and raptors. Late winter and early spring are the best times to visit this otherwise dry and dun-colored City of Napa park. The park's north end, described in "Dry Creek Trail" on pages 168–170, can be easily reached from the trailhead below, or from a separate parking area about 0.5 mile northwest on Dry Creek Rd. The trails in Alston Park are unsigned, but a crude map showing the park's eight named trails is available from the City of Napa Parks and Recreation Department, 1100 West Street, (707) 257-9529.

Directions: See the directions for "Dry Creek Trail" on p. 168. When you reach Dry Creek Rd., turn right and go 0.4 mile to parking area, left.

Facilities: Water, toilets

Trailhead: Southwest side of parking area.

Two trails leave from this trailhead: the Valley View Trail, a dirt path heading straight, and an unnamed dirt trail veering right. There is also a fenced dog exercise and training area, left, where dogs are allowed to run free. Elsewhere in the park, they must be leashed. Following the Valley View Trail, which connects the north and south ends of the park, you briefly enjoy the shade of a large valley oak, and then, passing a four-way junction, climb a set of wooden steps. Now on rocky ground, you climb past a picnic table, uphill and right, which is shaded by big, stately oaks. About 100 feet from the wooden steps, you reach a T-junction. Here the Valley View Trail turns right and heads to the north end of the park, but your route, the Prune Picker Trail, goes left.

As its name suggests, the Prune Picker Trail circles the remnants of an old orchard, mostly prune trees. Ken Stanton, in *Great Day Hikes in and around Napa Valley*, says this orchard also produced pears, cherries, peaches, and walnuts. The City of Napa purchased the property in the

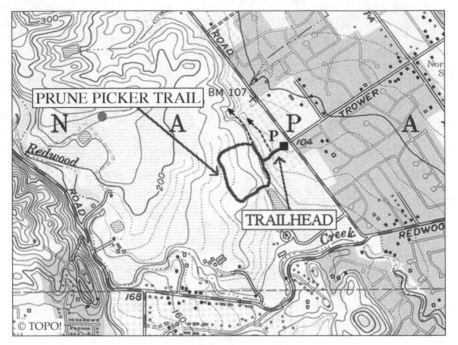

29. Orchard Loop

1970s and drew up plans to build a recreation complex, including sports fields and a community hall. Facing opposition from taxpayers, wine growers, and a group called Citizens for Alston Alternatives, the city's plans were defeated in 1981, and 10 years later Alston Park was opened to the public.

Now enjoying a clockwise circuit of the old orchard, you may notice songbirds flitting in the branches of the remaining trees, or raptors such as a white-tailed kite perched on a snag. Overhead, turkey vultures and hawks often describe lazy circles, especially on a warm day when rising air currents make it easier for these large birds. Other birds that call this park home include western meadowlarks, northern mockingbirds, a member of the mimic thrush family known for its imitative vocalizations, and northern flickers, a woodpecker. One day I caught a glimpse of a blacktail jackrabbit here as it bounded through the grass, wary of predators. Where the trail makes a gradual right-hand bend, you pass a vineyard, left, behind a fence.

As the trail rises gently, you can see a long, forested ridge topped with a water tank, left, on the southwest side of Redwood Creek, just beyond the park's boundary. Now past the orchard, the route makes a 90-degree bend to the right, crossing a weedy field full of colorful wild radish. Years of cattle grazing on this land have taken their toll, as evidenced by the presence of invasive, non-native plants, but restorative measures are underway and native species are slowly recovering. At a **T**-junction, unsigned, with the Valley View Trail, you turn right, and after 75 feet pass an unnamed trail (not shown on the park map) heading left. Soon you come to the junction with the Prune Picker Trail, where you began your loop around the orchard. From here, you turn left and retrace your steps to the parking area.

Scotch broom, although colorful, is an invasive pest.

◆ Bothe-Napa Valley State Park ◆

Located just south of Calistoga in the Napa Valley, California's premier wine-growing region, this park offers visitors a chance to counteract the effects of too much chardonnay or merlot by hiking, bicycling, riding horses, picnicking, camping, and swimming. Spring and fall are the best times to visit—it is during these seasons that the quiet redwood groves, the forested hillsides, and the rugged volcanic ridges are at their prime. The park's main trails run beside Ritchey Creek, a tributary of the Napa River that has a run of steelhead trout, a threatened species under federal law. Here are found towering coast redwoods, along with California bay, Douglas fir, madrone, valley oak, and bigleaf maple. Elevations in the park range from 300 to 2,000 feet. As you ascend, the vegetation changes from forest to chaparral, mostly manzanita and chamise. At the east end of the park, the 1.2-mile History Trail passes a pioneer cemetery and leads to Bale Grist Mill State Historic Park.

Who were Bothe and Bale? In the 1870s, Dr. and Mrs. Charles M. Hitchcock bought a 1000-acre parcel of land on Ritchey (or Ritchie) Creek for a country estate. Their daughter was Lillie Hitchcock Coit, a celebrated eccentric who loved fire engines and fire fighting. In her will, Lillie left money to the city of San Francisco for a monument to its firemen—Coit Tower. After Lillie's death in 1929, Reinhold Bothe and his wife Jeannie bought part of the Hitchcock estate and transformed it into Bothe's Paradise Park, complete with a lodge, a swimming pool, cabins, and an airstrip. The land became a state park in 1960.

Dr. Edward T. Bale came to California from England in 1837 and became a Mexican citizen, marrying the niece of Mariano Vallejo, the *comandante general* of Alta California. In the early 1840s, Bale was granted an 18,000-acre rancho that included much of the upper Napa Valley. He owned a saw mill on the Napa River and a grist mill on Mill Creek. Although he was probably the province's first surgeon and druggist, his noble calling did not prevent legal problems. He was jailed twice. The first time, in 1840, was for bootlegging, and the second time, in 1844, was for shooting at Salvador Vallejo, General Mariano Vallejo's brother.

The park has a small visitor center, which may be staffed only on weekends, with displays and publications. Interpretive programs are offered year-round, but most are in the summer—a schedule is usually posted on park bulletin boards. A Native American plant garden, located next to the visitor center, contains plants used by the Wappo people, the area's original residents. A day-use picnic area is at the end of the park entrance road, near the start of the History Trail. The park has a covered picnic area for group use, which can be reserved by calling the park. The park map, available at the visitor center, also covers Bale Grist Mill State Historic Park and Robert Louis Stevenson State Park/Mt. St. Helena. In addition, it contains a map of the wineries from Yountville to Calistoga, and town maps of Calistoga and St. Helena.

Year-round camping is available in 50 family sites, including 9 walk-in sites. There is also small group site for hikers and bike campers. Drive-in campsites can be reserved from April through October. During the rest of the year, they are available on a first-come, first-served basis. Reservations can be made up to seven months in advance, or as late as two days prior to arrival. There is also a group campsite for up to 30 people, which can be reserved year-round. A swimming pool, one of only two in the state park system, is open daily from mid-June through Labor Day. Pool hours are noon to 6 P.M. Campers and day-use visitors must purchase a ticket to use the pool.

Dogs are not allowed on the park's trails or in the pool area. Elsewhere, dogs must be leashed during the day and in a vehicle or tent at night.

VISITOR CENTER/PARK OFFICE: (707) 942-4575

CAMPING RESERVATIONS: (800) 444-7275

30

Bothe-Napa Valley State Park
COYOTE PEAK

Length: 4.5 miles

Time: 2 to 3 hours

Rating: Moderate

Regulations: CSP; parking fee; no dogs, no bikes, no horses.

Highlights: This semi-loop route, using the Ritchey Canyon, Redwood, Coyote Peak, and South Fork trails, explores the lush riparian habitat along Ritchey Creek and the wonderful upland forest and chaparral surrounding Coyote Peak. Spring and fall are the best times to visit. During the rainy season, it may be impossible to ford Ritchey Creek—as required on the return part of this route—and a detour using the Ritchey Canyon Trail and the Ritchey Creek Campground road may be required. However, *except* during the rainy season, the first parts of the Redwood and the Ritchey Canyon trails are heavily used by equestrians, mostly riders from the nearby horse concession, and may be carpeted with horse dung.

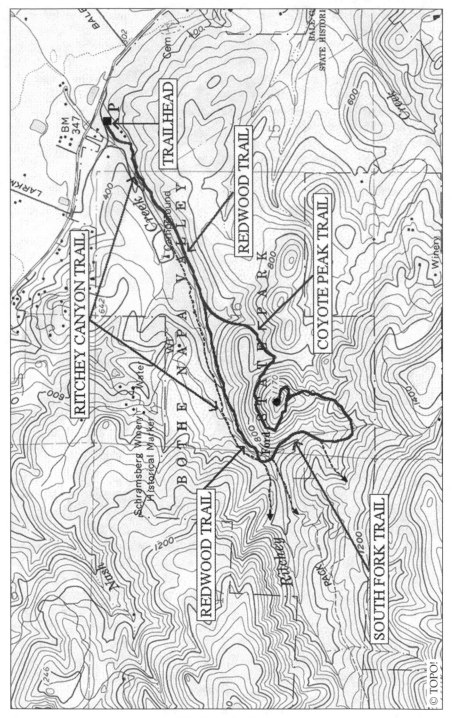

30. Coyote Peak

Directions: From Hwy. 29 northbound in St. Helena, go 5 miles from the first St. Helena stop light (at Pope St.) to the park entrance, left. After 0.1 mile you reach the entrance kiosk. If the entrance kiosk is not staffed, pay fee at the self-registration station in the parking area just ahead and right. Continue another 0.3 mile to the parking area for the Ritchey Creek trails, right.

From Hwys. 29 or 128 southbound in Calistoga, go 3.5 miles from their merger (Lincoln Ave.) to the park entrance, right. Then follow directions above.

Facilities: Visitor center, open most weekends, with books, maps; phone; water fountain on trail within first 0.5 mile; campground with 50 sites and a nearby swimming pool, (800) 444-7275.

Trailhead: West end of parking area.

The wooded area bordering Ritchey Creek, which your route will parallel at its start and finish, is home to a wonderful variety of trees, including California bay, coast redwood, Douglas fir, madrone, valley oak, and bigleaf maple. The creek itself holds a run of steelhead trout, listed as a threatened species under federal law. Heading west on the Ritchey Canyon Trail, a mostly level single track, you soon cross a paved road and then pass a junction with a trail, right. With an employee residence on your left, you merge with a dirt-and-gravel road coming from the left. A fountain here beckons you to top off your water bottle. Enjoying the sound of running water from Ritchey Creek, right, you begin to see some of the plants associated with a redwood forest, such as tanbark oak, hazelnut, thimbleberry, and western sword fern.

At about the 0.5-mile point, the Ritchey Canyon Trail branches right, descends, and crosses the creek, whose bed is rocky and crossed by many fallen logs. Your route, the Redwood Trail, continues straight and begins to climb on a moderate and then gentle grade. Adding to the mix of trees and shrubs in this dense forest are black oak, coast live oak, manzanita, toyon, and creambush. Steller's jay, a common Western species, but one much sought after by visiting birders from east of the Rockies, may greet you here with raucous calls. Soon you reach a junction with the Coyote Peak Trail, where you turn left and begin a winding uphill course on a moderate grade that changes in places to steep. As compensation for your efforts, the trail here is bordered with wild roses.

Dropping slightly to cross a small seasonal stream, the route curves right and climbs amid stands of bay trees. Bending left, the trail, now rocky and eroded, emerges from the trees and traverses an area of chaparral, with scrub oak, manzanita, chamise, and bush monkeyflower. Still gaining elevation, in some places steeply, you re-enter a dense forest of mostly Douglas fir, madrone, and spindly redwoods. Now a short descent preps you for more climbing, and soon you are admiring open vistas extending west and southwest across a deep canyon to a high, forested ridge. The trail here is a narrow track gouged out of a steep hillside falling away to your right. Magnificent manzanitas, tall, bulky, and twisted, grow in company with chaparral pea and yerba santa. The small dark birds you may see darting back and forth are swifts, described in one field guide as "cigars with wings." Swifts are rare in the park, and, except during migration, have been noted only in the vicinity of the cliffs in upper Ritchey Canyon.

Just shy of the 2-mile point the route forks. To your left is the trail to the summit of Coyote Peak (1170′), and to your right is the continuation of the Coyote Peak Trail. To visit the summit, bear left and climb steeply over rock outcrops, following the rough trail as it bends sharply left, heading almost due north. In the shade of Douglas fir and redwood, you negotiate a steep pitch and finally arrive atop Coyote Peak, hemmed in by trees, with only a few gaps where views of the Napa Valley peak through. Now retrace your steps to the previous junction, and bear sharply left onto the Coyote Peak Trail. If you forgo the summit, simply stay on the Coyote Peak Trail as it veers right at the junction with the summit trail.

Descending over loose dirt and rock through chaparral, you cross a level divide at the head of a canyon, and then begin to climb via a sharp left-hand switchback. Soon veering right, the shrub-lined trail affords you here and there a view back toward Coyote Peak. Returning to dense forest, you follow a rolling downhill course, accompanied perhaps by the sound of running water from a creek below and right. This drainage is home to tall trees, mostly redwood and Douglas fir. Crossing the creek, a tributary of Ritchey Creek, you now follow it downstream, generally north, to a junction with the South Fork Trail. Here the Coyote Peak Trail ends, but you continue straight, now descending the South Fork Trail on a grade that alternates between level, moderate, and steep.

Manzanita is one of the North Bay's earliest-flowering shrubs.

The trail, which may be wet and muddy, leads you to the creek. Stepping across it, you continue your descent, with the creek now on the left. At about the 3-mile point, a bridge takes you across the creek again. Once across you turn right, and in about 100 feet reach a junction with the Spring Trail, a dirt road. Here you turn right and follow the road as it crosses Ritchey Creek, which flows beneath it through a culvert. About 75 feet farther, you reach a junction with a confusing array of trails. From here, your route, the Redwood Trail, a single track, veers sharply right and heads back toward Ritchey Creek. Once beside it, you soon come to a spot where you can cross the creek on rocks. (During periods of high water, this crossing may be impossible. If so, return to the Spring Trail and turn right. Follow the dirt road, now called the Ritchey Canyon Trail, as it bends right and runs northeast, parallel to Ritchey Creek. When you reach Ritchey Creek Campground, follow the paved campground road to the park entrance road and turn right, returning to the parking area.)

If you are able to cross Ritchey Creek, follow it downstream with the creek on your left. At first on a flat track, the trail soon makes a steeply rising traverse across a hillside that drops left. After leveling and then descending, you are back beside the bubbling creek, enjoying a walk through groves of redwoods. After passing a trail, left, that leads across the creek to the Ritchey Canyon Trail, you soon reach the junction with the Coyote Peak Trail. From here, retrace your steps to the parking area.

31 Bothe-Napa Valley State Park
HISTORY TRAIL

Length: 2.5 miles

Time: 1 to 2 hours

Rating: Moderate

Regulations: CSP; no dogs, no bikes, no horses.

Highlights: This relatively short out-and-back hike, using the History Trail, covers much historical ground, starting with a visit to a cemetery containing the remains of Napa Valley pioneers, and ending at the partially restored Bale Grist Mill, a fixture in the valley since 1846. Following for much of its length a ridge that parallels Hwy. 29/128, the route explores dense forest, clearings filled with chaparral shrubs, and a riparian corridor along Mill Creek, making the route of interest to plant lovers as well as to history buffs. (This trip can be done as a shuttle by leaving a car at Bale Grist Mill State Historic Park, about 3 miles north of St. Helena, but note that the gate at the mill's parking area is locked at 5 P.M.)

Directions: See the directions for "Coyote Peak" on p. 177. Go 0.6 mile
                    past the entrance kiosk to a turn-around at the end of the
                    entrance road. Park on the shoulder of the turn-around.

Facilities: Picnic tables, water, toilet.

Trailhead: On the east side of the turn-around.

The History Trail, a mile-or-so of single track closed to horses and bikes,
connects Bothe-Napa Valley State Park with Bale Grist Mill State Historic
Park. Level at first, the trail heads south through a forest of coast live oak,
tanbark oak, California bay, Douglas fir, and black oak. After about 100
yards, a trail splits off to the left, but a trail post with an arrow advises
you to turn right. After turning right, you reach in a few paces a short
trail to Pioneer Cemetery, which is certainly worth a visit. Adjacent to the
cemetery is the site of Napa County's first church, built in 1853 and
named for a local reverend, Asa White. When I visited the park in the fall
of 1998, a project to restore the cemetery was underway. Among the pioneers and settlers buried here are members of the Tucker family. The
Tucker name lives on in connection with California's most famous sur-

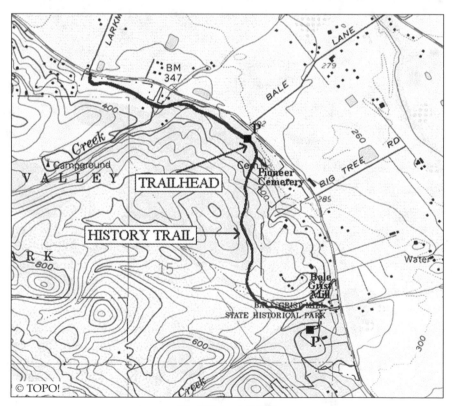

31. History Trail

vival story. As Ken Stanton writes in *Great Day Hikes in and around Napa Valley*, Reason Tucker, who traveled to California in 1846 and narrowly missed becoming snow-bound in the Sierra, made four trips to rescue members of the ill-fated Donner party.

Just past the cemetery, your route swings left and begins to climb on a moderate grade, winding its way uphill. Now on rough and rocky ground, the trail steepens, entering a forest dominated by madrone. These beautiful trees, with their broad green leaves and orange bark, are here growing tall and spindly, perhaps competing with other species for light. Soon the route nears the top of a ridge and the grade relaxes for a while, giving you a chance to listen for the sharp cry of a northern flicker, one of six species of woodpeckers to be found in the park. A clearing provides enough sunlight for manzanita, toyon, and coyote brush to thrive. Returning to dense forest, you continue zigzagging upwards. A trail post, right, marks the 0.5-mile point, with the Bale Grist Mill about 0.7 mile ahead.

Now on the ridgecrest at last, the trail follows it downhill on a gentle grade, past more clearings full of familiar chaparral plants such as manzanita, buckbrush, and chamise. Adding to the plant diversity, the setting soon changes to an oak savanna, made up mostly of blue oak or perhaps a hybrid oak, where small rock boulders line the trail. At about the 1-mile point, you cross a seasonal watercourse and enter a jungle-like area where the trees and shrubs are draped with vines of California wild grape and honeysuckle. Taking advantage of the occasional clearing are mountain mahogany and spiny redberry, more plants of the chaparral.

Pioneer Cemetery, near the start of the History Trail, contains the graves of early Napa Valley settlers.

At a junction marked by a trail post, a trail goes left to the old Mill Pond, now dry, but your route turns right and continues downhill, soon reaching a wooden bridge over a seasonal stream. After crossing the bridge, the trail veers right and finds level ground amid stands of California buckeye. A wooden fence, left, and a paved road beyond it show your goal to be near. Other signs of civilization include a water tank, a rest bench, and toilets. Passing a dirt-and-gravel path, left, you now find yourself on a paved path, which in about 50 feet brings you to a junction. From here, another paved path heads right, crossing a bridge over Mill Creek, to the Bale Grist Mill parking area, just off Highway 128/29. To reach the mill, continue straight ahead for a short distance.

The Bale Grist Mill was built in 1846 by employees of Dr. Edward Bale, an English surgeon and druggist who was granted an extensive rancho in the Napa Valley by General Mariano Vallejo. Grist mills, used for grinding wheat, corn, and other grains, were the community centers of early

Bale Grist Mill, partially restored, has been a fixture in the upper Napa Valley since 1846.

rural America. Farmers gathered to bring grain, and stayed to exchange news and gossip. Size and location made the Bale Grist Mill's granary an ideal place for meetings and social events. As you walk around the mill, you can see how it operates. The mill is driven by what is called an overshot wheel, powered by the weight of water falling from above. Water from Mill Creek was diverted by upstream dams and channels to the Mill Pond, and then delivered to the mill by a network of ditches and hollowed-out logs called flumes. Once you have circled the mill and granary, stopping to examine the old grinding equipment, gears, and shafts lying about, retrace your steps to the parking area.

Napa River Ecological Reserve
NATURE TRAIL

Length: 1.25 miles

Time: 1 hour or less

Rating: Easy

Regulations: California Dept. of Fish and Game; dogs on leash; no bikes, no camping, no alcohol, no collecting of plants, minerals, or wildlife; closed sunset to sunrise.

Highlights: This semi-loop hike follows the self-guiding Nature Trail into the heart of a small reserve wedged between the Napa River and Conn Creek near the Napa Valley town of Yountville. Traversing some of the last remaining old-growth riparian habitat in the Napa Valley, the trail brings you into a realm of oaks, birds, butterflies, and wildflowers. A pair of binoculars will help you locate and identify the reserve's many birds and butterflies. **Bold face** numbers in the route description refer to numbered markers along the trail, which are keyed to a trail guide published by the Napa-Solano Audubon Society. Copies of the guide are supposed to be in a box at the start of the Nature Trail, on the east side of the Napa River, but there may be none available when you visit. Access to the Nature Trail is impossible during the rainy season, because a footbridge over the Napa River, the trail's sole access, is removed. To find out if the bridge is in place, call the California Dept. of Fish and Game (707) 944-5500.

Directions: From Hwy. 29 in Yountville, take the Madison St. exit and go northeast 0.25 mile to Yount St. Turn left onto Yount,

and then immediately right onto Yountville Cross Rd. Go
0.9 mile to the reserve's parking area, left.

Facilities: Toilet

Trailhead: Northwest side of parking area.

This small reserve, purchased by the Wildlife Conservation Board in 1974
and administered by the California Department of Fish and Game in
cooperation with Napa County, sits in the flood plain of the Napa River,
and represents a habitat fast disappearing from the Bay Area—old-
growth riparian woodland. According to the Napa-Solano Audubon
Society, 146 species of birds have been seen here, including 67 that nest on
the reserve, such as wood ducks, woodpeckers, swallows, and owls.
Migration brings an influx of songbirds, and in spring, butterflies and
wildflowers add color to the landscape. Mammals that live here include
deer, raccoons, skunks, squirrels, opossums, and minks, although most of
these are active at night, when the reserve is closed.

The trail, a dirt track, heads northwest across an open, weedy field,
with a vineyard on the left and a dirt-and-stone levee, right. The levee
contains the Napa River during periods of high water and prevents
flooding. About 100 yards from the trailhead, you climb over the levee,
which has a trail running along its top, and descend toward the river. As
you descend, you pass a trail post with an arrow pointing you straight
ahead. Large valley oaks, one of the reserve's prime attractions, offer
shade here. The vegetation bordering the river—mostly thickets of willows and tangles of blackberry vines—is draped with California wild

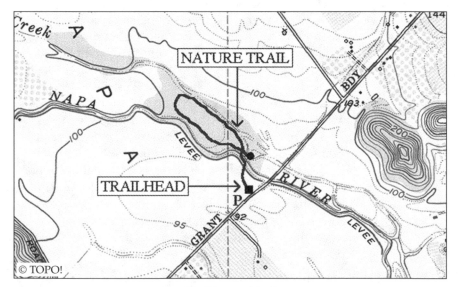

32. Nature Trail

grape, which turns yellow in the fall. Once on the gravelly riverbed itself, you lose the trail, and the signs here are not much help.

About 75 feet from the top of levee, you arrive at a clearing; here the next trail post, partially hidden by brush, directs you left. Turn left, walk about 125 feet upstream, and then turn right, toward the river. About 100 feet ahead is a wooden bridge, removed during the rainy season, which takes you across the Napa River. Once across, you veer left on a dirt trail and climb the riverbank, atop which is a junction. Here you turn right and follow a short spur trail that leads to marker **1**, overlooking Conn Creek, named in honor of John Conn, an early Napa Valley settler. The creek, dammed to create Lake Hennessey a few miles north of here, joins the Napa River just downstream. Lake Hennessey supplies water to the City of Napa, and Conn Creek's water flow is reduced to just a trickle by late summer. Birds found here include Wilson's warbler, a small yellow bird, and both Anna's and Allen's hummingbirds.

Now back at the junction, go right on a dirt trail for about 15 feet to a fork marked by a trail post, the start of the Nature Trail loop. A nearby box is supposed to contain trail brochures but may be empty. Robust valley oaks and tall California bays dominate the landscape. Nearby, you may notice large bird boxes with big holes: these are for wood ducks, a brightly colored species that prefers to nest in trees. Another local nester, the red-shouldered hawk, is known by its repetitive "keer, keer, keer" cry. Bearing right at the fork, you soon come to marker **2**, indicating poison oak. This shrub sports shiny leaves in threes, and, in fall, colorful foliage and small white berries. You can avoid it by staying on the trail. Another plant that produces white berries, called snowberry, is also found here. Its leaves look like they have been designed at random—each one is a slightly different shape.

The level trail meanders through lush woodland on a wedge of high ground between the Napa River and Conn Creek. One of the factors that make this reserve a great birding area is the presence of different habitats close together. For some reason, birding is often most successful on the border between habitats, such as the edge of a marsh, creek, or meadow. Here, a large meadow, left, may offer good viewing. Marker **3** describes lace lichen, the wispy, moss-like substance covering the valley oaks and giving the landscape a Southern feel. Lace lichen, sometimes called Spanish moss, is composed of two life forms, an alga and a

Sign along Hwy. 29 near Oakville.

fungus, growing in a symbiotic relationship, aiding each other. Lichen is sensitive to air quality, so it is heartening to see so much of it here.

Marker **4** refers to dead trees, called snags, used by acorn woodpeckers to store acorns for the winter. If you are lucky, you may see one of these black-and-white birds perched upright on a tree trunk, holding an acorn in its beak and pushing it into a pre-drilled hole in the tree's bark. Sometimes you come upon a tree with dozens if not hundreds of acorns tucked away. In addition to valley oak and bay, other trees found on the reserve include coast live oak, Oregon ash, bigleaf maple, white alder, and Fremont cottonwood.

Now the trail wanders out of the woods and into a large meadow dominated by Santa Barbara sedge, an evergreen grass-like plant about 2 feet tall. Dropping to cross a gully, the route returns to shade, arriving at marker **5**, deemed by the brochure a good place to listen for birds. From here you can look northeast across Conn Creek to the agricultural lands, vineyards, and posh homes near the Silverado Trail, a road that parallels Highway 29 from Napa to Calistoga. As the trail bends left, you come upon a rest bench and marker **6**. The nearby town of Yountville was named for George C. Yount, a North Carolinian who came to California in 1831. Five years later, Yount was granted a rancho, called Rancho Caymus, in the Napa Valley, on which the present town of Yountville is located. The land this reserve occupies was once called the Yountville Camp Grounds, and large religious camp meetings were held here from 1851 until 1879. The name of the rancho lives on as a vineyard in Rutherford that produces some of the Napa Valley's finest wine.

At marker **7**, be sure to stop and admire a large ropy vine of California wild grape, perhaps more than 100 years old. Also found here are two kinds of blackberry—California, a native, and Himalayan, an import from Europe. California blackberry has narrow, down-curving branches studded with slender thorns, whereas Himalayan blackberry has stiff, upright branches and stout, curving thorns. Now veering left again, in dense forest, you find marker **8** and a bed of periwinkle, another visitor from Europe, a spreading ground cover with blue flowers that may bloom year-round. Some non-native species can pose a threat to native plants, but others are harmless. Among the most unwelcome here are eucalyptus, French broom, English plantain, and Italian thistle. The few fruit trees you may see in the reserve, although not native, provide food for birds and deer, and are not considered harmful.

An overlook at marker **9** gives you a chance to view the Napa River. Here, at a wide spot, the rushing current during high water has undercut the far bank. When enough ground has been lost, trees will topple into the river, providing quiet pools for fish, among them migratory steelhead trout, listed under federal law as a threatened species. Walking downstream, but with the river now hidden, you come to an area favored by woodpeckers and other birds attracted to snags and trees with dead limbs. Even in death, trees provide places for birds to perch, feed, and nest. Beside the river again for a short distance, the trail soon bends left, returning to the edge of the large meadow you passed earlier, but now on its opposite side. This spot is a particularly active one for birds, and some of the trees here are riddled with woodpecker holes. The trail now bends right and reaches the south end of the meadow, where marker **10** indicates two shrubs, wild rose and snowberry. A rose relative, ninebark, may also be found on the reserve. When you reach the junction at the start of the Nature Trail loop, bear right and retrace your steps to the parking area.

Good birding draws visitors to the Napa River Ecological Reserve.

| 33 | Robert Louis Stevenson State Park
MT. ST. HELENA |

Length: 10.6 miles

Time: 4 to 6 hours

Rating: Difficult

Regulations: CSP; no dogs, no bikes on single-track trails.

Highlights: This out-and-back route, a "must-do" for lovers of high places, takes you to the 4,339-foot North Peak of Mt. St. Helena, the tallest summit in the North Bay. Gaining more than 2,000 feet from the parking area by means of an 0.8-mile single-track trail and a 4.5-mile section of the Mt. St. Helena Trail, a dirt road, the route is exposed for much of its length to sun, wind, and weather. The difficult rating comes from duration and elevation gain, not steepness, although the exposure at points along the way might upset someone with vertigo. Pick a cool day with unlimited visibility, and you will reap all the magnificent scenic rewards this hike has to offer.

Directions: From the junction of Hwys. 128 and 29 in Calistoga (at Lincoln Ave.), go northwest 8.7 miles on Hwy. 29 to a small parking area on the left side of the road at the highway's summit. If this area is full, park in the large area just across the highway. The trailhead for bikes is about 0.2 mile ahead on the left side of Hwy. 29, at a gated fire road. Parking for this trailhead is on the right side of the highway, just past the fire road.

Facilities: Picnic tables

Trailhead: On the west side of Hwy. 29, adjacent to the small parking area. If you need to cross Hwy. 29, do so carefully!

From the small parking area on the west side of the highway, you ascend a set of wooden steps to the trail, here a wide dirt track, and pass a sign-board with information about the park's namesake. In the summer of 1880, Scottish author Robert Louis Stevenson brought his new bride, Fanny Osbourne, here for their honeymoon. Stevenson was suffering from tuberculosis, and sought to regain his strength in the sunshine and pure air found on Mt. St. Helena. The couple had little money, so they camped in a cabin near the site of an abandoned silver and gold mine, about 0.7 mile up the trail. The tale of their experience, *The Silverado Squatters*, delighted American readers and helped launch Stevenson's career. Mt. St. Helena may have provided the author with a model for Spyglass Hill in his 1883 book, *Treasure Island*.

The trail rises gently in a dense forest of Douglas fir, tanbark oak, California bay, madrone, and bigleaf maple. From the mid-1800s to the turn of the century, the rugged hills of Napa County were studded with mines that produced cinnabar, an ore of mercury, as well as silver and gold. A toll road to Calistoga, the railhead, ran nearby, and as you begin your climb you may see what remains of the old toll house—its concrete foundation. State Park rangers say budget constraints have put trail maintenance on the back burner, and the first part of this route vividly demonstrates the result. Hikers have cut switchbacks and gouged out the hillside, causing massive erosion. In response, volunteer groups have placed signs urging hikers to stay on the trail. Unfortunately, as I witnessed firsthand, some well-meaning but ignorant hikers think the steep gouges between switchbacks *are* the trail. Instead of the current signs that say PREVENT EROSION or IMPIDE (sic) EROSION—probably meaningless to people unfamiliar with trails and switchbacks—the park needs signs that say KEEP OFF HILLSIDE and perhaps a split-rail fence on the downhill side of the trail.

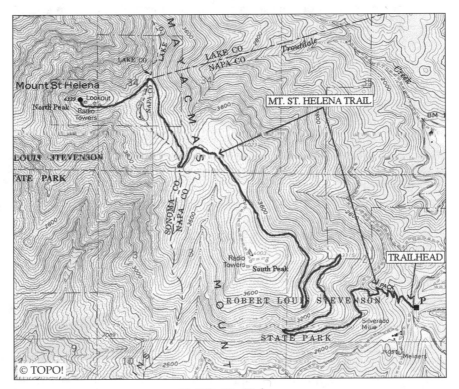

33. Mt. St. Helena

Mixed in with the taller trees are coffeeberry, hazelnut, poison oak, and California nutmeg, an evergreen with spine-tipped needles that resembles a young coast redwood. Following the switchbacks uphill over rocky ground, you soon reach a more open, sunny area where manzanita, chamise, and chaparral pea prevail. The oaks here are mostly canyon and interior live, and they are joined by knobcone pine, a three-needled species that favors hot, dry terrain. Chickadees, nuthatches, and wrentits may announce their nearby presence vocally, and woodpeckers may be heard drumming on dry tree trunks. Also keep an eye out for monarch and California sister butterflies. Back in dense forest, you soon pass a stone marker indicating the site of the Stevensons' honeymoon cabin, nothing of which remains. Just past the marker, the route makes a sharp right-hand switchback, and you climb a gently angled slab of rock, aided by footholds carved in its surface.

At a junction with the Mt. St. Helena Trail, a dirt road, you turn left, now with a good view of the rocky abutments and ramparts on the mountain's southeast flank. Although it is made of volcanic rock, Mt. St. Helena itself is not a volcano. But nearby volcanoes, quiet for several million years and no longer recognizable because of erosion and fault movement, spewed layers of ash that can been seen in roadcuts along Hwy. 29. The grade here is gentle, and as you gain elevation, the northern end of Napa Valley is revealed, along with the high, forested ridges that border it. No wonder this is one of the premier North Bay hikes for views! Bush poppy in spring and goldenfleece in summer and fall add daubs of bright yellow to the otherwise drab chaparral.

In a very rocky area, the road bends right and passes a trail post that gives the distance to North Peak, at 4,339 feet the highest of two summits that crown the mountain, as 4 miles. A few gray pines mixed in with the knobcones allow you to compare these species. Both have needles bundled in threes. The needles of the gray pine, gray-green in color, are from 8 to 12 inches long, and its round cones are large, from 6 to 10 inches across. This pine is also called foothill pine, indicating its preference for open slopes, where it is often found with oaks. Knobcone pine, usually shunning other tree species and preferring mountain soils, has dark-green needles 3 to 7 inches long. Its cones, 3 to 6 inches long, are egg-shaped and grow clustered in rings around the tree's trunk and its branches. Knobcone pines are adapted to fire: heat opens the cones and releases their seeds. Other traumas have the same effect, as you can see if you come upon a downed tree.

At a clearing beneath a dramatic, eroded cliff, the road makes an almost-180-degree bend to the right. A severe drop-off to the west requires caution—the views are just as good a safe distance back from the cliff's edge. From this point on, the feeling of isolation becomes more and more intense as you follow the well-graded road upward on a steepness that alternates between easy and moderate. Now the route bends left and passes stands of manzanita and a few stunted pines. The tap root anchoring each pine is incredibly long, sometimes out-growing the tree itself in its search for water. You can see examples of this where the road embankment has eroded away, exposing the roots. Passing under cliffs and ramparts rising steeply left, you enjoy protection from the wind on the mountain's eastern side. Creambush, often associated with the Bay Area's fog belt, has found a toe-hold here.

Just past the 2-mile point, a trail post, right, gives the distance to North Peak as 3 miles. At a wide clearing, crossed by power lines, you make a 180-degree turn to the left. Chinquapin, a frequent manzanita companion, is growing on a hillside, right. Its dark green leaves are dusted on their undersides with gold, giving it a resemblance to canyon oak. But instead of acorns, chinquapin, a chestnut relative, produces a nut encased in a spiny covering. The resemblance between canyon oak (*Quercus chrysolepis*) and chinquapin (*Chrysolepis chrysophylla*) is indicated by their Latin names, both of which refer to gold. Another sharp turn, this one right, aims you almost due north and soon brings you to very eroded ground. On your right, outcrops of rock fractured into columns may remind you of Devils Postpile in the Sierra. Now on a moderate grade, you have sweeping views east and northeast toward the series of ridges and summits that form the border between Napa and Yolo counties; beyond lies the Central Valley.

Just past the 3.5-mile point, you come to a junction, left, with the road to South Peak (4,003'). Ahead you can see most of the route to North Peak, another 1.7 miles. Both summits bristle with communication towers. Continuing straight, past mostly scrub vegetation, with a few pioneering Douglas firs and knobcone pines, you have a fine view of the Napa Valley, framed by a **V** notch formed by two intervening ridges. After a short descent, the first one today, the route levels briefly and then begins a gentle climb. At the next level spot, a saddle, the road curves right and rises on a moderate grade, passing a trail post, right, that gives the distance to North Peak as 1 mile. A false summit to the north is studded with rocky spires and pinnacles. Reaching a clearing, you pass a road, left, that heads toward several communication towers. Your route swings left and finds a level course, with North Peak in view at last. Soon a turn-around marks the spot where the well-graded road ends and a short, steep, rocky track to North Peak begins.

Passing several communication facilities, you arrive at last on the summit of North Peak—in the Bay Area, only Copernicus Peak on Mt. Hamilton is higher, by a mere 34 feet. You are now in Sonoma County, having traversed a corner of Lake County about 0.5 mile before reaching North Peak. The 360-degree views, on a clear day, are stunning, taking in all the familiar North Bay summits, plus Mt. Lassen and even Mt. Shasta, 192 miles away. How Mt. St. Helena got its name is uncertain. According to *California Place Names*, the first recorded climb took place in 1841 by a

Russian, J. G. Woznesenski, and many, including Josiah D. Whitney, director of the State Geological Survey, assumed the name had Russian origins. There is a replica of the plaque left on the summit by the 1841 Russian party to be found on the southwest side of the communication facilities. It was even said that Princess Helena de Gagarin, a niece of the Czar, climbed the mountain and bestowed upon it that name of her patron saint, *Saint Helena*, the mother of Constantine the Great. Perhaps a more likely derivation comes from a Russian ship, the Saint Helena, that may have spotted the peak from off the Northern California coast. After you have finished enjoying this spectacular vantage point, and perhaps pondering the mountain's name, retrace your steps to the parking area.

Skyline Wilderness Park
LAKE MARIE

Length:	6 miles
Time:	3 to 4 hours
Rating:	Moderate
Regulations:	Skyline Park Citizens Association; entrance fee; no dogs; bicyclists must wear helmets. Park hours: during daylight savings time, Monday–Thursday, 9 A.M. to 7 P.M.; Friday–Sunday, 8 A.M. to 7 P.M. During standard time, park opens same as above but closes at 5 P.M. Park closed on Thanksgiving and Christmas.
Highlights:	Wildflowers and scenic vistas are the attractions of this unique park, created in the late 1970s on 850 acres of land that were formerly part of Napa State Hospital and are now leased to the Skyline Park Citizens Association by Napa County. True to its name, the Skyline Trail, combined here with the Buckeye Trail to form a loop, clings to high ground for most of its length, as befits a segment of the Bay Area Ridge Trail, coming down only near Lake Marie, your destination. Park maintenance is a volunteer effort, so some trails may be in better shape than others— long pants are advised. The park welcomes equestrians and bicyclists as well as hikers, but parts of the Skyline Trail and all of the Buckeye Trail are closed to horses.
Directions:	From Hwy. 29 in Napa, take the Imola Avenue/Lake Berryessa/Hwy. 121 North exit and go east 2.9 miles on Imola Ave. to the park entrance, right. After paying a fee

at the entrance kiosk, bear right and go about 200 feet to a paved parking area.

Facilities: Picnic tables, rest rooms, water, maps at entrance kiosk. A campground adjacent to the parking area hosts RVs year-round, and tent camping during spring and summer. Also in the park are picnic and barbecue areas, an activity center, a cookhouse, a social center for meeting and indoor parties, and an equestrian arena.

Trailhead: Southwest corner of parking area.

In the shade of a beautiful valley oak, you walk downhill from the parking area on a dirt path, and in about 25 feet reach a junction. Here a trail post with a Bay Area Ridge Trail emblem urges you to turn right, and a sign warning you about rattlesnakes, wild pigs, poison oak, and ticks may make you feel like abandoning the hike altogether. Ignoring the trail post's advice, and deeming the sign's admonitions sensible but not terrifying, you continue straight, serenaded perhaps by California quail and red-winged blackbirds. On your right is the Martha Walker Native

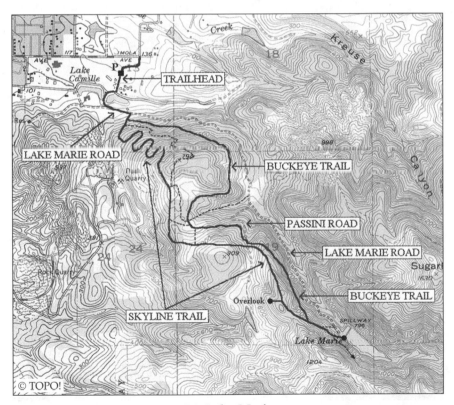

34. Lake Marie

Habitat Garden, a volunteer effort established in 1986 to honor its name-sake, a botanist who taught at the community college, hosted a radio pro-gram, and wrote a column in the Napa Valley Register. The garden, designed to attract birds, is worth a visit. It contains both native and non-native plants, bird feeders, a bird path, and a duck pond.

After about 400 feet, you come to a **T**-junction with a rough paved road, where you turn right. Passing the garden's entrance, right, you con-tinue another 400 feet, and at the next **T**-junction turn left onto a dirt road. After about 50 feet, the road crosses a bridge over Marie Creek, and in another 50 feet it merges with a paved road, where you veer left. Ahead is a locked gate, signed CAMP COOMBS, NAPA STATE HOSPITAL PROPERTY. Before reaching the gate, you turn right onto a dirt road, fenced on both sides, that passes between two man-made lakes—Lake Louise, left, and Lake Camille, right. After approximately 200 feet, the road bends left and soon reaches a junction. Here, Lake Marie Road heads straight, but your route, the Skyline Trail, a dirt-and-gravel road that is part of the Bay Area Ridge Trail, turns right and begins a moderate climb amid stands of coast live oak, California bay, blue oak, and California buckeye.

Like other Bay Area parklands snatched from the jaws of develop-ment, this park, located on land formerly used by Napa State Hospital, owes its existence to the efforts of concerned citizens, banded together as the Skyline Park Citizens Association, who were unwilling to see the State of California sell state land to private developers. With the help of groups such as the California Native Plant Society, the California Conservation Corps, the National Audubon Society, and the Sierra Club, a unique deal was struck: the state leased the land to Napa County, which

View north to the Napa Valley from the Buckeye Trail.

in turn leased it to the Skyline Park Citizens Association. The park, which opened in 1980, depends on user fees and volunteer efforts to keep it open.

After a few hundred feet, you pass the Buckeye Trail, your return route, left. In piles beside the road are hundreds of rusting tin cans, perhaps a legacy of the nearby state hospital, and through the trees, right, you can see a rock quarry—but you will soon leave these eyesores behind. In spring, the hillsides here are dotted with Ithuriel's spears, blue-eyed grass, California poppies, yellow Mariposa lilies, lupine, and other colorful wildflowers. A trail post, left, marks the Lower Skyline Trail, a route for equestrians and bicyclists. About 50 feet farther, the Skyline Trail, a single track for hikers only, veers left, leaving the dirt-and-gravel road. Turning left and following the steep, rocky trail as it makes a series of rising switchbacks, you are soon rewarded with a fine view northwest toward the City of Napa and the lower Napa Valley.

Climbing in the open, without much shade, you come to a rock wall and a barbed-wire fence marking the park's boundary. The wall, one of many in the park, was probably built by 19th century settlers and ranchers. Each switchback brings you back to the rock wall, behind which is a dense forest of bay and coast live oak. Bordering the trail are familiar shrubs—coffeeberry, snowberry, bush monkeyflower, and poison oak—and wildflowers such as Chinesehouses and bluedicks. A rising traverse eventually puts you atop an east–west ridge and brings you to a junction with the Bayleaf Trail, left. (The Lower Skyline Trail, the horse-and-bike route, joins the Bayleaf Trail about 50 feet to the left of this junction. Beyond that, the Bayleaf Trail is for hikers only.) Veering slightly right, you begin to descend on a moderate grade, in places stepping down over large rocks. Coming out of a wooded area, your view to the southwest now takes in the Highway 29 corridor, the Napa-Sonoma Marshes Wildlife Area and the northern end of San Pablo Bay.

At a fork marked by a trail post, a connector to the Bayleaf and Buckeye trails veers left, but you stay on the Skyline Trail, descending on a gentle grade into an oak-and-bay forest, with the rock wall still on your right. After reaching a low point, the trail rises gently, taking you through a gap in the wall and into a clearing, where a connector to the Buckeye Trail heads left. You continue straight, and soon begin a winding, moderate ascent through a brushy area of coyote brush, poison oak, and bush monkeyflower. After leveling briefly, the trail plunges headlong through a scrubby area and into an oak-and-bay forest, arriving at last at Passini Road, which begins at Lake Marie Road and exits the park through a locked gate, right. This junction, just past the 2-mile point, gives you access to several of the park's many trails. (To shorten today's hike, you can turn left onto Passini Road, follow it downhill several hundred feet, turn left onto the Buckeye Trail, and pick up the route description below. Or you can follow Passini Road downhill to Lake Marie Road, turn left, follow Lake Marie Road back to its junction with the Skyline Trail, and then retrace your steps to the parking area.)

To visit Lake Marie, you cross Passini Road and continue climbing on the Skyline Trail. Approaching a barbed-wire fence, the trail veers left and brings you onto an open, grassy hillside with fine views northwest into the lower Napa Valley. In a deep canyon, left, is Marie Creek, and rising on a hillside across the creek is the rocky ridge leading to Sugarloaf Mountain, West Peak. (You can explore this wonderful, rugged area on another day by following the route description for "Sugarloaf Mountain," beginning on p. 197.)

At an unsigned fork in the trail, you bear right. In about 15 feet the trail forks again, but this time you bear left. In dense forest, the route takes you up and over the crest of a north–south ridge, where occasional clearings give you views to the west. Passing a faint trace leading uphill through a grassy clearing, you follow a rolling course amid fields of wildflowers, and come to a more substantial path leading, in about 175 feet, to an overlook, right. The view southwest from this overlook is terrific, taking in the marshlands around the mouth of the Napa River, the northern end of San Pablo Bay, and, on a clear day, other Bay Area landmarks. Just past the junction with the trail to the overlook, the Skyline Trail begins descending on a moderate grade through a forest of oak and bay, and soon encounters your return route, the Buckeye Trail, left.

To reach Lake Marie, you continue straight on the Skyline Trail, soon passing the first of three access paths to the lake. When you reach the second, veer left and descend to the lake, built in 1908 to provide water for the state hospital farm. An earthen dam across Marie Creek forms the northwest edge of the lake, and a nearby rest bench invites you to stay awhile. When you are ready to set off again, retrace your steps to the junction of the Skyline and Buckeye trails. From this junction, you continue straight, now on the Buckeye Trail, a single track closed to horses. Maintaining a mostly level grade, the route soon takes you out of deep forest and across hillsides of California sagebrush, coffeeberry, toyon, and bush monkeyflower. Back in the woods, at an unsigned fork, you stay right, now descending to a clearing and Passini Road.

At the road you turn right, and in about 40 feet pick up the continuation of the Buckeye Trail, left. A moderate climb takes you past stands of manzanita and into a bay forest, then across open grassland ablaze in spring with wildflowers. A rock wall, right, runs parallel to the trail. Passing a connector to the Skyline Trail, left, you bear right and walk through a gap in the wall. In about 200 feet, you pass another connector to the Skyline Trail, left, and in 150 feet or so, reach a four-way junction, marked by a trail post, with the Bayleaf Trail. Continuing straight on the Buckeye Trail, you cross a large meadow where deer may be grazing, with a fine view of the Marie Creek drainage and Sugarloaf Mountain. At the northeast end of the meadow, the route rises to cross a rock rib, then begins to descend through a lovely forest of oak and buckeye, where clearings offer terrific views of the lower Napa Valley. After passing through a gap in a barbed-wire fence, the trail reaches a clearing that sweeps downhill to Lake Marie Road. Trail construction in 1998 rerouted the Buckeye Trail—it now holds a level course and in approximately 100 yards joins the Skyline Trail, here a dirt-and-gravel road. When you reach the road, turn right, then left at Lake Marie Road, and retrace your steps to the parking area.

35 Skyline Wilderness Park
SUGARLOAF MOUTAIN

Length: 7 miles

Time: 3 to 4 hours

Rating: Difficult

Regulations: Skyline Park Citizens Association; entrance fee; no dogs; bicyclists must wear helmets. Park hours: during daylight savings time, Monday–Thursday, 9 A.M. to 7 P.M.; Friday–Sunday, 8 A.M. to 7 P.M. During standard time, park opens same as above but closes at 5 P.M. Park closed on Thanksgiving and Christmas.

Highlights: This out-and-back route, best in spring when wildflowers are at their peak, uses Lake Marie Road and the Rim Rock Trail to ascend the 1630-foot west peak of Sugarloaf Mountain, the highest point in the park. Skyline Wilderness Park was created in the late 1970s on 850 acres of land that were formerly part of Napa State Hospital and are now leased to the Skyline Park Citizens Association by Napa County. Park maintenance is a volunteer effort, so some trails may be in better shape than others—long pants are advised. The park welcomes equestrians and bicyclists as well as hikers.

Directions: See the directions for "Lake Marie" on pages 192–193.

Facilities: Picnic tables, rest rooms, water, maps at entrance kiosk. A campground adjacent to the parking area hosts RVs year-round, and tent camping during spring and summer. Also in the park are picnic and barbecue areas, an activity center, a cookhouse, a social center for meeting and indoor parties, and an equestrian arena.

Trailhead: Southwest corner of parking area.

Follow the route description for "Lake Marie" on pages 193-194 to the junction of Lake Marie Road and the Skyline Trail. Paralleling its namesake creek, Lake Marie Road is a rough and rocky dirt track shared by hikers, bicyclists, and equestrians. Groves of California buckeye, blue oak, and California bay punctuate the open fields bordering the road, which in spring are brightly speckled with colorful wildflowers. Behind a fence, left, fruit and nut trees on the grounds of Camp Coombs, part of Napa State Hospital, bring color in the fall. Passing a horse trail, left, the road, rising on a moderate grade, is now just high enough to provide fine views toward the City of Napa and the lower Napa Valley. A grove of olive trees marks a fork in the road: the branches soon rejoin, but you can maintain elevation by staying right. A rest bench, right, and a watering trough for horses, left, mark a junction. Here, a closed trail heads steeply right, and the Marie Creek Trail, which may be overgrown and not maintained, veers left. Just past the junction is a cave—a number of which can be found in the park—gouged from the rocky hillside, right. These may have been dug to find sources of water for the hospital, or perhaps they were the beginnings of mine shafts.

Still gaining elevation on a moderate grade, Lake Marie Road enters the realm of black oak, madrone, manzanita, chamise, and bush monkeyflower. Across a deep valley, left, you may see a man-made rock wall, one of many in the park which were probably built by 19th century ranchers and settlers. On exposed flats of dry, rocky soil, look for yellow

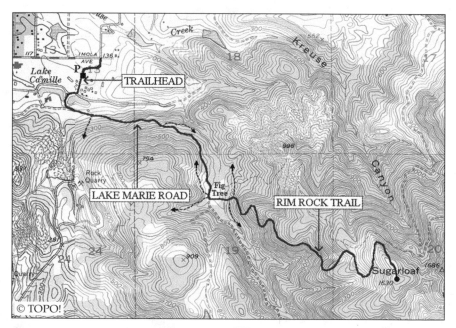

35. Sugarloaf Mountain

Hikers on the Rim Rock Trail enjoy the view from near the summit of Sugarloaf Mountain's west peak.

johnnytuck, sometimes called butter-and-eggs, a relative of the paint-brushes and owl's-clovers, sporting purple-tipped leaves and three yellow sacs at the end of each flower. Now descending on a moderate grade, the road soon reaches a level area with a large grassy meadow, right. Here, the Oakleaf Trail joins sharply from the right, and as you continue to descend, you pass a closed trail, left, and the Bayleaf Trail, right. About 75 feet ahead and left is one of the park's most remarkable features, a giant fig tree whose branches droop to the ground, forming a living tree house. The joists and rafters are twisting, curving fig limbs, and the roof and sides are made from hand-sized fig leaves. In the center of the one-room dwelling, anchoring the structure, are two sturdy trunks. A fence surrounds the fig tree to protect it.

Just past the fig tree, you leave Lake Marie Road and turn left onto a single track trail, heading toward Marie Creek. Uphill and right is a picnic table, one of the few in the park's backcountry. This is a wonderful place for a picnic, as you may be entertained by a covey of California quail or dive-bombed by a hummingbird. Continuing east from the fig tree, a single-track trail wanders about 100 yards to Marie Creek, and just before reaching it, merges with a trail coming from the picnic table. A bridge provides an easy way across the creek, and about 60 feet farther you come to a junction with the Marie Creek Trail, right. Continue straight, passing two signs, one for the Manzanita and Toyon trails, the other for your route, the Rim Rock Trail (called Thatcher's Rim Rock Trail on the park map.)

In about 15 feet, where the trail starts to bend left, you come to another junction, this one unsigned. Here you turn right, onto the Rim Rock Trail, which passes through a gap in a rock wall and then reaches a fork, where you bear right. A series of moderate uphill switchbacks soon puts you high above Marie Creek, hugging the park boundary. Manzanita, toyon, chamise, and bush monkeyflower all tolerate the hot, dry conditions found here during summer and early fall. After a rainy winter, spring wildflowers such as wine-cup clarkia and globe gilia, are a delight here, distracting you from the work at hand as you huff and puff your way up the mountain. Now the trail crosses a rocky hillside, home to a succulent plant called common dudleya, a member of the stonecrop family that resembles a fleshy artichoke with red and green leaves. These produce yellow-to-red flowers in late spring and early summer.

The route curves east, following a tributary of Marie Creek, far below and right. The grade eases as you reach the head of a canyon, but then rises steeply via a series of switchbacks that brush the park boundary, marked by a barbed-wire fence. In addition to wildflowers, spring brings colorful butterflies to decorate the scenery. One of the most common is the chalcedon checkerspot, varying from brown to yellow to red. Suddenly you come upon a heart-stopping viewpoint, where Mt. Tamalpais, Burdell Mountain, Big Rock Ridge, and San Pablo Bay are presented for you to admire. Other things that may give your heart pause, especially if you are on the lookout for rattlesnakes, are lizards rustling through dry leaves, or a flock of band-tailed pigeons fluttering noisily aloft from a towering oak.

The route zigzags up a grassy hillside dotted in spring with mule ears, California poppy, Johnny jump-up, blue-eyed grass, purple owl's-clover, and California buttercup. Passing through a grove of bay and coast live oak, the route descends slightly, and now you can see Sugarloaf Mountain, East Peak (1686'), topped with several communication towers, due east. In the midst of another oak-and-bay grove, you reach a clearing centered around a low rock. This undistinguished spot, ringed by trees, marks the 1630-foot summit of Sugarloaf Mountain, West Peak. From here, a faint trace leads right, to another clearing, and a more substantial trail heads left and downhill. This trail, not on the park map, is a rough, undeveloped track that drops steeply from Sugarloaf Mountain and joins the Skyline Trail about 0.3 mile east of Lake Marie. Someday, it is hoped, an improved version of this route will allow a grand loop to be made around the entire Skyline Wilderness Park. For now, after you have enjoyed relaxing on the summit, retrace your steps to the parking area.

36	## Westwood Hills Park ## NORTH KNOLL LOOP

Length: 2 miles

Time: 1 hour or less

Rating: Easy

Regulations: City of Napa Parks and Recreation Department; no dogs, no bikes.

Highlights: Using the Valley View, Rocky Ridge, Meadow, Oak Knoll, North Knoll, and Deer trails, this semi-loop route explores most of Westwood Hills Park, a small patch of eucalyptus forest, oak woodland, and open grassland west of Hwy. 29, on the outskirts of the City of Napa. The park was opened in January 1976, and later that year a fire burned many of the park's eucalyptus trees and some coast live oaks. To help reduce fuel, cows are permitted to graze in the park from April through October, and the mess they make is hard to avoid. To avoid cow pies and flies, plan your visit during some other month. A crude map showing the park's eight named trails is available from the City of Napa Parks and Recreation Department, 1100 West Street (707) 257-9529.

Directions: From Hwy. 29 northbound in Napa, take the First Street/Downtown Napa exit. After exiting, turn left and go over the highway, now on Browns Valley Road. Go 1 mile to the parking area, left.

From Hwy. 29 southbound in Napa, take the First Street/Downtown Napa exit, then turn left onto Browns Valley Rd. and follow the directions above.

Facilities: Picnic tables, water; Caroline Parr Nature Museum, open Saturdays and Sundays from 1 P.M. to 4 P.M., is just west of the parking area; (707) 255-6465.

Trailhead: Southeast corner of parking area.

The paved park-entrance road continues south past the parking area, and just to its right is your route, the Valley View Trail, a dirt path. Along the route, you may notice numbered markers indicating various plants. They are keyed as follows: **1**, **2**, and **3** (in the picnic area adjacent to the parking area), California buckeye, bigleaf maple, and California bay; **4**, cherry plum (*Prunus cerasifera*); **5**, poison oak; **6**, Himalayan blackberry; **7**,

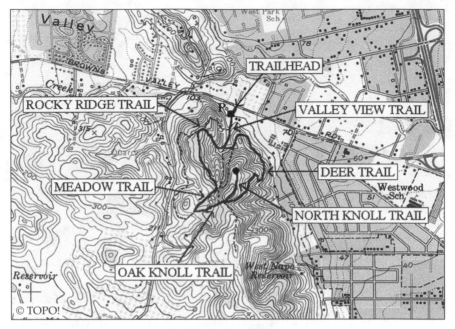

36. North Knoll Loop

eucalyptus, blue gum; **8**, French broom; **9**, coast live oak; **10**, turkey
mullein; **11**, madrone; **12**, valley oak. Passing a water fountain about 150
feet south of the parking area, you go another 100 feet to a gated dirt
road, the continuation of the Valley View Trail. Stepping around the
wooden gate on the right, you walk uphill on a moderate grade, surrounded by tall eucalyptus. Left is a house and barn, the home of a rancher whose heirs sold his land to the City of Napa to create this park.

About 200 feet uphill from the gate, you pass an unsigned trail, right.
Here the eucalyptus is joined by coast live oak, cypress, California bay,
toyon, and thickets of French broom, poison oak, and blackberry vines.
Another couple of hundred feet bring you to a metal gate, which you pass
around on the right. Soon you come to a four-way junction with a rest
bench and two unsigned trails, left and right. The left-hand trail is part of
your return loop, but for now, you turn right and begin climbing on a
wide dirt path that wanders through a forest of eucalyptus, coast live oak,
and bay. Moderate at first, the grade soon eases. When you reach a
barbed-wire fence with a wooden gate, open it and walk through. As the
route bends left and continues its climb, you pass a trail, right, and then
reach a fork where you stay left. Now on the Rocky Ridge Trail, the track
widens as it passes back through the barbed-wire fence and follows a
level, then descending, course past moss-covered rock outcrops to a five-
way junction where the Rocky Ridge, Valley View, Gum Canyon, and
Meadow trails converge.

Turning right onto the Meadow Trail, a dirt road, you descend on a moderate grade, listening perhaps to the call of a northern flicker, a western scrub-jay, or a red-tailed hawk circling overhead. The terrain is more open here, featuring rolling hills studded with oaks. When you reach the next junction, where a confusing array of unsigned trails come together, turn left onto the Oak Knoll Trail, a single track. A grove of oak and bay soon gives way to a clearing, where a trail post (but no sign) marks a fork. Here you bear left and begin a moderate climb through a weedy area that seems to delight members of the park's squirrel population. At a T-junction with a dirt road, signed TRAIL, you turn right and continue uphill. A few paces more and you reach a four-way junction, at about the 1-mile point, where a dirt road crosses your path, and the Deer Trail, a single track, takes off across the road, veering left by a picnic table.

Agricultural clearing has drastically reduced California's population of valley oaks.

To visit the summit of North Knoll, where views of the lower Napa Valley and the City of Napa await, turn left onto the dirt road and follow it uphill, soon reaching a trail, left, to a picnic table atop the summit. After enjoying the views, retrace your steps to the previous junction and find the Deer Trail, about 50 feet north of the picnic table, by marker **11**. This trail skirts the east side of North Knoll on a steep hillside falling away right. Sprouting here and there are clumps of California sagebrush, bush monkeyflower, California fuchsia, and turkey mullein. When you come to a fork in the trail, bear right, making a level traverse and then descending via switchbacks. Where a trail merges from the right, you continue straight, dropping to cross a watercourse, right, and then regaining level ground. Soon you come upon a trail post, again with no sign, marking the Gum Canyon Trail, a dirt road joining sharply from the left. In a clearing about 100 feet ahead, you find a trail post with two arrows, one pointing ahead, the other back. Here, under some large eucalyptus and cypress trees, you begin to veer left and walk uphill over rough ground. A right-hand turn brings you to a dirt road, the Valley View Trail, at the junction you passed near the start of the loop. Here you turn right and retrace your steps to the parking area.

◆ Sonoma County ◆

37

Annadel State Park
LAKE ILSANJO

Length: 9 miles

Time: 5 to 6 hours

Rating: Difficult

Regulations: CSP; no dogs; obey signs in the parking area, which is not part of the state park.

Highlights: Length, not terrain, earns this trip its difficult rating. Using the Cobblestone, Orchard, Rough Go, Canyon, and Spring Creek trails, this semi-loop route encounters dense forest, oak savanna, and a wonderful, albeit man-made, lake during its tour of the northwestern part of Annadel State Park. A massive and ongoing restoration effort, begun in 1998, completely transformed many of the park's eroded dirt roads into winding multi-use paths shared by hikers, equestrians, and bicyclists. Many of the trails are subject to seasonal closure during wet weather. Please observe all closure signs, and use only named and maintained trails. Because the park is in a state of flux, it is wise to call before visiting: (707) 539-3911.

Directions: From Hwy. 101 in Santa Rosa, take the Sebastopol/ Sonoma/Hwy. 12 exit and follow Hwy. 12 east toward Sonoma. At 1.4 miles, turn left onto Farmers Ln., go 0.8 mile, and turn right onto Montgomery Dr. Go 2.7 miles and turn right onto Channel Dr., signed for Annadel State Park and Spring Lake. Go 0.6 mile to a large dirt-and-gravel parking area, left.

From Hwy 12 going northwest from Kenwood to Santa Rosa, turn left on Los Alamos Rd. and go 0.2 mile to Melita Rd. Turn right on Melita Rd. and then immediately left onto Montgomery Dr. Go 0.5 mile to Channel Dr., turn left, and go 0.6 mile to a large, dirt-and-gravel parking area, left.

Facilities: None at parking area; ahead, inside the park, are a ranger station, drinking fountain, picnic tables, and toilets.

Trailhead: Opposite the east end of the parking area, across Channel Dr. on its south side.

(previous page) The yellow flower of the mule ears.

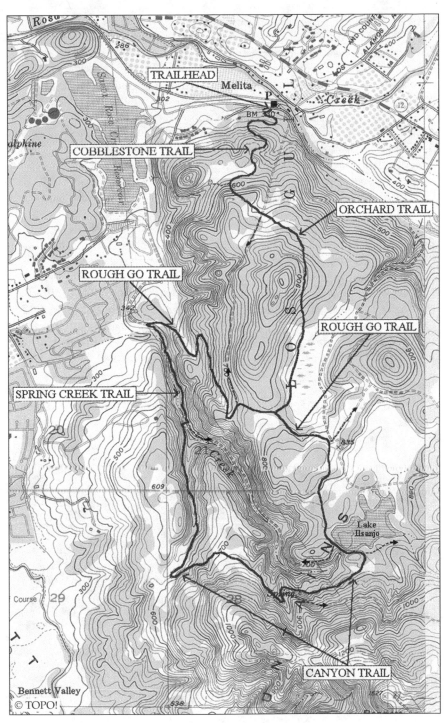

37. Lake Ilsanjo

Your route, the Cobblestone Trail, starts in a wooded area of eucalyptus, coast live oak, and California bay, overgrown with French broom and honeysuckle vines. Alternating between moderate uphill and level sections, the trail works its way generally south through rocky terrain that may become muddy during wet weather. Stands of tall manzanita, some of them top-heavy and bent toward the ground, line the trail. This park is one of the best places in the North Bay to see wild turkeys—look in damp ravines or along the edges of clearings for large flocks of these dark, iridescent birds, which are slightly smaller than their domestic cousins. Veering sharply left but still climbing, you enter the realm of black oak, passing a rocky hillside, left, strewn with rust-colored rock boulders. Clinging to the oaks are clumps of mistletoe and strands of lace lichen, sometimes called Spanish moss. In fall, black-oak leaves offer a colorful display of yellow and orange. Due east, across Highway 12, rises the forested summit of Mount Hood (2730'), a destination for another day.

After traversing an open, grassy field, where you may see the remains of a dirt road, the route bends sharply left and is crossed by a trail that has been closed for restoration. Back in forest, you catch glimpses, through the trees, of the housing developments bordering Highway 12 in Oakmont—visible evidence of why creating and protecting open space is so important. At about the 1-mile point, you reach a junction. Here the Frog Pond Trail goes straight, but your route, the Cobblestone Trail, curves left. Gaining elevation on a gentle grade, you enjoy a pleasant stroll through oak groves and across open fields, one holding the remains of an old orchard. Now passing a trail on the right, you enter a forest of Douglas fir and bay. At a junction with a dirt road—closed on your left but open on your right as the continuation of the Cobblestone Trail—you

A dam on Spring Creek forms Lake Ilsanjo, named for Ilsa and Joe Coney, who formerly owned this property.

go straight, now on the Orchard Trail. After passing an unsigned trail, right, you make a long traverse across a wooded hillside that falls away left, then climb to an open area where manzanita thrives in company with oaks, whose outstretched limbs arch over the trail.

Looking east, you can see landmarks in Sugarloaf Ridge State Park, including the volcanic ridge itself and also Red Mountain (2548'), site of a communication tower. The park's highest peak, Bald Mountain (2729') is hidden behind Mt. Hood. Passing the remains of a several cobblestone quarries, right, you soon reach a fork marked by a trail post, where you stay left, still on the Orchard Trail. Ahead, in the distance to the southeast, rises Bennett Mountain, at 1887 feet the highest point in Annadel State Park, its slopes dappled in fall with colorful foliage. Now crossing a beautiful oak savanna, you come to a T-junction with the Rough Go Trail, where you turn left. The great expanse of open fields here favors aerial hunters such as red-tailed and red-shouldered hawks. Hard to distinguish from one another against a bright sky, they are best told apart by their calls: a single whistled "keer" for the red-tailed hawk, and a repeated crying "keer, keer, keer" for the red-shouldered.

Climbing on a gentle grade, the Rough Go Trail soon meets the Live Oak Trail, left, and then bends right, finding a level course in the shade of coast live oaks. At last nearing Lake Ilsanjo, named for the former property owners, Ilsa and Joe Coney, you bear right at a fork, and then pass a trail, left. The area ahead is used as a spillway for the lake during periods of high water. If the spillway is flooded, you can detour around and over it by means of a trail, right, and a bridge about 100 feet to your right. About 25 feet ahead, your route becomes paved, and 100 feet or so farther it arrives at a T-junction with a dirt road. Turning left, you walk about 200 feet to a picnic table in the shade of a large oak, where a short path leads down to the lake, a lovely body of water. Just past the picnic table is the concrete dam on Spring Creek that forms the lake.

Bearing left across the 100-yard-long dam, you pass the Spring Creek Trail, right, a wonderful route but closed during the rainy season. On the far side of the dam, another picnic table beckons, and here the route, a dirt road, swings left and begins a gentle climb. The still waters of the lake form a perfect mirror, especially entrancing when the sky is blue and filled with puffy white clouds. American coots and ruddy ducks may drift lazily near the shore. Topping a low rise, the road descends to a junction, where your route, the Canyon Trail, a dirt road, turns right. Watch here for the dark, fleeting form of a Cooper's hawk, a crow-sized raptor of the forest. As the road climbs southwest, with the canyon holding Spring Creek to your right, you begin to get fine views into the Santa Rosa area through a gap in the nearby hills. In a dense, fern-floored forest of Douglas fir, coast live oak, bay, and bigleaf maple, you pass Hunter's Spring, a favorite haunt of wild turkeys. How different this jungle-like area is from the oak savanna you visited just a short while ago!

At about the 4-mile point, you reach a junction having a picnic table, left, and a rest bench, right. The dirt road heading left is the Marsh Trail, part of the Bay Area Ridge Trail. You continue straight on the Canyon Trail, now also part of the Bay Area Ridge Trail, and still a dirt road. The route drops to cross a watercourse, which drains through a culvert under the road, then comes into an open area where you can see just the tip of Mt. St. Helena rising slightly east of north. You continue to descend over very rocky ground on a gentle grade, following the road as it makes a sweeping right-hand bend, passing a trail, left, that goes through a locked gate. Leaving open grassland graced with valley oaks, you enter a forest of coast live oak, black oak, and madrone, soon turning sharply right to cross a bridge over Spring Creek. Just across the creek, the Canyon Trail ends at a T-junction with the Spring Creek Trail. To your right the Spring Creek Trail is a single track, and to your left it is a dirt road, part of the Bay Area Ridge Trail.

Turning left, you enjoy a level walk along Spring Creek, home to white alder and Oregon ash, and soon pass a junction where a gravel road heads left to a flood-control dam and levee. Entering an oak savanna, the road continues parallel to Spring Creek, but just before it veers left to cross a wooden bridge, at about the 6-mile point, you turn sharply right onto the Rough Go Trail. Now climbing southeast on a gentle grade, the trail, a multi-use path, makes several switchbacks, each one bringing better and better views of the Santa Rosa area. Near the crest of a ridge, you encounter a large circular maze built of small rocks, perched on the edge of a steep hillside—a tribute perhaps from some local Druids. Veering left here, a bit more climbing brings you to a junction with the Cobblestone Trail, left. Continuing straight, you wind uphill past stands of oak and manzanita to the junction with the Orchard Trail you arrived at earlier. Now turn left and retrace your steps to the parking area.

Still waters of Lake Ilsanjo reflect a tranquil sky.

◆ Armstrong Redwoods State Reserve ◆
◆ Austin Creek State Recreation Area ◆

These two side-by-side parks, located about 75 miles northwest of San Francisco near the Russian River town of Guerneville, encompass more than 6,400 acres of deeply cut canyons, forested ridges, chaparral bands, and grassy meadows. Along Fife Creek, in Armstrong Redwoods State Reserve, are groves of magnificent old-growth coast redwoods, some dating back more than 1400 years. This species, *Sequoia sempervirens*, is the world's tallest tree, some specimens on the northern California coast reaching more than 350 feet. Found only on the coasts of California and Oregon, redwood forests were once extensive, but logging has taken its toll. Today, only isolated pockets of virgin redwood forest remain on federal, state, and private lands.

The redwood groves along Fife Creek are still standing thanks to the foresight of one man, James B. Armstrong, and the perseverance of his daughter Lizzie. Armstrong, a native of Ohio and a colonel in the Union Army, came to Sonoma County in 1874 and was involved in lumbering and real estate. In 1875 he purchased 440 acres bordering Fife Creek, thick with redwoods. Armstrong owned a nearby mill that produced 5 million board feet of lumber each year, but his intention was to create an arboretum on the Fife Creek land to preserve its groves of ancient trees. Armstrong died in 1900 without achieving his goal, but in 1916, through the efforts of his daughter Lizzie, voters in Sonoma County approved purchase of the land. The reserve remained in county hands until 1934, when it became part of the state park system. A redwood tree named in Armstrong's honor is near the start of the Discovery Trail. Colonel Armstrong's daughter Lizzie married William Ladd Jones, a clergyman from Maine who settled in California. He is memorialized by the Parson Jones redwood near the start of the Pioneer Trail. Lizzie Armstrong Jones has a plaque in her honor beside the Discovery Trail parking area, on a rock just right of the trailhead.

The reserve has a fine visitor center, on the east side of the main day-use parking area, staffed by helpful volunteers. Here you can find books, maps, park information, and suggestions for walks and hikes. Be sure to check with the visitor center staff for any scheduled interpretive programs that may coincide with your visit. The visitor center is open daily from 10 A.M. to 4 P.M. in summer, and from 11 A.M. to 3 P.M. in winter. A ranger station that serves both the reserve and the recreation area is on the west side of Armstrong Woods Road, across from the entrance kiosk. Parking in the day-use parking area is free. There is a self-guiding nature trail in the reserve, and also a trail designed for blind or visually impaired visitors, called the Discovery Trail. The Redwood Forest Theater, a Depression-era project in the heart of the reserve that was the site of artistic performances from 1936 to 1995, is a quiet place for contemplation. Picnic tables and fire grates are available at several sites near Fife Creek; one is available for groups and may be reserved by calling the reserve office. There is a fee for driving into the reserve.

Austin Creek State Recreation Area has more than 20 miles of hiking trails in rugged terrain that ranges from 150 feet to nearly 1900 feet in elevation. Douglas fir, California bay, and several species of oak are the dominant trees here, and there are also zones of chaparral and grassy meadows filled with wildflowers. The recreation area has four backcountry trail camps, located a few hundred feet above sea level in rugged terrain near East Austin Creek. To reach them, hikers must descend more than 1000 feet on the Gilliam Creek or Austin Creek trails. The trailheads are found by following Armstrong Woods Road, a steep, narrow, and winding paved track, into a remote part of the recreation area. The road is closed to vehicles more than 20 feet long and to those of any length towing trailers. The camps are available on a first-come, first-served basis. A backcountry permit is required and can be obtained at the ranger station during business hours. There are also 23 family campsites in the Bullfrog Pond Campground near the end of Armstrong Woods Road. These too are available on a first-come, first-served basis. There are fees for driving into the recreation area and for camping.

All of the recreation area's trails are open to horses, and there is a pack station concession offering guided day and overnight trips. The pack station is located about 0.4 mile west of the Discovery Trail parking area in Armstrong Redwoods State Reserve. In both the reserve and the recreation area, bicycles are permitted only on the paved roads and the service roads, not on the trails. Dogs are not permitted on any of the trails, or in the backcountry trail camps. Elsewhere, they must be leashed during the day, and in a vehicle or tent at night.

RANGER STATION: (707) 869-2015

PACK STATION: (707) 887-2939

DISTRICT OFFICE: (707) 865-2391

THE STEWARDS OF SLAVIANKA: a volunteer organization that works with the state parks in the Russian River/Mendocino district; (707) 869-9177

38   Armstrong Redwoods State Reserve
East Ridge

Length:	2.3 miles
Time:	1 to 2 hours
Rating:	Moderate
Regulations:	CSP; no dogs, no bikes.
Highlights:	This loop, using the East Ridge and Pioneer trails, explores the high ground east of Fife Creek, then drops to the canyon floor to wander amid serene groves of ancient coast redwoods, the main attraction of this 805-acre reserve. A longer, more demanding variation of this route, extending north into the Austin Creek State Recreation Area, is described in "Grand Loop" starting on p. 216.
Directions:	From Hwy. 116 in Guerneville, 0.1 mile west of the bridge across the Russian River, go north on Armstrong Woods Rd. 2.3 miles to the visitor-center parking area, right.
Facilities:	Visitor center with interpretive displays, books, maps, helpful staff; ranger station, rest rooms, picnic tables, water, phone.
Trailhead:	About 75 feet south of the visitor center.

The East Ridge Trail, your route, starts as a paved path just south of the visitor center. After passing the rest rooms and a drinking fountain, left, the trail changes to a dirt-and-gravel track—and soon to dirt only—finding a moderate course via well-graded switchbacks up the steep east wall of the canyon holding Fife Creek, the reserve's main watercourse. Most of the reserve's towering coast redwoods are found along Fife Creek, but there are many on this hillside too, mixed in with Douglas fir, California bay, tanbark oak, evergreen huckleberry, hazelnut, and bigleaf maple. The ground cover consists mainly of western sword fern and redwood sorrel, both common where redwoods are found. At night, cold air pools in the canyon, and it can be chilly starting off on an early morning hike. But as you ascend, the air keeps getting warmer, and soon you may be shedding a layer or two.

After about 0.5 mile of relentless climbing, the trail gains the crest of a ridge and turns north, following it uphill. The forest here is less dense, making way for species such as coast live oak, madrone, black oak, and Oregon oak. Now on a rolling course with some steep sections, you stay right at a fork, then rejoin the left-hand branch in about 150 feet. Passing a rest bench, left, the trail veers left and leaves the ridgecrest, which rises

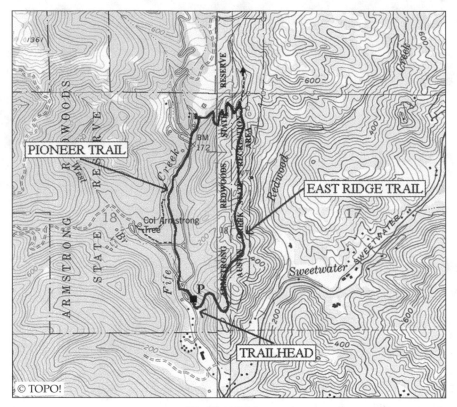

38. East Ridge

to the right. The warmer, drier microclimate on this ridge encourages shrubs such as manzanita, toyon, coffeeberry, and coyote brush. Staying left at the next fork, you reach a junction marked by a trail post, about 50 feet ahead. Here the East Ridge Trail continues straight, but you turn sharply left onto a single track and descend a series of switchbacks over rough ground. Passing a rest bench and a path to a viewpoint, right, the trail enters the redwood realm as it nears Fife Creek, giving you a chance to enjoy these massive giants from a slightly elevated perspective.

Now on the canyon floor, the route crosses Fife Creek on a wooden bridge, and arrives at a picnic area. Bearing left here, you follow a paved road through a parking area, with the creek on your left. After a couple of hundred feet, your road is joined by one from a service area, right, and in another 50 feet or so, you reach Armstrong Woods Road, the reserve's main road, which is paved. Here you bear left, passing the first of two paved roads to another picnic area, right. When you reach the second one, in about 50 feet, you cross it by angling right, and just ahead find your route, the Pioneer Trail. From here to the visitor center, the Pioneer Trail, a dirt path carpeted with duff—redwood needles and other forest debris—runs parallel to Armstrong Woods Road, passing through some of the North Bay's finest redwood groves. Immediately to your left is Fife Creek. After crossing it on a wooden bridge, you enjoy a level walk though the redwoods, stopping to crane your neck upward and marvel at their towering height.

Passing a trail, left, that jogs over to the Armstrong Woods Road, you skirt a large fire-hollowed tree, called a goosepen, and soon reach a junction with the Nature Trail, right. Here you continue straight, marveling at a huge ring of trees called Burbank Circle, named for Luther Burbank, a famous Santa Rosa horticulturist. When you reach a paved road, cross it and rejoin the Pioneer Trail. Soon you come to a display created from the cross-section of a redwood that began its life in 948 A. D. Some important dates in world history are marked on its surface, including the signing of the Magna Carta in 1215, the landing of Columbus in 1492, the

The Pioneer Trail along Fife Creek enters the realm of the redwoods.

Declaration of Independence in 1776, and the earthquake of 1906. Sadly, the last date, 1978, is the year the tree was felled by vandals. A few feet beyond this display is a another paved road. Left is the Parson Jones Tree, 310 feet high, 13.8 feet in diameter, and more than 1300 years old. Crossing the paved road, you rejoin the Pioneer Trail, and soon reach Armstrong Woods Road, with the reserve's entrance kiosk to your right. After crossing the road, you turn right and in a few paces reach the visitor center and the parking area.

39 ## Armstrong Redwoods State Reserve/Austin Creek State Recreation Area
GRAND LOOP

Length:	5.6 miles
Time:	4 to 5 hours
Rating:	Difficult
Regulations:	CSP; no dogs, no bikes.
Highlights:	This athletic loop, using the East Ridge, Pool Ridge, Discovery, and Pioneer trails, explores the high ground east of Fife Creek in Armstrong Redwoods State Reserve, and then continues north into the Austin Creek State Recreation Area, gaining nearly 1000 feet in elevation. Groves of old-growth coast redwoods are the prime attraction in the reserve, but the recreation area boasts fine forests of Douglas fir, oak, and California bay, along with sweeping vistas from the route's high point. The last 0.5 mile of the loop takes you past the Colonel Armstrong and Parson Jones trees, both more than 300 feet high.
Directions:	See the directions for "East Ridge" on p. 213.
Facilities:	Visitor center with interpretive displays, books, maps, helpful staff; ranger station, rest rooms, picnic tables, water, phone.
Trailhead:	About 75 feet south of the visitor center.

Follow the description for "East Ridge" on pages 213–214 to a junction at the 1.2-mile point with a trail heading sharply left and downhill to the picnic area. Here you continue straight, with the crest of a ridge uphill and right, and a steep drop to your left. On a rolling course, the trail emerges from forest to cross a clearing, then re-enters the trees, where a

Steller's jay may scold you for trespassing. Dropping into a ravine that holds a tributary of Fife Creek, the trail turns left to cross a bridge, and then comes to a four-way junction with a dirt road, just west of the tributary. You have just left Armstrong Redwoods State Reserve and are now in Austin Creek State Recreation Area. Across the road is the continuation of the East Ridge Trail, but you may wish to linger for a few minutes, enjoying the shade and solitude of a wonderful redwood grove beside the road.

Now climbing uphill on a moderate grade, the route, a dirt road, curves left and traverses a large clearing at about the 2-mile point. At a junction with a dirt road, left, you continue straight, passing Pond Farm, the site of an artists colony active from 1949 to 1952, and home of Marguerite Wildenhain, a famous Bauhaus-trained potter who left

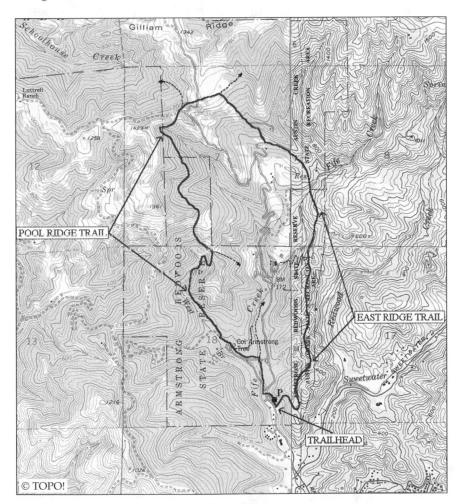

39. Grand Loop

Europe and emigrated to the US to escape Nazi persecution. About 60 feet beyond where a road from the farm pond joins from the left, you reach a fork. Here the dirt road bends left, but your route, the East Ridge Trail, a single track, veers right and uphill. (The distance given on a sign here, 0.7 mile to Bullfrog Pond, should be 1.7 miles, maybe more.) Now in a forest of Douglas fir, climbing past the ranger's residence, you soon join a dirt road that curves right, and then begin a steep climb that eases to moderate. Passing an overgrown dirt road, left, your route swings left to cross a seasonal creek, and then resumes its relentless climb on a rocky, eroded track. Crossing a shallow ravine, left, the trail, now a single track, works its way steeply uphill.

Leaving the forest, you make a rising traverse across an open slope, where a fine view extends south across the Russian River all the way to Mt. Tamalpais. Spurred on by this scenic reward, you soon reach a flat spot and a grove of trees, left, that makes a perfect picnic spot. Here your trail makes a T-junction with a dirt road, across which are several trails into an area signed as closed. If you follow the dirt road right, you are on the continuation of the East Ridge Trail, which reaches Bullfrog Pond and the Bullfrog Pond Campground in 1.3 miles (here signed correctly). Your route follows the road left and downhill to the Gilliam Creek and Pool Ridge trails. But before you leave this wonderful eyrie, turn right and walk a few paces uphill for another vista, this one stretching southeast from Jackson Mountain, topped with communication towers, to Sonoma Mountain, and, on a clear day, to Mt. Diablo.

Now descending the dirt road toward the Gilliam Creek and Pool Ridge trails, you have a view northwest into the rugged country surrounding Fox Mountain (1378') and the East Austin Creek drainage. Four remote backcountry camps—Manning Flat (two camps), Tom King, and Gilliam Creek—are located near East Austin Creek in a remote corner of the recreation area, a few hundred feet above sea level. To reach them, hikers use the Gilliam Creek Trail, just ahead, or the Austin Creek Trail, and descend about 1,000 feet to the camps. Soon your trail reaches paved Armstrong Woods Road, which you cross, and then resumes its downhill course, aided by a few wooden steps. Upon reaching a small parking area adjacent to a dirt road, you pass the trailhead for the Gilliam Creek Trail, a single track leading downhill and right. To find your route, the Pool Ridge Trail, bear right on the dirt road and follow it west a few hundred feet to a junction, where you turn left.

The single-track Pool Ridge Trail heads south and descends on a moderate grade over loose dirt and gravel, crossing an open, grassy hillside graced by a large valley oak. Finding level ground, the trail hugs a hillside that falls away left, passing stands of manzanita, and then pursues a rolling course which takes you across several ravines and back into Armstrong Redwoods State Reserve. A few downhill switchbacks bring you to a sunny area of chaparral—chamise, scrub oak, toyon, coffeeberry, and bush monkeyflower—and then back into a dense forest of Douglas fir, bay, coast live oak, tanbark oak, and hazelnut. After a moderate descent, the route levels and reaches a junction at about the 4-mile point, not shown on the park map. A trail, signed here as the Loop Trail, rises to the right, but you continue straight on the Pool Ridge Trail, now a wide path of loose dirt, in places badly eroded. At the next junction, marked by a trail post, you pass a trail signed PICNIC AREA, and follow the Pool Ridge Trail, signed ARMSTRONG TREE, as it curves right.

A steep canyon, right, into which you descend via switchbacks, holds a tributary of Fife Creek. After several crossings of the watercourse, which may be dry, you enjoy a mostly level and then downhill walk among massive redwoods, illuminated on sunny days by shafts of light filtering through the forest canopy. Reaching a dirt-and-gravel road that leads to a pack station, right, you turn left and soon come to a paved road, part of a turn-around circle. To the right are rest rooms and the Depression-era Redwood Forest Theater, once used for artistic performances but now a place of quiet contemplation, surrounded by redwoods and big-leaf maples. To the left is the parking area for the Discovery Trail, designed for the physically and visually disabled. Here you turn left and walk through the parking area, which has space for about six cars. Leaving the parking area, you begin a level walk on a dirt hiking path. On the right is a nylon rope, stretched between posts, to serve as a guide for blind or visually impaired visitors, and there are markers along the way in English and Braille describing features of the reserve and its magnificent trees.

Giant Redwood along the Pioneer Trail dwarfs hiker.

After about 100 feet, you come to the Colonel Armstrong Tree, 308 feet high, 14.6 feet in diameter, and more than 1400 years old. Just past the Armstrong Tree is a fork marked by a trail post, where you bear right. Most members of the redwood-forest community can be found here, including tanbark oak, hazelnut, wild rose, and redwood sorrel. Reaching a paved road, you bear left and cross Fife Creek, which flows under the road. Once on the east side of the creek, turn right, cross the road, and join the Pioneer Trail heading south. From here, follow the route description for "East Ridge" on pages 215–216 back to the parking area.

40 Armstrong Redwoods State Reserve NATURE TRAIL

Length: 1.2 miles

Time: 1 hour

Rating: Easy

Regulations: CSP; no dogs, no bikes, no horses.

Highlights: This semi-loop route, using part of the Pioneer Trail and the Discovery Trail, takes you through the heart of the redwoods, past the Colonel Armstrong and Parson Jones trees, both more than 300 feet high. **Bold face** numbers in the route description refer to numbered markers along the self-guiding trail, which are keyed to a brochure available in the visitor center.

Directions: See the directions for "East Ridge" on p. 213.

Facilities: Visitor center with interpretive displays, books, maps, helpful staff; ranger station, rest rooms, picnic tables, water, telephone.

Trailhead: In front of the visitor center.

From the visitor center, you head north on a paved road, with the ranger station on your left, following a line of whimsical white footprints painted on the pavement. About 150 feet from the visitor center, you come to paved Armstrong Woods Road, which you cross. On the other side of the road, your route, the Pioneer Trail, marked by a large sign, follows a level course into a forest of coast redwoods bordering Fife Creek, the reserve's main watercourse. Following a trail carpeted with redwood needles and other forest debris, you soon meet a paved road. To your right is the Parson Jones tree, 310 feet high, 13.8 feet in diameter, and more than 1300 years old. Across the road is the continuation of the Pioneer Trail, which you follow past a rest bench to a display made from a cross-section of a redwood that dates from 948 AD. By counting its rings, researchers have established and marked on its surface some important dates in world history: 1000, Leif Erickson lands in North America; 1436, invention of the printing press; 1579, Sir Francis Drake lands in California; 1861, American Civil War; and, sadly, 1978, the year the tree was cut by vandals.

Marker **1**, right, and marker **2**, ahead about 100 feet on the left, refer to how the redwoods regenerate themselves, and the role in this process played by the protective carpet of plant material on the forest floor, called duff. Capturing moisture from rain and fog, duff helps supply water to the redwoods. Duff is also a barrier, preventing redwood cones and seeds from reaching soil. Only when this barrier is destroyed, as by fire, do the seeds have a chance to germinate. Most of the time, redwoods reproduce by sprouting new growth in a circle around the trunk of a damaged or fallen tree, sometimes called a fairy ring or a family circle. Other plants associated with a redwood forest include tanbark oak, California bay, hazelnut, wild rose, western sword fern, red bead lily, and redwood sorrel, which is indicated by marker **3**, left.

Crossing a paved road, you rejoin the Pioneer Trail and enter Burbank Circle, named for horticulturist Luther Burbank, whose home and gardens you can visit in Santa Rosa. According to a fact sheet provided by the reserve, what formed this large circle of giant redwoods is a mystery—it is too large for a fairy ring, and no central root system has been found. Marker **4**, right, refers to the beneficial effects of wildfires and how they help regenerate the forest by reducing duff and converting its

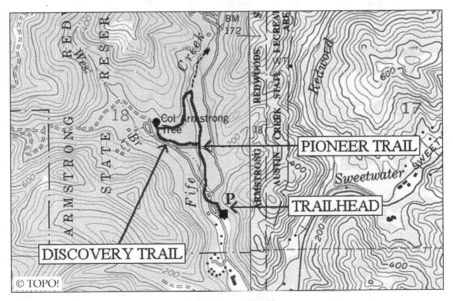

40. Nature Trail

remaining plant material to nutrients. Redwoods insulate themselves with thick, fibrous bark and are immune to most fires. Even redwoods that have been hollowed by fire, which forms a so-called goosepen or cavity, can continue to live. The last fire here, in 1926, was probably caused by man, not nature.

Marker 5, left, on the bank of Fife Creek, describes why redwood trees thrive along the wide banks of creeks and rivers: rich soil deposited by annual floods provides nutrients for the trees. Beginning in the 1930s, flood-control projects here widened channels and reinforced stream banks, thus depriving parts of the forest of an important food supply. Marker 6, right, indicates Douglas fir, and marker 7, left, is for tanbark oak. At about the 0.5-mile point, you leave the Pioneer Trail and turn left, continuing your self-guiding walk. This trail, also a duff-carpeted path, is signed for the Armstrong Tree, the Discovery Trail, and the Forest Theater. Ahead the trail splits to pass around the Icicle Tree, marker 8. On this tree, clusters of dormant buds, called burls, have formed fantastic shapes that resemble icicles. Burls are yet another way for a redwood to reproduce itself—when a tree falls, new growth often sprouts from its burls. Left of the Icicle Tree is marker 9, bracken fern, a highly adaptable species that is at home in many different environments. About 100 feet past the Icicle Tree, you cross a bridge over Fife Creek, which will now be on your left.

After crossing the creek, you curve left and pass a grove of immense redwoods, marker 10, a few of which have toppled in the wind. As you can see by examining the underside of an uprooted redwood, it has no tap root. Instead, a network of shallow but interlocking roots underlies the redwood-forest floor, with each tree helping to support its neighbors. Marker 11, just ahead and right, is for western sword fern, a species that, like the redwoods, dates back millions of years. Now the route bends right and comes to marker 12, California bay, and, after a series of wooden steps, to marker 13, hazelnut. About 25 feet ahead is a junction: the Discovery Trail is left, but you turn right and walk about 25 feet to marker 14, the Colonel Armstrong Tree. This living monument to the reserve's namesake is 308 feet tall, 14.6 feet in diameter, and more than 1400 years old.

From the Armstrong Tree, retrace your steps to the previous junction, and then bear right on the Discovery Trail, designed for the physically and visually disabled. On the right is a nylon rope, stretched between posts, to serve as a guide for blind or visually impaired visitors, and there are markers along the way in English and Braille describing features of the reserve and its magnificent trees. Reaching a paved road, you bear left and cross Fife Creek, which flows under the road. Once on the east side of the creek, turn right, cross the road, and join the Pioneer Trail heading south. From here, follow the route description for "East Ridge" on pages 215–216 back to the parking area.

• Jack London State Historic Park •

At 28, he was world famous and one of the highest-paid authors of his time. Twelve years later, he was dead from gastrointestinal uremic poisoning, a possible suicide. As fiction, *The Life and Death of Jack London* would have been right at home on the bookshelf, next to his beloved adventure novels *The Call of the Wild*, *The Sea Wolf*, and *White Fang*. As fact, it trumped them. London, who was born in 1876 in San Francisco, escaped a poverty-ridden childhood at age 17 by shipping as an able seaman bound for the Bering Sea and Japan. He went north to the Klondike during the Gold Rush of 1897, reported for a newspaper during the Russo-Japanese War, and in 1914 served as a war correspondent in Mexico during the Villa-Carranza revolt. London also found time to build a boat, the *Snark*, which he and his wife Charmian sailed to Australia and the South Pacific.

The refuge in the midst of London's stormy life was a run-down ranch he bought at the foot of Sonoma Mountain near Glen Ellen. He called it "...a quiet place in the county to write and loaf in and get out of Nature that something which we all need, only the most of us don't know it." Over the years he expanded the original holdings into a 1400-acre property known as Beauty Ranch. Some of the ranch buildings were formerly part of the Kohler & Frohling winery, and others London had built. The most ambitious of these was known as Wolf House, conceived and erected between 1911 and the summer of 1913. On the night of August 22, 1913, just before the Londons were to move in, a fire of mysterious origin swept through the ornate, 26-room mansion, leaving it a smoking ruin. London tried to overcome his terrible disappointment through writing, working on his ranch, and traveling. His consumption of alcohol increased, and his health deteriorated. On November 22, 1916, London died at age 40 in his wood-framed cottage, not far from the remains of Wolf House, which was never rebuilt.

After her husband's tragic death, Charmian stayed on, building The House of Happy Walls, where she lived until her death in 1955. As she had directed, after her death the house became a memorial to her husband and a museum dedicated to his work. Jack London State Historic Park was created in 1959, partly through a gift from London's nephew and heir. The park's original 40 acres included The House of Happy Walls, the ruins of Wolf House, and London's grave site. Later additions brought the park up to 837 acres, and visitors today can take a self-guiding walk among the farm buildings of Beauty Ranch, tour London's cottage, and hike to London's Lake, where the Londons entertained guests. A trail continues above the lake to near the top of Sonoma Mountain, which lies just beyond the park boundary. A short trail leads from the museum, which also houses a visitor center, to Wolf House and the grave site. The museum is just east of the park's entrance kiosk. Guided walks in the park are offered by the Valley of the Moon Natural History Association. Dogs are not allowed on the park's trails, nor in the museum. In all other areas they must be leashed.

MUSEUM: open daily 10 A.M. to 5 P.M. Closed Thanksgiving, Christmas, and New Years Day; (707) 938-5216

VALLEY OF THE MOON NATURAL HISTORY ASSOCIATION: (707) 938-4827

41 Jack London State Historic Park
LONDON'S LAKE AND MAYS CLEARING

Length:	2.9 miles
Time:	2 to 3 hours
Rating:	Moderate
Regulations:	CSP; parking fee; no dogs, no smoking.
Highlights:	Jack London's ranch, a beautiful redwood forest, and a vista point with superb views are the attractions of this semi-loop trip that uses the Lake, Upper Lake, and Mountain trails. After your hike, be sure to visit the park's fine visitor center and museum, open daily 10 A.M. to 5 P.M., devoted to the work of its namesake author. From the museum, located next to a parking area just east of the entrance kiosk, you can walk to London's grave site and the remains of his elaborate mansion, called Wolf House, which was destroyed by fire in 1913, a month before the Londons were scheduled to move in.
Directions:s	From Hwy. 12 just north of Sonoma Valley Regional Park, take Arnold Dr. southwest to Glen Ellen. At 0.9 mile, Arnold Dr. crosses a bridge over Calabazas Creek and begins to turn left. Here you bear right onto London Ranch Rd., which is heavily used by bicyclists. Go 1.3 miles to the park's entrance kiosk; turn right just past the kiosk into a large paved parking area. If the entrance kiosk is not staffed, pay fee at the self-registration station in the parking area.
Facilities:	Picnic tables, fire grates, water, toilet; visitor center and museum, with displays, books, and helpful staff, located

next to a separate parking area, just east of the entrance kiosk.

Trailhead: On the parking area's southwest side, just behind the self-registration station. Horses must use a trailhead located a few hundred feet to the right.

Stepping into history is one of the attractions of this state park, the former home of author Jack London. Another is hiking through a wonderful redwood forest on your way to London's Lake. And yet another is seeing the expansive view from Mays Clearing above the lake. Your journey begins on a paved path that soon changes to a dirt-and-gravel road leading through a shady picnic area. Between 1911 and 1915, London planted more than 80,000 eucalyptus seedlings on his land, hoping to produce lumber for construction. When the trees proved unsuitable for this purpose, they were felled for firewood, but many re-sprouted and are now considered a nuisance by the park. A plan is underway to confine the trees to their historical area around London's farm buildings.

Passing the three stone barns, left, you come to a T-junction with another dirt-and-gravel road, part of the Bay Area Ridge Trail. London used two of the three barns to stable horses and one as a manure pit. Turning right at the T-junction, you soon pass a trail, left, to London's cottage, which the author purchased in 1911 and where he died in 1916. The cottage is open to visitors on weekends from 12 to 4 P.M. Many of the

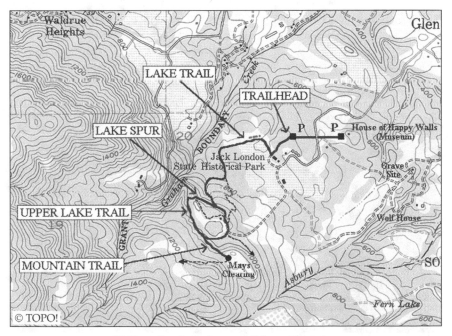

41. London's Lake and Mays Clearing

buildings here, including one heavily damaged in the 1906 earthquake and then by a 1965 fire, were part of the Kohler & Frohling Winery, active in the late 1800s. The vineyard to the southwest was kept by London's heirs when they sold the rest of the property to the state in 1978. Rising dramatically behind the vineyard is Sonoma Mountain, a long ridge capped by a 2463-foot summit that is on private land just west of the park boundary. You may see signs for the Pig Palace—this was an elaborate piggery designed by London and built in 1915.

About 75 feet from the **T**-junction, you bear right at a fork onto a dirt road, signed LAKE and PIG PALACE. Several hundred feet ahead, the trail from the equestrian trailhead, labeled Lake Trail on the park map, joins from the right. You continue straight, now on the Lake Trail, and in 100 feet pass a hikers-only trail to the Pig Palace. Follow the road as it curves left, with a beautiful view of the vineyard, left. Soon you pass another trail, right, to the Pig Palace—this trail also passes two stone silos used by London to store fodder for his animals. Beside the road are stands of black oak, blue oak, coast live oak, madrone, and manzanita. As the road bends sharply left around a corner of the vineyard, you pass a closed trail, right, and now walk beneath tall Douglas fir and bigleaf maple. When you approach a gate across the road, look for the hikers-only Lake Trail heading downhill and right. Both the road, beyond here called Lake Service Road, and the Lake Trail carry the Bay Area Ridge Trail emblem. Bikes and horses must stay on the road, passing to the side of the gate.

Veering right onto the Lake Trail, you soon enter a magical forest of coast redwood, California bay, tanbark oak, and hazelnut, the latter especially beautiful when its green, felt-like leaves are backlighted by the sun.

Stone barn is one of the ranch buildings near the start of the Lake Trail.

The trail climbs moderately at first, then levels, then climbs again. Some of the huge redwood stumps you pass, the remains of old-growth giants, are surrounded by descendants sprouting from the base of their ancestor, a so-called fairy ring or family circle. Thimbleberry, gooseberry, wild rose, and poison oak line the trail, and the forest floor, carpeted with leaves and redwood needles, may be dotted here and there with wildflowers. Reaching a closed trail, right, your route turns left and continues to climb. Just shy of the 1-mile point, you come to a rest bench and a junction with a trail taking off sharply right, signed here as the Upper Lake Trail, but listed on the map as Lake Spur. Here you turn right, gaining elevation on a moderate and then steep grade. Soon you come to a T-junction where you turn right, now without doubt on the Upper Lake Trail.

After a couple of hundred feet, your route turns sharply left, and now you enjoy a level walk among towering redwoods. Below and left, through the trees, you can begin to see a marshy area at the northwest corner of London's Lake. Created by a stone dam built in 1915, the lake was designed as an irrigation reservoir, but soon became a swimming hole where London and his wife Charmian entertained their guests. Sediment and vegetation have cut the lake's original size in half. The London's bathhouse, which you can visit later, is made of redwood and sits back from the shore on the lake's northeast corner. Just after an abandoned road joins your trail sharply from the right, you reach a junction with the Mountain Trail, a wide dirt road. Turning right, you pass a wet area where water may be cascading over the road. Climbing on a grade that alternates between gentle and moderate, you leave the redwood realm and are now surrounded by bay, bigleaf maple, madrone, and coast live oak.

Suddenly the forest ends, and you are confronted with a big grassy meadow called Mays Clearing, which in spring is full of blue-eyed grass, California buttercup, vetch, and false lupine. A rest bench just ahead beckons you to pause and enjoy the stunning view, which extends southeast all the way to Mt. Diablo. When you are thoroughly satiated with scenery, retrace your steps to the junction of the Upper Lake and Mountain trails. At this junction, the Mountain Trail makes an almost-180-degree bend to the right, and you follow it downhill on a gentle and then moderate grade. As you approach the lake, which is ringed with cattails and other marsh plants, you pass a path leading left to the stone dam, and then the Quarry Trail, right. Just ahead is a T-junction with a dirt road, drawn incorrectly on the park map.

The road heading right is labeled Vineyard Road on the map, and here you turn left and walk toward the lake, with the stone dam in front of you. Your route then turns right and runs parallel to the dam. Once on its far side, you can see London's bathhouse and a picnic area with tables, left. Now you are on Lake Service Road, but only briefly. Where the road begins to descend, you leave it and bear left, coming in about 50 feet to a

trail post signed with the Bay Area Ridge Trail emblem and the words
PARKING LOT, 1 MILE. This is the Lake Trail, a wide dirt path for hikers only.
As you follow it downhill, you pass a faint trail, left, to the bathhouse,
shown on the map as the Upper Lake Trail. Continuing straight, you pass
a wonderful fairy ring with 14 distinct trees, some joined at the bases, circling a huge redwood stump. Your trail soon narrows and then reaches
the junction signed for the Upper Lake Trail (Lake Spur on map) where
you turned off the Lake Trail to begin this loop. From here, continue
straight on the Lake Trail and retrace your steps to the parking area.

*The remain's of London's mansion, Wolf House, can be
visited via a short trail from the museum.*

Jack London State Historic Park
MOUNTAIN TRAIL

Length:	8 miles
Time:	4 to 5 hours
Rating:	Difficult
Regulations:	CSP; parking fee; no dogs, no smoking.
Highlights:	This out-and-back route, difficult because of its length, follows the Lake, Upper Lake, and Mountain trails to the park's high point just northeast of Sonoma Mountain's summit, which lies on private land. Along the way, you pass Jack London's ranch, his vineyard, and the redwood-circled lake where he and his wife Charmian entertained friends. Above the lake, the route alternates between forest, meadow, and savanna. In spring, this is one of the best wildflower treks in the North Bay and the vista from trail's end is not to be missed.
Directions:	See the directions for "London's Lake and Mays Clearing" on p. 224.
Facilities:	Picnic tables, fire grates, water, toilet; visitor center and museum, with displays, books, and helpful staff, located next to a separate parking area, just east of the entrance kiosk.
Trailhead:	On the parking area's southwest side, just behind the self registration station. Horses must use a trailhead located a few hundred feet to the right.

Follow the route description for "London's Lake and Mays Clearing" on pages 225–227 to Mays Clearing. From here you follow the Mountain Trail, a dirt road, as it bends sharply right, passing the Fallen Bridge Trail, left. Many of the trails joining the Mountain Trail are subject to seasonal closures, indicated by signs, that apply only to bikes and horses. Now back in the shade of the redwoods, you resume a moderate uphill grade, looking beside the road for spring wildflowers such as iris, woodland star, red larkspur, and wild geranium. Soon you pass another branch of the Fallen Bridge Trail, labeled on the map as the Upper Fallen Bridge Trail. Although this is a popular state park, relatively few people venture beyond London's Lake, so you may have the route mostly to yourself. Now the road levels in the midst of a Douglas-fir forest, and then reaches a beautiful clearing called Pine Tree Meadows. At about the 2-mile

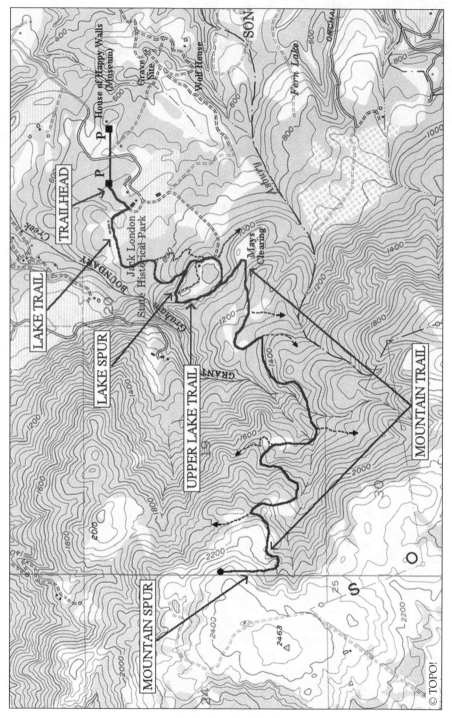

42. Mountain Trail

point, you pass Treadmill Road, labeled Lower Treadmill Road on the map.

The route steepens as it passes over rocky ground, and then drops into a ravine to cross a creek that flows under the road through a culvert. The character of this hike changes from minute to minute: now you are in a damp, jungle-like area carpeted with a variety of ferns, silent except for birdsong and the rustle of leaves in the wind. At the next creek crossing, where South Graham Creek may be flowing over the road, pick your way across on rocks, looking upstream to see a series of wonderful miniature waterfalls. Now you climb steeply beneath the outstretched limbs of bigleaf maple and California buckeye, soon reaching a Y-junction with Treadmill Road, labeled Upper Treadmill Road on the map. Here you bear right, staying on the Mountain Trail and, just ahead, crossing lovely Middle Graham Creek, which flows under the road through two culverts. This spot, which may be very muddy because of streams meandering across the road, has some very tall redwoods, with an understory of creambush and gooseberry.

With a picnic table on your left, you reach the end of the dirt road. The Mountain Trail, now a single track, heads uphill through an open meadow, which in spring is carpeted with meadowfoam and California buttercup. This meadow may be flooded and very muddy during winter and

Redwoods tower over the trail near London's Lake.

spring. At its north edge, you re-enter forest and come to a fork. Here the Cowan Meadow Trail, for hikers only, heads right, but you stay on the Mountain Trail, once again a dirt road, and veer left through a savanna of California bay and black oak. Soon the path becomes rocky and eroded as you make a steep climb past a viewpoint to another open meadow. The moss-covered oaks beside the trail here may be loaded with mistletoe. A short descent brings you to a T-junction. Here the Hayfields Trail, part of the Bay Area Ridge Trail, goes right, but you turn left, still on the Mountain Trail. This area, open and park-like, can be cold and windy, but you have a wonderful view east across the Sonoma Valley toward the high ridge that forms the border with Napa County.

A moderate climb across a steep grassy hillside brings you to yet another meadow with a creek running through it. The surrounding oak-clad hills are absolutely beautiful to behold. Entering forest again, the trail winds back and forth, gaining elevation, until you reach a trail post with an arrow pointing right. Ahead is the summit of Sonoma Mountain (2463') but alas it is on private property behind a barbed-wire fence. So you must make do with a high point just shy of the 2400-foot mark, reached by turning right onto the Mountain Spur, and following its steep grade uphill through tall grass dotted with lupine, fiddleneck, bird's-eye gilia, and California poppy. A rocky scramble brings you to the end of the trail, where you can revel in views that extend north to Mt. St. Helena and south to Mt. Tamalpais and San Pablo Bay. The summit of Sonoma Mountain rises just left of the three communication towers that are just west. When you have taken it all in, retrace your steps to Mays Clearing, and then follow the route description for "London's Lake and Mays Clearing" on pages 227–228 back to the parking area.

◆ Sonoma Coast ◆

A nuclear power plant on Bodega Head. A 5,200-home subdivision on the coastal bluffs near Black Point. A four-lane freeway leading north from Jenner. Gravel mines in the estuaries of the Russian and Gualala rivers. Limited public access to miles of coastline. These were some of the plans underway during the 1960s and 70s to radically transform the Sonoma coast, a remote and idyllic region that had, up to then, remained unspoiled by development. Thanks to tireless efforts of concerned citizens, and the proximity of the San Andreas fault to the power-plant site, all but one of these projects were stopped, and the subdivision, Sea Ranch, was greatly reduced in size and required to allow public access from Highway 1 to the Pacific shoreline.

As Martin Griffin writes in his book, *Saving the Marin–Sonoma Coast*, the group responsible for some of these victories was called COAAST— Californians Organized to Acquire Access to State Tidelands. Its efforts led in 1972 to passage of Proposition 20, the Coastal Initiative. This legislation set up a commission to oversee coastal development. In 1976, the California Coastal Act established a permanent California Coastal Commission, whose job is to conserve and manage resources along the entire 1100-mile coast. In 1987, the commission published *California Coastal Resource Guide*, its report on the natural and manmade resources found along California's coast. According to the *Guide*, the last few centuries have taken a heavy toll on our coast's natural resources. Hundreds of thousands of acres of coast-redwood forest have been logged. Rivers and creeks have been dammed, and 90 per cent of the state's coastal wet lands have been destroyed, thus ruining habitat for plants, birds, and fish. Seals, sea otters, and whales have been slaughtered for their fur or oil. Species which once flourished have been pushed to the brink of extinction, and even beyond.

Is the news all grim? Decidedly not! At least in the areas under their jurisdiction, state parks along the Sonoma coast have ensured public access, prevented development, protected habitat, and given plants and animals a fighting chance at survival. What is more, they offer visitors some of the most beautiful hiking trails and magnificent scenic vistas in the North Bay. Among the parks here are Salt Point State Park, a 6,000-acre park about 20 miles north of Jenner; Fort Ross State Historic Park, about 11 miles north of Jenner; and Sonoma Coast State Beach, actually a series of beaches stretching from Russian Gulch to Bodega Head.

Salt Point State Park has trails for hiking, horseback riding, and bicycling. A pygmy forest of stunted trees and shrubs on the upland side of the park is one of its main attractions. The park includes Gerstle Cove

Reserve, one of the first underwater parks in the state, enjoyed by SCUBA divers. There are two year-round campgrounds, one with 30 sites, the other with 80. From April through October, hikers and bicyclists can take advantage of 20 walk-in campsites and 10 ride-in campsites. Camping reservations may be made up to eight weeks in advance. Nearby, Kruse Rhododendron State Reserve has 5 miles of hiking trails on its 317-acre property.

Fort Ross State Historic Park is an outpost that was used in the 19th century by Russian fur traders. Established in 1812, the fort grew to include several houses, a barracks, a chapel, an orchard, and a cemetery. In addition to the restored buildings, visitors can enjoy daily guided tours, a museum and visitor center, a picnic area, hiking paths, and beach access. Each year, costumed volunteers participate in a Living History Day, usually one of the last two Saturdays in July, recreating life in the outpost. The nearby Fort Ross Reef Campground has 20 sites available on a first-come, first-served basis, open April through October.

Sonoma Coast State Beach consists of 21 units encompassing approximately 5,000 acres and 13 miles of shoreline. Hiking, picnicking, birding, fishing, beachcombing, and tide-pooling are just some of the activities available. Among the most scenic areas are Bodega Head, Shell Beach, Blind Beach, and the highlands overlooking Willow Creek and the Russian River. A campground at Willow Creek has 11 sites near the Russian River, and the neighboring Pomo Canyon Campground has 21 sites in a redwood grove. Both campgrounds are open April through October. For year-round camping, there are 30 sites at Wright's Beach, and 98 at Bodega Dunes.

As a general rule, bicycles are allowed only on paved and dirt roads, not on single-track trails. Bicyclists should check with each park for specific rules and closures. Dogs are not allowed on any state park hiking trails, nor in any of the Willow Creek area. Elsewhere, they must be leashed during the day, and in a vehicle or tent at night.

CAMPING RESERVATIONS: (800) 444-7275

SALT POINT STATE PARK: (707) 847-3221

FORT ROSS STATE HISTORIC PARK: (707) 847-3286

SONOMA COAST STATE BEACH: (707) 875-3483

RUSSIAN RIVER DISTRICT OFFICE: (707) 865-2391

43	Salt Point State Park
	PYGMY FOREST

Length: 3.8 miles

Time: 2 to 3 hours

Rating: Moderate

Regulations: CSP; parking fee; no dogs.

Highlights: This wonderful loop, using the North and Central trails, visits three distinct coastal habitats: a mixed evergreen forest, a prairie, and a unique pygmy forest where poor.soil has stunted the growth of trees and shrubs. With its lovely rhododendron, California rosebay, that blooms in spring, this area is a paradise for native-plant enthusiasts, but birders will be busy too, especially those trying to learn to "bird by ear," because the mostly dense foliage keeps the birds well hidden.

Directions: From Hwy. 1 at its junction with Hwy. 116, just south of Jenner, go northwest 19.5 miles to the Woodside Campground entrance, right. Go 0.1 mile to the entrance kiosk. If the entrance kiosk is not staffed, pay fee at the self-registration station in the parking area about 100 yards ahead, past the campground road, right.

Facilities: Rest rooms, picnic tables; water and phone near entrance kiosk.

Trailhead: Northeast end of parking area, at a metal gate.

From the parking area, a dirt-and-gravel road heads uphill through a botanical wonderland, where you may find coast redwood, Douglas fir, bishop pine, tanbark oak, madrone, rhododendron, wax myrtle, evergreen huckleberry, salal, western sword fern, and many other coastal plants. A trail post, left, tells you this is the Central Trail, but the state-park map leaves it—and many others in the park—unnamed. Gaining elevation on a moderate grade via S-bends, you soon reach a dirt road, left, signed NORTH TRAIL. This is the lower of two connectors to the North Trail. Here you turn left and wander through a redwood grove, often cool and foggy, that has a rain-forest feel. In spring, look for tiny yellow flowers of the evergreen violet, a redwood companion, on the forest floor.

Crossing several wet areas, and then Warren Creek, which flows under the road, your route rises to an unsigned fork. Now you bear right onto the North Trail. Resuming a moderate and relentless ascent, with Warren Creek on your right, you emerge after a while from dense forest into a

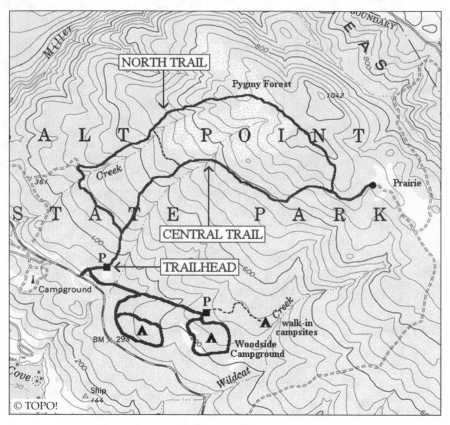

43. Pygmy Forest

magical realm of manzanitas, some of them 10 to 15 feet tall. Folds of lace lichen hanging from the trees and shrubs enhance the beauty of this place. At about the 1-mile point, the upper connector to the Central Trail joins from the right. Now back in a dense forest, where many of the trees are riddled with woodpecker holes, you tread softly on a carpet of leaves, mostly tanbark oak. Although not a true oak, this primarily coastal species produces acorns which Native Americans ground into flour, and was once the main source of tannin in the West.

   As the route levels, the soil becomes sandy, and you enter the Pygmy Forest, a fascinating area of dwarf trees and shrubs, including cypress, manzanita, chinquapin, evergreen huckleberry, and Labrador tea. Even the pines here are stunted, reaching a height of only 20 or 30 feet in the poor soil. Few other areas in the North Bay have such a dramatic transition from one habitat to another. Now on a gravelly path which may be wet, you thread your way through a corridor—almost a tunnel—of vegetation, perhaps accompanied by the sharp cry of a northern flicker or the scolding note of a winter wren. Soon the trees and shrubs regain their normal heights, and you may notice chinquapin growing here as a tall tree with brown and gray bark split into ridges. The trail descends gently and then joins the Central Trail at a junction marked by a trail post signed SOUTH TRAIL, PRAIRIE.

From here, the Central Trail continues 0.4 mile east and then southeast to a junction with the South and Sea View trails. To view the Prairie, a vast grassland on the left side of the trail, turn left onto the Central Trail, a dirt road, and follow it for about 0.2 mile to the prairie's northwest edge. After you have finished enjoying the expansive scene, return to the junction of the Central and North trails. From here, continue straight on the Central Trail, descending on a gentle grade through a forest of Douglas fir and tanbark oak. As the grade changes to moderate, around the 3-mile point, you pass an area that may be wet. Coffeeberry and blackberry vines line the road, and deep-blue wild irises poke up from the forest floor. Evergreen huckleberry is joined here by its cousin, red huckleberry, a rangy shrub with alternate circular leaves, tiny spherical flowers, and red berries in late summer. Bishop pines and a few interior live oaks add to the almost overwhelming plant diversity.

Soon you reach a junction, right, with the upper connector to the North Trail. Just beyond the junction on the right are four large water tanks. You continue straight, now on a gravel road that soon curves left and passes more lovely rhododendrons. Enjoying an easy descent, you reach the lower connector to the North Trail that you used earlier at the start of this loop. From here, retrace you steps to the parking area.

Tiny urn-shaped manzanita flowers are characteristic of the heath family.

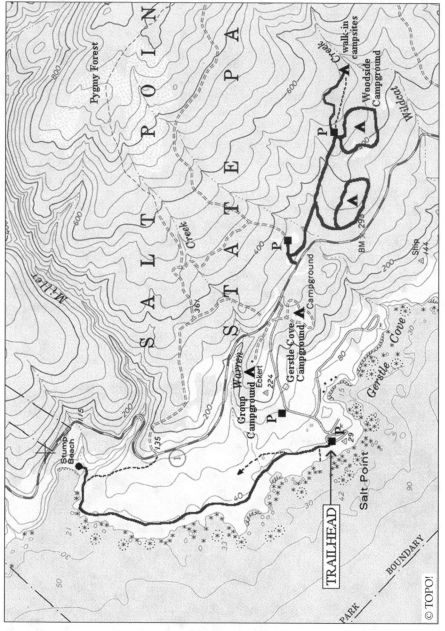

44. Stump Beach

44   Salt Point State Park
STUMP BEACH

Length: 2.5 miles

Time: 1 to 2 hours

Rating: Easy

Regulations: CSP; parking fee; no dogs.

Highlights: This out-and-back route visits Stump Beach, a secluded sandy strand at the mouth of Miller Creek. The coastal prairie you walk through to get there is mostly open grassland, with scattered trees and shrubs. The view of the Pacific Ocean along the way is magnificent, and you may find yourself mesmerized by the plumes of froth billowing skyward as wave after wave crashes against the rocky shore.

Directions: See the directions for "Pygmy Forest" on p. 235. At the Woodside Campground entrance, continue northwest on Hwy. 1 for 0.1 mile to the Gerstle Cove Campground entrance. Turn left and go 0.1 mile to the entrance kiosk. If the entrance kiosk is not staffed, pay fee at the self-registration station in the parking area ahead. Go another 0.5 mile to a junction with a road, left, signed SOUTH GERSTLE COVE, VISITOR CENTER, PICNIC AREA. Continue straight for another 0.1 mile to a large day-using parking area.

Facilities.   Rest rooms, water, shower; visitor center open only on weekends; phone beside entrance kiosk.

Trailhead: Northwest end of parking area.

This parking area serves two trails: a trail heading northwest to Stump Beach, and a much shorter trail leading south to Salt Point. The rugged, rocky coastline around Salt Point, and the sheltered curve of Gerstle Cove, an underwater reserve stretching southeast from Salt Point, will tempt you to linger here before starting your hike. To find the trail to Stump Beach, walk northwest from the parking area on the paved entrance road. In about 200 feet the entrance road bends right, and here your route, a dirt road, continues northwest through a vast coastal prairie dotted with boulders, rock outcrops, and low hillocks. The Pacific Ocean is on your left, and the route to Stump Beach runs parallel to it. Vegetation here is mostly grasses and shrubby clumps of coyote brush and lupine, which form attractive perches for one of the Pacific coast's most common birds, the white-crowned sparrow. Found often in flocks,

Trail to Stump Beach is great for wave watching.

these sparrows of open county can be told immediately by their high-pitched note, almost a squeak.

About 50 feet past the paved road, a trail heads left, but you continue straight to a fork, where you bear right on a level course. A beautiful cove, downhill and left, can be viewed from an overlook. Divers sometimes put in here, and you can watch them getting ready for their undersea adventure. Beside the trail look for salal, a member of the heath family whose flowers resemble those of its cousins madrone and manzanita. Many side paths diverge from the main trail; ignore them. Your route crosses Warren Creek, which flows through a culvert, and then passes an area where evergreen huckleberry bushes and a scattering of hearty pines have gained footholds on the otherwise vacant prairie. A 1993 fire, started by an illegal camp fire, burned 450 acres of parkland between Woodside Campground and Stump Beach, crossing Highway 1 in several places. During your visit, you may see evidence of this fire—in the form of barkless trees bleached white by salt and sun—and also of its rejuvenating effects on certain plant species.

At a fork in the road, you stay left, keeping a seaward eye peeled for brown pelicans cruising low over the breaking waves. Geyser-like spumes of ocean spray erupt along the rocky shore: their crashes and the cries of birds are perhaps the only sounds to reach your ears. Exposed bands of rock leading down from the prairie to the water's edge—cream-colored at top, changing to chocolate brown at sea level—tell a geological tale involving the San Andreas fault, which is just inland from here, and layers of sediment deposited over millions of years shifting steadily northwest. In fact, like Point Reyes, the coastline here probably started its fault-propelled journey somewhere on the southern California coast. In the distance to the northwest are Fisk Mill Cove and Horseshoe Point, also part of Salt Point State Park. In a little gully, look for succulents like iceplant and dudleya.

Now the road that earlier forked right rejoins your route, and just after it does you cross a gully with a rusted culvert. Song sparrows, western meadowlarks, and perhaps a mourning dove or two may add their voices to nature's chorus. At about the 1-mile point, the route nears the seaward edge of the prairie, and you have a fantastic vantage point to watch the waves breaking on shoreline rocks near the entrance to Stump Beach Cove. When you reach an unsigned fork, stay left; the right-hand branch goes uphill to Highway 1. As you skirt the cliff's edge, high above the shore, you begin to curve right, tracing a long finger of water pointing east toward Stump Beach, a sandy strand at the mouth of Miller Creek. The pines along the creek have had their tops pruned at a sloping angle by the wind, whereas those a bit farther from the shore grow tall and straight. Now you make a steep and rocky descent to the mouth of Miller Creek, which flows into a lagoon just behind Stump Beach. Here the shoreline is protected from the full force of the ocean's fury, and the secluded beach, covered in places with rocks, gravel, and ropes of kelp, makes a fine picnic spot. When it is time to leave, retrace your steps to the parking area.

Fort Ross State Park preserves a unique Russian settlement on the California coast.

Sonoma Coast State Beach
BODEGA HEAD

Length: 1 mile

Time: 1 hour or less

Rating: Easy

Regulations: CSP; no dogs, no bikes, no horses.

Highlights: The jutting promontory of Bodega Head is a fine place to come face to face with the elemental forces—sun, sea, and sky—that preside over California's coast, and the easy loop trail that circles the head presents you with fine vistas almost every step of the way. This hike can easily be combined with others on the Sonoma coast to make a full-day outing.

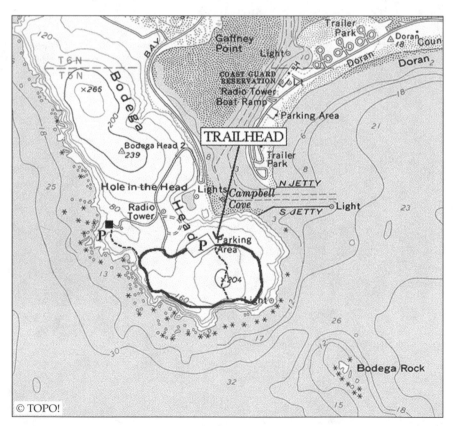

45. Bedega Head

Directions: From Hwy. 1 just north of the town of Bodega Bay, turn
west onto East Shore Rd., signed here for Bodega Head
and Westside Park Marinas. Go 0.3 mile to a stop sign at
Bay Flat Rd. and turn right. Continue straight—first on
Bay Flat Rd., then on West Shore and Westside roads—for
a total of 3.7 miles to a large dirt-and-gravel parking area
at the end of the road.

Facilities: Toilets.

Trailhead: On the southeast edge of parking area.

A low wooden fence borders the parking area, and after passing through
a gap in it, you set off on a level, single-track trail heading almost due
east. Before you reach the toilets, a trail cuts uphill and right, and in about
100 yards another veers left and downhill. Directly below are Campbell
Cove and the two rock jetties that form the entrance channel to Bodega
Harbor. Just across the channel is a sandy finger of land called Doran
Beach, a popular county park. Bodega Head itself is the tip of a large,
mostly treeless peninsula jutting south from the Sonoma coast mainland.
The hilly terrain around you is covered with grasses and scrub vegetation
such as coyote brush, blackberry vines,
and yellow bush lupine. This can be a
beautiful, sunny paradise or a bleak,
windswept barren—the only constant
here is the mournful note of the channel
marker warning boaters of the narrow
harbor entrance.

After passing another trail heading
left, your route begins its clockwise
curve around Bodega Head, and soon, if
the day is clear, you can make out
Tomales Point and the entrance to
Tomales Bay to the southeast, Point
Reyes to the south, and even the Farallon
Islands. Bodega Bay is the enormous
semi-circle of water between Bodega
Head and Tomales Bay. Flocks of sparrows may keep just ahead of you as you
walk, flitting from one lupine bush to
another. A trail plunges left down a steep
ravine, but your route continues to bend

*Although most lupines are blue,
this yellow form is common on the
coast.*

right. Just offshore to the southeast is a big rock used as a roost by sea
birds and as a haul-out for seals, whose barking you may hear. The southeast face of Bodega Head is a sheer cliff, so use caution as you approach
it. Avoid mishaps by stopping to admire the view and paying attention to

where you place your feet. A large nautical marker of red and white squares topped by a light is uphill and right. Below and left, waves crash against the head's rocky foundations. As the trail turns west and rises on a gentle grade, you are confronted with the wide Pacific Ocean, magnificent no matter what the weather or the season.

As your trail crests a rise, you pass a trail, right, and then swing left and downhill. Daubs of color are added to the scene by the yellow-and-red flowers of seaside paintbrush, and the magenta blooms of iceplant, a succulent that carpets California's coastal dunes and sandy roadside embankments. Just offshore, lines of brown pelicans or cormorants may be cruising low over the waves. Where a trail heads downhill and left to a promontory, your route bends right, hugging the cliffs, with no fence to keep you from the abyss. Jagged knife-edge ridges jut proudly toward the ocean and slice down to the water's edge. Enjoying a level walk, you begin to get views to the northeast, across Bodega Harbor to the town of Bodega Bay and the Sonoma coastal hills. Passing another trail to a promontory, left, your route swings right and descends, soon passing within about 6 feet of a dirt road, right. Cross over to the dirt road and follow it downhill for about 100 yards to a low metal gate and a wooden fence. Step over the gate, bear right across a dirt-and-gravel turn-out, and then get on the paved road that leads uphill to the parking area.

46   Sonoma Coast State Beach
KORTUM TRAIL

Length: 3.7 miles

Time: 2 to 3 hours

Rating: Moderate

Regulations: CSP; no dogs, no bikes, no horses.

Highlights: This out-and-back trip on part of the Kortum Trail parallels the Pacific Ocean on a coastal prairie just west of Hwy. 1. For most of the way the route is within sight of the crags and cliffs that rise from the water's edge. For a more ambitious outing, try starting at Wright's Beach, about 1.5 miles south; in that case the round-trip distance would be 7.6 miles. The Kortum Trail is often done as a car-shuttle trip—the entire route from Wright's Beach to Goat Rock is 3.8 miles. This hike can easily be combined with others on the Sonoma coast to make a full-day outing.

Directions: From Hwy. 1 northbound just north of the town of Bodega Bay, use the junction of Hwy. 1 and East Shore Rd., the turn-off to Bodega Head, as the 0.0-mile mark. Go north 7.1 miles to the entrance to Shell Beach. Turn left and go 0.1 mile to the parking area.

From Hwy. 1 southbound just south of Jenner, use the junction of Hwy. 1 and Hwy. 116 as the 0.0-mile mark, and go south 1.9 miles to the entrance to Shell Beach, right. Turn right and go 0.1 mile to the parking area.

Facilities: Rest rooms

Trailhead: Northwest corner of parking area.

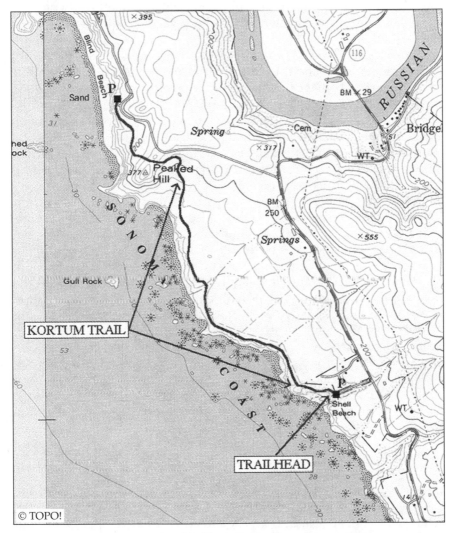

46. Kortum Trail

This trail, which stretches nearly 4 miles from Wright's Beach to Goat Rock, honors Bill Kortum, a dairy veterinarian and coastal-preservation advocate who helped defeat a proposed nuclear power plant at Bodega Bay. Kortum, who served in the 1970s as a Sonoma County supervisor, was also active in the fight to preserve public access to lands acquired by Sea Ranch, and this effort led to passage of the Coastal Act of 1972 and the creation of the Coastal Commission and the Coastal Conservancy.

Leaving the parking area, you head northwest on a single track through coastal scrub—mostly coyote brush—and across the open, flat coastal prairie. This wide and grassy expanse stretches from Highway 1 to the rocky cliffs that border the Pacific. The scenic cove of Shell Beach is downhill and left. A gully with willow thickets is also left, and you pass a trail heading in that direction that goes to a vantage point at the edge of the seaside cliffs.

Ahead, as you proceed, you can see two large rocks, one in the ocean, a roost for sea birds, and the other on dry land. At some time in the not-too-distant past, both were underwater, but geological forces uplifted the marine terrace you are standing on and put the rocks in their present alignment. The San Andreas fault, chief architect of California's coastline, is just offshore here. Beyond the two rocks rises Peaked Hill, and beyond it are the Sonoma coastal mountains north of the Russian River, which empties into the ocean near the town of Jenner. (Peaked Hill, by the way, has a counterpart across the continent in the dunes of Provincetown, Massachusetts.) A path, left, leads to a promontory, and if you turn and look southeast, you can see the hulking form of Bodega Head in the distance. Now a trail veers left, but your route goes right and through a gap in a barbed-wire fence. Just beyond the fence, a trail branches right, but you continue straight, stepping across a narrow fissure in the ground. The trail forks again, and you stay right. Many paths lead toward the ocean, and soon your route does too, coming to the edge of a cliff above a lovely cove with a sandy beach. Now you are joined by a trail coming sharply from the right, and soon you descend into a vegetation-choked gully which may be wet. The next gully has a bridge over it. After crossing it the route turns left, and then comes to a fork, marked by a trail post, where you bear right.

Just beyond where a trail joins sharply from the left, you pass through a gap in a barbed-wire fence. Immediately you come to a narrow trail heading left, but you continue straight on the wider path. Here and there beside the trail are great impenetrable tangles of blackberry vines and beach grasses. Pillars of rock, at one time sea stacks in the ocean, jut upward from the coastal prairie. Offshore rocks, the largest and farthest offshore called Gull Rock, are painted white with bird droppings. Now the trail drops into a wildly overgrown shallow ravine that holds a creek, which you cross on a short bridge. As the trail rises from the ravine bottom, you pass a trail, left, but your route continues uphill over wooden steps and bends right. In the open fields around you may be sparrows and western meadowlarks, and the off-shore rocks may hold pelicans, cormorants, and common murres. At about the 1-mile point the trail dips into and out of another shallow ravine, and then swings right, toward a jumble of rock pillars. These pillars were used during World War II as bombing-practice targets. The northernmost one, called Sunshine Rocks, is today used for practice by local climbers because it offers a bomb-proof belay spot.

At an unmarked fork, where a blank trail post provides no help, you stay right, passing the rock pillars. The tenacity of nature's creations is illustrated here by clumps of vegetation desperately clinging to crevices in the rocks. Just past the pillars, a path heads right, but you continue straight, now climbing on a moderate grade. The trail markers here are round wood posts with the tops cut at a 45-degree angle. Fine views, which get better with each step, extend southeast along the coastline toward Bodega Head, and beyond to Point Reyes. A trail leads left toward Peaked Hill, the high point on a ridge you will soon surmount. Ignoring that trail, you continue straight up the ridge, pass through a gap in a barbed-wire fence, and then turn left. Now you have a paved road uphill and right, and a short trail branches to it. You stay on the main trail, which runs parallel to the road, and head for a saddle between Peaked Hill and a lesser summit. When you reach the saddle, where a trail heads left, an entirely new vista is waiting for your enjoyment, this one sweeping northwest along the Sonoma coast north of the Russian River.

Now descending from the saddle on a moderate grade, you have a beautiful view ahead to Goat Rock, a flat-topped giant joined to the mainland by a narrow strip of sand. Beyond it are the mouth of the Russian River and the town of Jenner. To your left is Arched Rock, a wave-eroded outpost. Be careful not to look and walk at the same time, as the trail is rocky and needs your complete attention. Soon the route levels and traverses a grassy hillside, coming to a barbed-wire fence with a gap, and then the paved road you approached a few minutes ago. Walking along its shoulder, you reach the parking area for Blind Beach, which is just southeast of Goat Rock. From the parking area you have another opportunity to study and to marvel at the surrounding landscape, or you can descend a dirt-and-gravel road via series of switchbacks to Blind Beach itself. On the northeast side of the parking area are rest rooms. When you are ready to return, retrace your steps to the parking area at Shell Beach.

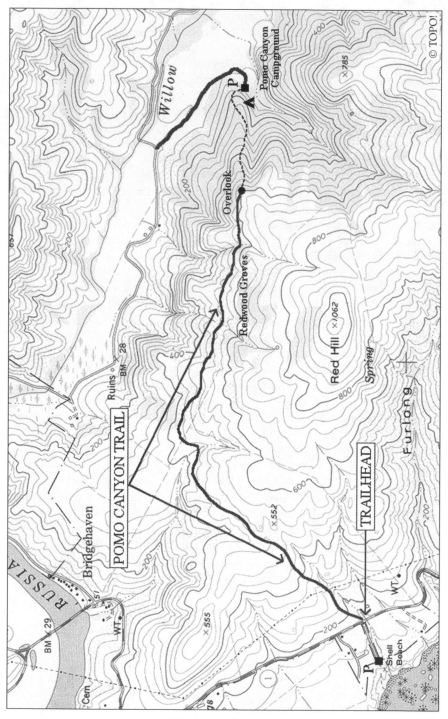

© TOPO!

47. Pomo Canyon

47 | Sonoma Coast State Beach
POMO CANYON

Length: 4 miles

Time: 2 to 3 hours

Rating: Moderate

Regulations: CSP; no dogs, no bikes, no horses.

Highlights: The Pomo Canyon Trail, part of an ancient Indian trade route, runs from Hwy. 1, just east of Shell Beach, to Pomo Canyon Campground, off Willow Creek Rd. The scenic out-and-back trip described here, using a 2-mile leg of the trail, takes you across open grassy hills, past two hidden redwood groves, and then to a vantage point atop a rocky ridge. For a longer hike, you can continue to the campground; you can also make this a car shuttle trip. This hike can easily be combined with others on the Sonoma coast to make a full day outing.

Directions: See the directions for "Kortum Trail" on pages 244–245.

Facilities: Rest rooms

Trailhead: On the east side of Hwy. 1, opposite the entrance to Shell Beach, about 0.1 mile east of the parking area.

Although the leading actor on the Sonoma coast is clearly the Pacific Ocean, important supporting roles are played by the rolling hills and deep canyons just east of Highway 1. From the trailhead, you pass to the right of a metal gate and get on the Pomo Canyon Trail, which starts as a paved road rising northeast on a moderate grade through open grassland dotted with clumps of coyote brush and tangles of blackberry vines. A slight gain in elevation is all it takes to give you, on a clear day, magnificent views southeast to Bodega Head and south to Point Reyes. After passing under a set of power lines, you come to a junction. Here the road, now mostly dirt and broken pavement, turns left, but you continue straight on a wide dirt path over level ground. A few hundred feet ahead is a fork, marked by a trail post, where you bear left. This is prime hunting ground for aerial predators such as red-tailed hawks, northern harriers, and American kestrels. Each has its own hunting style. Red-tailed hawks describe lazy circles high in the sky, using their sharp eyesight to spot rodents and other small mammals. Northern harriers cruise low over the ground, swooping and banking to follow the terrain. The kestrel, North America's smallest falcon, is one of the few birds to truly hover, diving suddenly on its prey.

Soon the barren nature of the landscape is tempered by the addition of a few Douglas firs and tanbark oaks, and thickets of hazelnut, cream-bush, coffeeberry, poison oak, and wild rose. A line of willows indicates the presence of a nearby stream. In the distance to your left, the Russian River runs a snaky course toward its rendezvous with the Pacific near the town of Jenner. Now the route drops into a cool, shady gulch that holds a creek flowing under the trail through a culvert. Beyond the creek, the route rises and bends left, reaching in a couple of hundred feet a junction marked by a trail post. Here an overgrown trail heads straight, but your route turns sharply right. The Douglas fir trees beside the trail are only 20 or 30 feet tall, but they have grown amazingly stout and twisted, mute testimony to the power of the wind. The trail here is a corridor lined with shrubs, including thimbleberry, snowberry, bush monkeyflower, and coast silk tassel.

With a barbed-wire fence marking the park boundary, right, the trail bends right and descends to a creek, which you cross on a plank bridge. A couple of hundred feet ahead is another plank bridge, this one to take you across a wet area. The route loses elevation on a moderate grade, bends right, and then regains the lost ground. Ahead is a weirdly shaped coast redwood—its huge trunk has two main divisions, and each of these supports three tall trees. This peculiar sentinel guards a magical redwood grove, extending uphill to the right of the trail, that lines the banks of a small creek. The understory is a riot of western sword ferns, and through them runs a narrow path into the heart of this silent, perhaps even spooky, place. You can use the path to reach a fallen log a couple of hun-dred feet uphill, a fine spot to sit and contemplate this majestic remnant of a once-vast ancient forest that stretched along the California and Oregon coasts. Continuing past the grove on the main trail, you begin a moderate ascent through an overgrown area and soon reach another red-wood grove, larger than the first, with its own creek.

Leaving the redwoods behind, you descend through a willow thicket and then enjoy a level walk across open grassland, where you see a third redwood grove uphill and right. Crossing a creek on a plank bridge, you follow the trail through corridors of shrubs as it seeks higher ground, and pass at about the 2-mile point a wonderful circular grove of California bay trees, left. With a huge tree in the middle and lesser ones ringing it, this grove resembles a redwood fairy ring—a circle of descendents around an ancestor. About 100 feet past the bay grove, a low rocky ridge rises left of the trail. Two trails climb it: take the second one and scramble up loose gravel to the summit. From here you can see the mouth of the Russian River, the Pacific Ocean, the redwood groves you just passed, and the heart of the Russian River country to the north and northeast. After surveying the 360-degree scene from this fine vantage point, retrace your steps to the parking area.

◆ Sonoma County Regional Parks ◆

Sonoma County operates 37 regional parks, many of which contain fine trails for hiking, bicycling, and horseback riding. The variety of terrain encompassed by these parks is remarkable, ranging from the chaparral-cloaked summit of Mt. Hood, near the Sonoma–Napa border, to the sandy shoreline of Bodega Bay. Some of the best trails are found in parks near Highway 101, including Helen Putnam, Crane Creek, Shiloh Ranch, and Foothill. The largest park, Hood Mountain, is adjacent to Sugarloaf Ridge State Park, near the town of Kenwood on Highway 12. The best access is through the state park. Hood Mountain is open only on weekends and holidays, and is closed during the fire season.

Besides hiking, bicycling, and horseback riding, other activities in the parks include picnicking, nature study, fishing, and team sports. Five of the parks have campgrounds, and four of these are on the coast: Doran and Westside, both in Bodega Bay; Stillwater Cove, between Jenner and Sea Ranch; and Gualala Point, on the Sonoma–Mendocino border. The fifth, Spring Lake, is just east of Santa Rosa. Eight of the parks have marina and boat-launch facilities.

Sonoma County Regional Parks has established the West County Trail, which one day will run from downtown Santa Rosa to Steelhead Beach Regional Park on the Russian River north of Forestville. Right now the route is piecemeal, using existing trails, bike lanes, road shoulders, and paths. This is primarily a bicycle route, best for mountain bikes but good for road bikes too. Many of Sonoma County's regional parks are disabled-accessible, and the park map and guide, available from the administrative offices, rates each for its level of difficulty. In all of the parks, dogs must be securely leased on a maximum 6-foot leash and in immediate control of a person at all times. In campgrounds, dogs must be within a tent or vehicle at night. Dogs are not allowed on the trails in Shiloh Ranch Regional Park. There is a dog-exercise area at Sonoma Valley Regional Park.

ADMINISTRATIVE OFFICES: (707) 527-2041

SPRING LAKE VISITOR CENTER: (707) 539-2865

| 48 | Sonoma County Regional Parks
CRANE CREEK |

Length: 1.4 miles

Time: 1 hour or less

Rating: Easy

Regulations: Sonoma County Regional Parks; parking fee; dogs on leash.

Highlights: This enjoyable semi-loop, made from the Creek, Fiddleneck, and Poppy trails, is a short and easy jaunt through wildflower-dotted grassland and shady woodland. Although the park is small, a wonderful diversity of habitats is represented here, especially near Crane Creek, the park's main watercourse. Cattle graze in parts of the park for a limited time after the rainy season, so please close all gates you pass through.

Directions: From Hwy. 101 in Cotati, take the Rohnert Park/Sebastopol/Hwy. 116 exit and go east 0.1 mile to Old Redwood Hwy. Turn right and go 0.4 mile to E. Cotati Ave. Turn left and go 2.4 miles to Petaluma Hill Rd. Turn right and go 0.5 mile to Roberts Rd. Turn left and go 1.4 miles to end of Roberts Rd., at its junction with Lichau Rd., right, and Pressley Rd., straight. Continue straight, now on Pressley Rd., and go 0.6 mile to the park entrance, left, and a paved parking area with a self-registration station.

Facilities: Rest rooms, picnic tables.

Trailhead: North end of parking area.

This parking area serves two trailheads. The one at the parking area's north end, which you will use, gives access to the Creek, Poppy, Buckeye, Lupine, and Sunset trails. The other, at the parking area's northwest corner, is for the Hawk Ridge, Overlook Loop, and Fiddleneck trails, the latter a dirt road used by bicyclists and equestrians to circle the park. Most of the terrain here is either open grassland, where cattle may be grazing, or oak woodland. But this diverse park also contains examples of an oak savanna, a riparian woodland, vernal swale wetlands, a vernal pool wetland, and a bunchgrass/wildflower meadow. Heading north and passing to the right of the rest rooms, you follow a gravel path which changes to dirt and gravel in about 75 feet. Just ahead, a connector coming from the other trailhead joins on your left. Now on the Creek Trail, you enjoy easy travel on a level grade, with some beautiful valley oaks in a marshy area, right, and also on a hillside, left. A black phoebe, a flycatcher, may watch you pass from its perch on a fence post.

At a junction with the Poppy Trail, which goes straight through a gate, you turn right to follow the Creek Trail across a wooden bridge. In a few hundred yards, you come to a four-way junction. Here the Buckeye Trail veers right to cross Crane Creek, a watercourse lined with willow, white alder, and California bay. (Bikes and horses must use this route to connect to the Fiddleneck Trail.) Another trail heads to a shady spot beside the creek. And your route, the Creek Trail, turns left and runs parallel to the creek, passing a thicket of blackberry vines and a rest bench in the shade of a California buckeye. Soon you reach a junction where the Lupine Trail forks left through a gate in a barbed-wire fence, but you take the right-hand fork, passing another rest bench, right, and an array of large coast live oaks. Now you meet the other end of the Lupine Trail, left, and not too far ahead, the Creek Trail ends and the Fiddleneck Trail merges from the right. Now on the Fiddleneck Trail, a dirt road, you turn left and pass through a gate in the barbed-wire fence. At a junction marked by a trail post, the Northern Loop Trail goes uphill and right, but you continue curving left, now walking southeast through an oak savanna.

After the other end of the Northern Loop Trail merges from the right, the Fiddleneck Trail crosses a seasonal creek and then passes a junction with the Lupine Trail, left. After about 150 feet, a path to the Lupine Trail veers left, but your route bends right and crosses rocky ground near

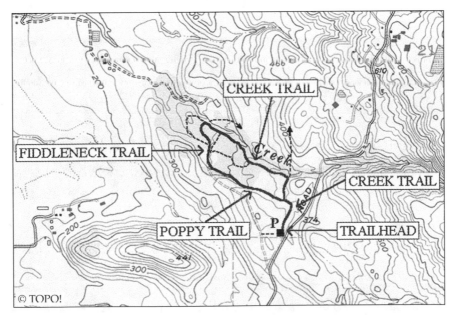

48. Crane Creek

another seasonal creek. Just before the creek, you come to a junction marked by a trail post, left. (Bikes and horses must stay on the Fiddleneck Trail.) From here the Fiddleneck Trail crosses the creek and continues generally southeast toward the parking area, but you turn left onto the Poppy Trail, with the creek on your right. Soon reaching the creek, you step across it and gain elevation on a gentle and then moderate grade. Here the oaks wear a cloak of lace lichen, sometimes called Spanish moss, and croaking frogs may serenade you from a gully, left. An old snag riddled with woodpecker holes makes a fine perch for birds of prey. Reaching a gate in a barbed-wire fence, you pass through it and arrive at the junction with the Creek Trail you passed earlier. Now continue straight and retrace your steps to the parking area.

Hikers returning to the parking area on the Creek Trail.

49 | Sonoma County Regional Parks
FOOTHILL

Length: 2.3 miles

Time: 1 to 2 hours

Rating: Easy

Regulations: Sonoma County Regional Parks; parking fee; dogs on leash.

Highlights: Using the Westside, Oakwood, and Three Lakes trails, this short and easy loop wanders through Foothill Regional Park, nestled in a residential area on the northeast corner of Windsor, not far from Healdsburg and the Russian River. The park's inland location makes it ideal for a spring or fall hike. For a longer outing, combine a visit here with one to nearby Shiloh Ranch Regional Park, described on pages 261–263.

Directions: From Hwy. 101 in Windsor, take the Old Redwood Hwy. exit and go southeast 0.6 mile to Hembree Ln. Turn left, and go 1.2 miles to a stop sign at Foothill Dr. Continue straight, now on Arata Ln., for 0.1 mile to the park entrance, right. Park for free on Arata Ln., or use the parking area just inside the park entrance for a small fee.

Facilities: Toilet, phone.

Trailhead: Northeast side of paved parking area, at a green metal gate.

A wooden fence surrounds the parking area, and a gated dirt-and-gravel road heads northeast into this lovely park, tucked away in the hills between busy Highway 101 and quiet Chalk Hill Valley. You pass to the left of the gate, through a gap in the fence next to an information board and the parking area's self-registration station. The dirt-and-gravel road, called the Three Lakes Trail, gives access to the park's three fishing ponds and a picnic area. Just past the gate, a single-track trail heads left, but you continue about 100 feet to the next junction, where two trails veer left and the road bends right. A trail post here lists the Three Lakes and Westside trails. Now you turn sharply left, and, with the trail post on your right, begin a gentle uphill climb that soon brings you to a rough dirt road. This road, which starts at a locked gate on the parking area's northwest corner, is the Westside Trail.

Turning right onto the Westside Trail, you continue uphill, and in about 150 yards pass a single-track trail merging from the right. This park is an oasis of rolling hills and oaks in the midst of suburbia, and as you climb you begin to get views of the surrounding housing developments. For most of the route, however, civilization lies hidden behind a screen of trees and shrubs, giving the park a remote, secluded feel. Downhill and right is Pond A, the smallest of the park's three ponds. The vegetation— blue oak, black oak, and manzanita—marks this part of the North Bay as a sunny and relatively dry area. Also here are coast live oak and madrone. Passing a gravel road to several water tanks, left, the road crests a ridge and follows it on a rolling course. Two unofficial trails, about 100 yards apart, head right, but you continue straight, soon reaching a junction with the Oakwood Trail, where you veer left.

The Oakwood Trail swings left and gains elevation on a gentle and then moderate grade, taking you through an oak savanna with a few picnic tables scattered here and there. The park boundary, marked by a fence, is just left, and behind it are some lovely cypress trees. After a short, moderate descent, you pass a trail going left through a gap in the fence, but you stay on this side, curving right. With power lines overhead, the trail rises to an open area where a rest bench and an overlook await. The view from here stretches south across Pond B to the Highway 101

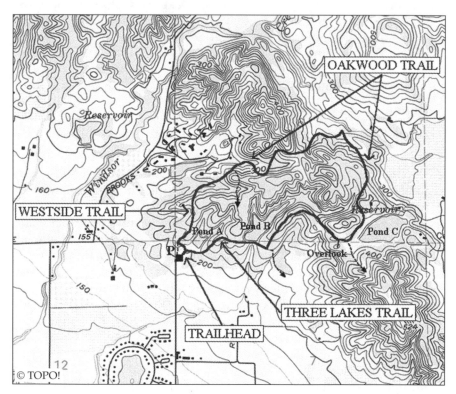

49. Foothill

Black oak leaves turn yellow and orange in fall.

corridor. Reaching the head of a ravine, the route swings around it to the right, then switchbacks left and climbs over the crest of a ridge. Reaching a level area at about the 1-mile point, you suddenly have a fine view to the northeast of Mt. St. Helena, framed by oak limbs in the foreground and the Bald Hills in the middle distance.

Now your route swings left and descends via switchbacks through an open area, with a split-rail fence bordering the trail on your right. A wooden bridge takes you across a seasonal watercourse, and then you turn sharply right, entering a dense forest on a gently rising grade. A narrow path joins from the right, and another leads left to a small pond. Also left, beyond the park boundary, is another pond, this one large. Floating on its surface may be American coots, plump black birds that resemble ducks but are actually related to marsh birds such as the clapper rail. You may see a large bird box on a tree—this is to attract nesting wood ducks, extremely colorful birds that look hand-painted. With power lines again overhead, you come to a trail, left, that climbs uphill directly under them. A short detour left on this trail brings you to a wonderful vantage point in the middle of a meadow, with Mt. St. Helena rising in the distance behind the large pond. Back on the main trail, you immediately reach another junction, where a path goes left and uphill to a knoll with two picnic tables and more great views.

Descending from this junction, you follow the Oakwood Trail, now a rocky and eroded dirt road, as it curves right and passes a trail and a rest bench, both left. Views from here to the southwest take in Pond C and the sprawling subdivisions that make up Windsor. The road follows the crest of a ridge on a rolling but generally downhill course to a T-junction with a gravel road, the Three Lakes Trail. For a closer look at Pond C and a visit to the picnic area, turn left. Otherwise, go right and stay on the road, ignoring all side paths. From here the road climbs on a very gentle grade, soon crossing the earthen dam that formed Pond B, which is on your right. Now climbing on a moderate grade, the road curves right, and in about 100 yards comes to a junction, right, with the Westside Trail, a rocky dirt road. Descending the crest of a ridge, past stands of manzanita, you arrive at Pond A, right. As you continue downhill past the pond, your route swings sharply left, and then you pass the junction where you began this loop. Now retrace your steps to the parking area.

50   Sonoma County Regional Parks
HELEN PUTNAM

Length: 2.1 miles

Time: 1 to 2 hours

Rating: Easy

Regulations: Sonoma County Regional Parks; parking fee; dogs on leash.

Highlights: This enjoyable ramble through a lovely county park southwest of Petaluma consists of two different loops, an approximately 1.5-mile circuit through rolling grassland, and a 0.6-mile visit to an oak-clad hill, where a clearing affords fine views. The shorter loop begins at about the 0.5-mile point on the larger one. Although named on the park's master plan, the trails are not signed. The first 0.5-mile, on a paved road called the Victoria Trail, is part of the Bay Area Ridge Trail.

Directions: From Hwy. 101 northbound, just south of Petaluma, take the Petaluma Blvd. South exit, crossing under the highway at 0.9 mile, and reaching Western Ave. at 2.5 miles. Turn left onto Western Ave., go 1.9 miles to Chileno Valley Rd., and turn left. Go 0.8 mile to the park entrance, left, and a paved parking area with a self-registration station.

From Hwy. 101 southbound in Petaluma, take the Washington St. exit., which brings you to E. Washington St. Turn right onto E. Washington St.—which becomes Washington St. at Lakeville St.—and go 1 mile to Petaluma Blvd. N. Turn left and go 0.1 mile to Western Ave. Turn right onto Western Ave. and follow the directions above.

Facilities: Rest rooms, water, phone; covered picnic area with tables, fire grates; children's play area; horse-trailer parking.

Trailhead: Northeast end of parking area, at a yellow metal gate.

Helen Putnam, the park's namesake, was mayor of Petaluma from 1965 to 1978, and a Sonoma County supervisor from 1979 to 1984. The park, situated on the county's southeast edge a few miles from the Marin border, consists of rolling, open hills punctuated by groves of oak. The park's main thoroughfare, a paved road, begins at a yellow metal gate on the parking area's northeast end, and winds its way to Oxford Court, a street off Windsor Drive in a housing development on the park's northeast edge. The first 0.5 mile of this road is part of the Bay Area Ridge Trail, a mere sliver of what will someday be a 400-mile loop around the San Francisco Bay area. Passing left of the metal gate, you follow the paved road past the picnic area, right, and the rest rooms, left. Just beyond the rest rooms, a dirt trail, your return route, heads left, but you stay on the road as it swings right and crosses a culvert holding a seasonal watercourse. With the ranger's residence on your right, you continue gently uphill, with fine views of the coastal hills extending toward the Chileno Valley and Bolinas Ridge. A grassy hillside rising left may hold a flocks of goldfinches and western meadowlarks.

As the paved road begins to curve left, a dirt-and-gravel road heads straight to the park boundary. You stay on the paved road, soon passing a rough dirt track taking off uphill and left to a water tank. A moderate ascent past coyote brush, willows, and blackberry brambles brings you to

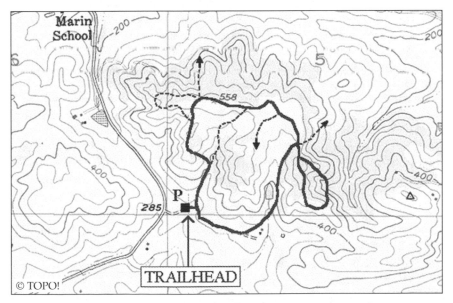

50. Helen Putnam

a small fishing pond, left, ringed by a narrow trail. The pond was creat-ed by an earthen dam, and a dirt road joining yours goes across it to the water tank. Leaving the pond behind, you pass an area being planted with valley oaks. Uphill and right is a hilltop, densely covered with coast live oaks, which you will visit in a few minutes via a loop trail. After the road levels, you reach a four-way junction marking the end of the Bay Area Ridge Trail segment. On your right is a single-track trail to the oak-covered hilltop, and on your left is a wide dirt trail heading into a grassy field, which you will use later.

Now turning right and climbing on a moderate grade, you soon pass a trail, left, the returning end of the loop that crosses the hilltop. Suddenly you are in a serene and shady grove of oaks, a haven for birds, and a home for other creatures you may hear scurrying through the leaf litter. Ahead is a clearing with a rest bench and fine views of Burdell Mountain to the southeast and the Petaluma valley to the east. Behind Burdell Mountain rises Big Rock Ridge, the high divide between the City of Novato and Lucas Valley, topped by two communication towers. Soon the route crosses the hilltop, descends, and bends left, passing a few black oaks. At the next rest bench, with San Pablo Bay shimmering in the dis-tance, a rough track heads downhill and right, but you continue straight toward a barbed-wire fence. Just before the fence, your trail bends left, passing another rough track, right. Now in the shade of coast live oak, California bay, and valley oak, you traverse a hillside that falls away right. When you arrive at the junction with the start of the loop, bear right to the four-way junction with the paved road.

Now you cross the paved road and head north on a wide dirt path through an open, weedy field. Along the way, several paths diverge from the main trail: ignore them. After a gentle climb, you are rewarded with terrific views to the northeast across Petaluma and toward Sonoma Mountain. Reaching a level spot, the route curves left and you pass a trail going left. At the next junction, a dirt road heads downhill and left, but you continue straight, with a line of trees on your right that may hold a northern flicker or a western scrub-jay. Arriving at a five-way junction, you turn left, passing a rest bench and then a junction with a trail, right. Reaching the crest of a hill, where a path leads to a viewpoint, right, you enjoy 360-degree views of the ridges and rolling hills that characterize this corner of Sonoma County. Staying left at a fork, you make a moder-ate descent over eroded ground, soon merging with a wide dirt trail. Here you turn sharply right and follow the trail downhill, with a water-course on your left. Ignoring a few rough trails heading right, you con-tinue to descend, reaching the paved road used at the start of this route. Now turn right to the parking area.

51

Sonoma County Regional Parks
SHILOH RANCH

Length: 3.8 miles

Time: 2 to 3 hours

Rating: Moderate

Regulations: Sonoma County Regional Parks; parking fee; no dogs.

Highlights: This loop, using the Big Leaf, Ridge, Pond, and Creekside trails, explores a forested enclave north of Santa Rosa on the east side of Hwy. 101. For a longer outing, combine a visit here with one to nearby Foothill Regional Park, described on pages 255–258.

Directions: From Hwy. 101 in Windsor, take the Shiloh Rd. exit and go east 1.5 miles to Faught Rd. Turn right and go 0.1 mile to the park entrance, left, and a paved parking area with a self-registration station.

Facilities: Rest rooms, water, phone, picnic tables, fire grates.

Trailhead: At north end of parking area.

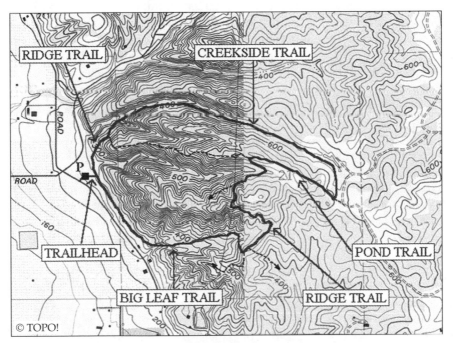

51. Shiloh Ranch

Heading north on the Big Leaf Trail, a rocky dirt road, you soon pass the Ridge Trail, left, which you will use on the return part of this loop. The road now curves sharply right and follows a shady course under the arching limbs of large coast live oaks, valley oaks, and madrones. Beside the road are common shrubs such as manzanita, toyon, coyote brush, poison oak, and bush monkeyflower. After several hundred feet, you pass an alternate trail from the parking area, right, and soon a horse trail from the parking area merges on your right. A vineyard rises from Faught Road, right, to just beside your road. As the road bends left and begins a moderate climb, you encounter tall Douglas fir and bigleaf maple, the latter combining with the vineyard's grape and nearby poison oak to create a dazzling display of fall foliage. A ravine, right, holds a seasonal creek, and the road swings right to cross it. Soon the vegetation thins and you are in a savanna of mostly blue oak, where a power-line tower and a rest bench mark a junction and the end of the Big Leaf Trail.

Now you bear left on the Ridge Trail and continue a moderate climb that soon eases, with views extending south across agricultural land to the Highway 101 corridor. The next junction is with the Mark West Creek Trail, right. Here you continue straight on a narrow crest running generally north. Re-entering a densely wooded area, the road crosses the seasonal creek it crossed earlier and lower down, and then veers left. Coming out of the trees, you have a steep climb under a set of power lines, which brings you to a T-junction. Here a trail post has arrows pointing both left and right. Turning right, still on the Ridge Trail, you descend a dirt road on a gentle grade under the power lines, and soon reach an area shaded by California buckeye, Douglas fir, and madrone, where honeysuckle vines, in fall loaded with berries, thrive. A deep canyon is left, and your route angles down into it, switchbacks left, and climbs out.

Around the 2-mile point, at a junction marked by a trail post, the Pond Trail, a dirt road, heads right. You follow it on a gently rising grade, with views now of Mt. St. Helena northeast through the trees. Now the road loses elevation, gently at first, then on a moderate grade. As the road begins to bend left, you turn sharply left onto the Creekside Trail, a single track marked with a trail post. Now you head north toward a lovely pond ringed with willows and cattails. Several rest benches invite you to contemplate this small man-made oasis in the midst of mostly open, rolling hills. A marsh wren may begin its scolding chatter as you approach. There is an earthen dam at the northwest end of the pond and a junction with a trail going across it. When you reach this junction, continue straight, following a northwest course that soon puts you back in a dense forest, mostly black oak, with a few examples of Oregon oak, madrone, bigleaf maple, and Douglas fir. Ferns and moss give this place a rain-forest feel. The trail threads its way between two steep-sided hills, with a narrow ravine downhill and right.

Now the trail descends on a moderate grade, aided by wooden steps, into the ravine. Here, two creek beds, which may be dry, merge. Where they do, your route drops briefly into their joined bed, and then climbs out. With the ravine still on your right, you climb on a moderate grade to a **T**-junction with the Ridge Trail, a dirt road. Turning right and walking downhill, you soon pass a junction with an overgrown dirt road, right. Here your road curves left and comes to a seasonal creek, which you cross. Now you meet the Big Leaf Trail at the junction you passed earlier at the start of this loop. Here you turn right to the parking area.

View west from the Big Leaf Trail takes in a vineyard adjacent to Shiloh Ranch Regional Park.

52 Sonoma County Regional Parks
SONOMA VALLEY

Length: 2.6 miles

Time: 1 to 2 hours

Rating: Easy

Regulations: Sonoma County Regional Parks; parking fee; dogs on leash.

Highlights: This small park is big on rewards: a fine picnic area shaded by oaks, a surprisingly varied loop trail that runs through a streamside corridor and then climbs a forested ridge to a high point with great views, and a 1-acre dog-exercise enclosure. For a full-day outing, combine a hike here with a visit to any of the nearby state parks: Jack London, Sugarloaf Ridge, or Annadel.

Directions: From Hwy. 12 northbound in Sonoma, use the junction of Broadway and Napa St., on the south side of the Plaza, as the 0.0-mile point. Follow Hwy. 12 west and then northwest for a total of 6.6 miles to the park entrance, left.

From Hwy. 12 southbound, south of Kenwood, use the junction with Arnold Dr. as the 0.0-mile point. Continue 0.4 mile to the park entrance, right, and go 0.2 mile to a paved parking area with a self-registration station.then follow the directions above.

Facilities: Picnic tables, fire grates, water, toilet.

Trailhead: South end of parking area, at a metal gate.

A paved path, shared by hikers, bicyclists, and equestrians, leaves the parking area and wanders through a large open field graced here and there with a few venerable native oaks and some planted trees. After about 150 feet, you pass a gravel road leading uphill to two large water tanks. Now your path curves right, and, in another 100 feet or so, reaches a junction, left, with a dirt-and-gravel road that you will use on the return part of this loop. You continue on the paved path, which descends gently past several oak-shaded picnic tables and then finds a mostly level course. Many of the oaks and other trees and shrubs in this park are draped with beautiful strands of lace lichen, sometimes called Spanish moss. Entering a savanna of mostly blue oak, you follow a seasonal creek that crisscrosses under the trail through culverts. Joining the blue oaks are black oak, valley oak, California buckeye, California bay, and manzanita. Soon a hikers-only trail departs left, and then an unsigned single track rises right.

A few more picnic tables and a rest bench invite you to stay awhile and enjoy the sights and sounds, which may include a woodpecker's drumming on a dead tree trunk, or a spotted towhee's scratching for food in leaf litter on the ground. Growing from the creek bed is Oregon ash, a tree that turns brilliant yellow in fall. Several more trails take off left and uphill: ignore them all. Soon a dirt path joins from the right, and then your path bends left. To your right, beyond a screen of trees and a ravine, is Arnold Drive and the town of Glen Ellen. Sonoma Mountain, a high forested ridge that forms the backbone of Jack London State Historic Park, rises to the southwest. Past the 1-mile point, you come to a junction. Here the paved path continues straight, but you turn left onto a single-track trail that heads uphill. In about 75 feet you come to a fork, marked by a trail post, where you bear left onto a rocky track that climbs across a steep hillside. Here the manzanitas are draped with folds of lace lichen, a

52. Sonoma Valley

lovely sight. A tall madrone invites comparison with its smaller cousins. Madrone has orange bark and large, shiny green leaves, whereas manzanita has burgundy bark and small, pointed leaves that range from gray to dark green.

Curving right through an oak savanna, the trail approaches the crest of a hill, the top of which is on private land behind a barbed-wire fence. A path, right, goes through a gap in the fence, but you continue straight, soon dropping steeply over rough ground. Now a level traverse across a steep hillside brings you to a junction, where a trail goes downhill and left. At about the 2-mile point, the hikers-only trail you passed earlier joins from the left, and now your route runs along the top of a ridge and then crosses to its left side. At the next junction, a trail goes right and uphill to a metal gate in the barbed-wire fence. About 20 feet ahead, another trail also goes right. Ignore both of these, and instead follow your trail as it bends sharply left, then jogs back to the right. With the two water tanks near the parking area in view, you come to a four-way junction, where you turn left. Now out in the open, the trail passes near the top of a hill, where a short path leads to a rest bench and a vantage point with fine views from northwest to southeast.

Past this spur, the main trail widens as it descends steeply over a bed of loose rock and gravel. Reaching a T-junction with a dirt road, you turn left. Then, after about 75 feet, you merge with a dirt-and-gravel road and bear left. Ahead is the paved path you used at the start of this loop. Bear right on it and retrace your steps to the parking area.

In spring before the trees get their leaves is a good time to look for birds.

◆ Sugarloaf Ridge State Park ◆

One of Sonoma County's finest parks, Sugarloaf Ridge State Park takes its name from a rolling ridge of volcanic rock that rises just south of Sonoma Creek near the park's border. The hills and ridges that surround Sonoma Creek, including the park's high point, Bald Mountain (2729), and neighboring Mt. Hood (2730'), are part of the Mayacmas Mountains, a range that divides the Clear Lake and the Russian River drainages and forms the border between Sonoma and Napa counties.

There are 21 miles of trails, a combination of dirt roads and single tracks, in the 2,700-acre park. These give visitors access to a variety of plant communities, including redwood forest, valley and foothill woodland, grassland, and chaparral. These different habitats, and especially the margins between them, provide excellent opportunities for birding—the park's bird checklist has nearly 100 species. The park can be hot in summer and cold in winter, so spring and fall are the best times to visit. The park's grassy meadows are ablaze with wildflowers in spring, and there is a 25-foot waterfall on Sonoma Creek that is fed by winter rains. The creek holds a run of steelhead trout, which are listed under federal law as a threatened species.

The upper stretch of Sonoma Creek was once home to a Wappo Indian Village called Wilikos. These people lived in long, domed huts framed with poles and thatched with grass. They survived by hunting, fishing, gathering acorns, and trading with other groups of Indians. When the Spanish arrived in the 18th century, the Wappo resisted missionization and other colonial efforts, and it was disease—cholera and smallpox—rather than Spanish arms, that finally defeated them. The survivors were sent to the Mendocino Indian Reservation. In the mid-1800s, the hills near Sugarloaf Ridge, though not nearly as fertile as the nearby valleys, saw limited ranching and farming. In 1920, the State of California bought the property along Sonoma Creek to dam it as a water supply for Sonoma State Hospital. The plan was stopped by local property owners, and for many years use of the land was confined to grazing and recreation. In 1964 the area became part of the State Park System.

A large day-use parking area just beyond the entrance kiosk serves many of the park's trails, including a self-guiding nature trail. Two other parking areas, on Adobe Canyon Road, serve trails to the waterfall and to Mt. Hood, which is in the adjoining Hood Mountain Regional Park, operated by Sonoma County. A campground with 50 sites is near the entrance kiosk, as is a small visitor center, which may be open only on weekends. There is also a group camp area, for up to 50 people, at the end of the park entrance road. Nearby is the Sonoma Cattle Company, a pack station offering trail rides. The Valley of the Moon Natural History Association, a volunteer group working with three state parks—Sugarloaf Ridge, Annadel, and Jack London—offers guided walks in the park. Dogs are not allowed on the park trails. In the campground and the picnic area they must be leashed during the day and kept inside a vehicle or tent at night.

RANGER STATION: (707) 833-5712

DISTRICT OFFICE: (707) 938-1519

CAMPING RESERVATIONS: (800) 444-7275

FERGUSON OBSERVATORY: (707) 833-6979

VALLEY OF THE MOON NATURAL HISTORY ASSOCIATION: (707) 938-5216

SONOMA CATTLE COMPANY: (707) 996-8566

53 Sugarloaf Ridge State Park
BALD MOUNTAIN

Length:	6.7 miles
Time:	4 to 5 hours
Rating:	Difficult
Regulations:	CSP; parking fee; no dogs, no bikes, no horses.
Highlights:	This semi-loop route, using the Lower Bald Mountain, Bald Mountain, Vista, Headwaters, Red Mountain, and Gray Pine trails, is a challenge, but well worth the effort. A superb array of trees, shrubs, and wildflowers, along with some of the best views in the North Bay, are the rewards for tackling the 1500-foot climb to the summit of Bald Mountain. The mountaintop is exposed to wind and weather, and should be avoided if thunderstorms or other adverse conditions threaten.
Directions:	From Hwy. 12 just north of Kenwood, take Adobe Canyon Rd. and go northeast 3.4 miles to the entrance kiosk. If the entrance kiosk is not staffed, pay fee at the self-registration station here. Continue 0.1 mile to a dirt parking area, left.
Facilities:	Picnic tables, fire grates, toilet; visitor center, water, and phone just southeast of entrance kiosk.
Trailhead:	Northeast corner of parking area.

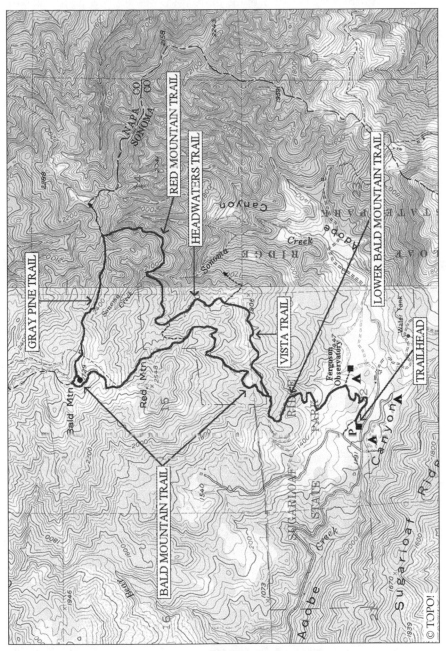

53. Bald Mountain

The Lower Bald Mountain Trail, a single track, heads from the parking area through a wet area into open grassland and finds a gentle uphill course. In spring, the fields beside the trail are dotted with wildflowers, including blue-eyed grass, yarrow, bluedicks, lupine, vetch, and blow wives. High on your left are rolling hills and forested ridges, but your goal, Bald Mountain (2729') remains hidden behind them. In places, the trail enters groves of coast live oak, California bay, and madrone, where you will also find shrubs such as manzanita, coffeeberry, toyon, and poison oak. At a junction with the Meadow Trail, you veer left and soon begin a moderate uphill climb via a series of switchbacks in a densely wooded area. As you emerge from forest into chaparral, the change in vegetation is dramatic and fascinating for lovers of native plants—here, in addition to manzanita, you may find chamise, buckbrush, spiny redberry, bush monkeyflower, and leather oak, an indicator of serpentine soil.

Just before the 1-mile point, your trail merges with the Bald Mountain Trail, a paved road that is part of the Bay Area Ridge Trail. This junction is a fine vantage point, with views west along Sonoma Creek Canyon, northwest to Mount Hood, south to Sugarloaf Ridge, and north to Red Mountain. Bearing right on the paved road, which is attractively lined with silver lupine, you follow it steadily uphill on a moderate grade, with views to the right of the park campground, visitor center, and horse stables, all far downhill. Where the road angles sharply left, you turn onto the Vista Trail, a single track leading right and downhill. This trail is

View south toward San Francisco from the summit of Bald Mountain. On the far skyline is Mt. Tamalpais.

closed to bikes year-round and closed in winter to horses. A small pond in a marshy area welcomes you to a lovely but fragile area. Deer frequent this area, and wild pigs have been seen nearby. In the distance to the southeast rises another Bald Mountain, its open slopes planted with vineyards. According to *California Place Names*, more than 100 peaks in California are named Bald, but it is certainly confusing to have two so close together. Only Black and Red are more popular mountain names, and this park has one of those, too.

Now in a shady corridor of oak, toyon, and manzanita, you enjoy a level walk, soon reaching several small streams crossed by wooden planks. This wet area supports bigleaf maple trees, ferns, and wildflowers. The trail dips to cross a seasonal creek and then climbs on a moderate grade across an open, grassy hillside. With a view ahead of chaparral-clad Brushy Peaks, you pass a large rock outcrop, right, that makes a fine vantage point or picnic spot. But the best views are still to come: as you pass a trail post, left, Mt. Diablo rises in the distance to the southeast, and Mt. Tamalpais appears to the southwest. The route turns left and then descends steeply over loose, rocky ground to a junction with the Headwaters Trail, left. Turning left, you walk in the shade of Douglas fir and coast live oak, looking beside the single-track trail for wild iris, California buttercup, and red larkspur.

After making a short, steep descent, your route wanders among moss-covered boulders in a magical, fern-filled area that has a rain-forest feel. Reaching Sonoma Creek but staying on its west side, the trail bends left and rises on a moderate grade past tangles of wild rose, creambush, and honeysuckle. Water tumbles from pool to pool, forming miniature waterfalls in the creek, and the nutrient-rich forest floor hosts a variety of wildflowers, including mule ears, common star lily, and Solomon's seal. After struggling uphill over rough ground, the trail meanders past stands of bay, black oak, canyon oak, manzanita, and mountain mahogany, at last reaching a **T**-junction with the Red Mountain Trail, a single track. Here you turn right and descend to a crossing of Sonoma Creek near its upper reaches. This is a beautiful place, where the only sound may be the splash of water over rocks. Golden globe lilies and wild iris decorate the landscape, which, as you ascend on a moderate grade, begins to take on a park-like aspect.

Finding a rolling course, the trail takes you back into dense forest, but soon the scene changes, with open vistas that again take in Mt. Diablo and Mt. Tamalpais, with Veeder Mountain to the southeast and Red Mountain, topped by a communication facility, to the west. As the trail swings north, a deep canyon downhill and right holds a seasonal tributary of Sonoma Creek. Now you descend steeply to a creek and cross it on a wooden bridge. Once across, the trail switchbacks right and climbs on a moderate grade, crossing a steep hillside and soon resorting to more switchbacks to surmount a steep grade. Suddenly you are atop a manzanita barren—the sandy, rocky soil here is perfect for these hearty, pioneering plants. From this barren you have a wonderful 360-degree view that, at last, reveals the summit of the park's Bald Mountain, slightly north of west, along with the other Bay Area summits already seen. The trail passes just south of the barren's high point, then curves counterclockwise around it.

The sight of gray pines is welcome, because it means you are approaching the Gray Pine Trail, the last leg to Bald Mountain. You join the Gray Pine Trail, a dirt road, at a T-junction just past the 3-mile point. Now turning left, you continue uphill on a moderate grade, in places shaded by Douglas fir, bay, madrone, and black oak. The road, which here follows the Napa–Sonoma line, is lined with shrubs—manzanita, chamise, buckbrush, blue blossom, and silver lupine. Far to the south, you may just make out the shimmering waters of San Pablo Bay, the rounded hulk of Angel Island, and the skyline of San Francisco. After several steep pitches, you leave the Gray Pine Trail where it bends right, and continue west over windswept open ground a few hundred feet to the summit of Bald Mountain. The views on a clear day, needless to say, are extraordinary, ranging from the Sierra Nevada to Point Reyes, and from Snow Mountain, north of Clear Lake, to San Francisco. Two display panels—one facing north, the other south—help you identify landmarks in addition to the ones already noted. From here, Mt. Hood is due west, and Mt. St. Helena, at the corner of Napa, Sonoma, and Lake counties is slightly west of north. Sonoma Mountain, the backbone of Jack London State Historic Park, is southwest, and the Napa Valley is east.

When it is time to head down, retrace your steps to the Gray Pine Trail, turn left onto it, and follow it steeply downhill for several hundred feet to a T-junction with the Bald Mountain Trail, a dirt road. Here you turn left, climb briefly, and then circle the west side of Bald Mountain. A series of S-bends helps you lose elevation, and the grassy slopes beside the road are sprinkled with California poppies and lupine. With Red Mountain ahead, you drop steeply to a T-junction with a paved road. Here

Small seasonal waterfall just off the Vista Trail.

the Bald Mountain Trail continues on pavement, left, and the right-hand branch of the **T** climbs to the communication facility atop Red Mountain. Use caution while descending the road, because it is also used by service vehicles. Turning left, you head downhill on a gentle and then moderate grade into a forest of oak, California buckeye, madrone, and bigleaf maple.

Passing a picnic table, right, the route levels and begins a gentle climb, in places passing exposed bands of red rock that perhaps gave the mountain its name. Where the Red Mountain Trail departs left, you continue straight, passing through a zone of chaparral where fine views extend southwest to Sugarloaf Ridge and Sonoma Mountain. Just shy of the 5-mile point, you pass a rest bench, left, and then the road follows a curvy course downhill, crossing a creek that flows through a culvert. The display here of bush monkeyflower, when in bloom during spring and summer, is stunning. Seeing an open meadow, left, means you are nearing the junction with the Vista Trail. When you reach it, continue downhill on the Bald Mountain and Lower Bald Mountain trails, retracing your steps to the parking area.

54   Sugarloaf Ridge State Park
MEADOW LOOP

Length: 2.6 miles

Time: 1 to 2 hours

Rating: Moderate

Regulations: CSP, parking fee, no dogs, no bikes.

Highlights: Using the Creekside Nature, Hillside, and Meadow trails, this lovely loop explores a forested hillside south of Sonoma Creek at the foot of Sugarloaf Ridge, and then circles back through mostly open meadows full of spring wildflowers just north of the creek. Along the way, you pass the Ferguson Observatory, which offers public astronomy programs; for information call (707) 833-6979.

Directions: See the directions for "Bald Mountain" on p. 268.

Facilities: Picnic tables, fire grates, toilet; visitor center, water, and phone just southeast of entrance kiosk.

Trailhead: South of the parking area, across the park entrance road.

Just right of a picnic area is the trailhead for the park's self-guiding nature trail, built in 1977 by the Youth Conservation Corps and labeled

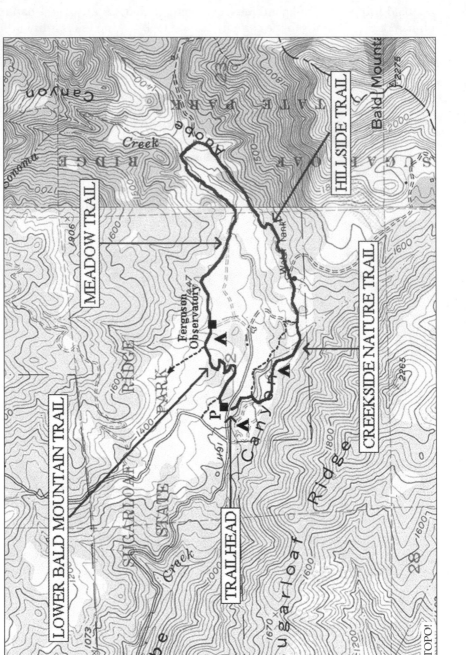

54. Meadow Loop

Creekside Nature Trail on the park map. Following this single-track trail into a forest of Douglas fir, coast live oak, and California bay, you have a wooden fence on your right, guarding the steep drop-off to Sonoma Creek. After several hundred feet you reach a fork. The right-hand branch leads downhill to a picnic area by the creek, but you stay left and on level ground, soon reaching a clearing and the park's camp-fire center, where evening programs are held. When you reach a four-way junction with a cement path, turn right and cross Sonoma Creek on a large wooden bridge. About 50 feet past, you come to a T-junction with a paved road, where you turn left. Now in the park's campground, you follow the road southeast, passing a junction with another paved road, right. A big grassy meadow is left, offering inspiring views to Mt. Hood, northwest, and Red Mountain, north, and there are camp sites scattered in a wooded area, right.

A turn-around marks the end of the road, and between camp sites 25 and 26 is your route, the Creekside Nature Trail, a dirt and gravel path heading southeast. The trail crosses an open area dotted in spring with wildflowers, including California poppies, blue-eyed grass, mule ears, and bluedicks. Reaching Rattlesnake Creek, a seasonal stream, you ford it and then begin a moderate climb, with the rocky ramparts of Sugarloaf Ridge towering above you to the right. At a T-junction, the Creekside Nature Trail continues left, and the Hillside Trail leads both left and right. You turn right, climbing on a gentle and then moderate grade past thickets of willow, coyote brush and blackberry. A wet area, right, provides nesting habitat for red-winged blackbirds, and your passing may be noted, even disputed, by these territorial birds. Passing a picnic table and then two water tanks, the trail changes to a dirt-and-gravel road and soon begins to descend via sweeping S-bends. Tributaries of Sonoma Creek flow under the road through culverts, and the moisture they bring encourages great tangles of wild rose.

Your descent is interrupted by several brief uphill pitches, but soon you reach a meadow graced with oaks and wildflowers, and arrive at a junction with the Brushy Peaks Trail, right. Your road continues straight from here with a new name, the Meadow Trail. After several hundred feet, as the road makes a left-hand bend, you pass the Gray Pine Trail, right. Reptile enthusiasts should keep a sharp eye peeled for the California whiptail, a coffee-brown lizard with a tail as long as its body, and the rubber boa, a plain brown snake, 1 to 3

Yarrow's white flower clusters dot grassy fields in springs.

feet long with a small, pointed head. A wood bridge takes you across beautiful Sonoma Creek, where a picnic table invites you to sit and be serenaded by birdsong in the shade of bigleaf maple and white alder. Now emerging from the trees, your route crosses open ground where deer may be grazing in the tall grass. A large meadow, left, holds Sonoma Creek, and behind it rises Sugarloaf Ridge, its steep sides densely clad with trees and chaparral. After crossing a seasonal tributary of Sonoma Creek, which flows under the road through a culvert, you pass a gate and then reach a paved parking area.

Located here is the Ferguson Observatory, named for the late Bob Ferguson, a Petaluma astronomer dedicated to involving young people in astronomy. Operated by the Valley of the Moon Observatory Association, the facility houses both a 40-inch and a 20-inch telescope, along with smaller telescopes, and is open to the public for observation, classes in telescope making, and group meetings. Across the parking area to the west are picnic tables and a toilet. Between them and the observatory is the continuation of your route, the Meadow Trail, here a rocky dirt track climbing on a moderate grade. Soon your reach a fork marked by a trail post, where the Lower Bald Mountain Trail heads right and the Meadow Trail veers left. You follow the Meadow Trail, and in about 200 feet pass a connector, right, to the Lower Bald Mountain Trail. Now the route wanders through meadows filled with wildflowers—including blue-eyed grass, yarrow, bluedicks, lupine, vetch, and blow wives—and shady groves of coast live oak, California bay, madrone, manzanita, coffeeberry, toyon, and poison oak. A gentle descent through a wet area returns you to the parking area and your starting point.

55

Sugarloaf Ridge State Park
MT. HOOD

Length: 7 miles

Time: 4 to 6 hours

Rating: Difficult

Regulations: CSP; parking fee; no dogs, no bikes, no horses. Hood Mountain Regional Park, which this route enters at the 2.1-mile point, is open to day use only on weekends and holidays, and is closed during fire season. For more information, call Sonoma County Regional Parks, (707) 527-2041.

Highlights: Many of the tallest peaks in North Bay are traversed by well-graded roads and topped with communication towers—not so Mt. Hood. The only way to reach its 2730-foot summit is via steep and rugged trails, making this the most difficult—but in many ways the most rewarding—summit hike covered in this guide. Using the Goodspeed Trail from Sugarloaf Ridge State Park, this out-and-back route leaves a wooded canyon, rises through forest and chaparral, and crosses steep, wildflower-dotted hillsides exposed to sun and wind. The best views are from Gunsight Rock, just below the mountain's summit.

Directions: See the directions for "Bald Mountain" on p. 268. At the 2.3-mile point on Adobe Canyon Rd., there are a parking area and a self-registration station, left.

Facilities: None

Trailhead: On the west side of parking area.

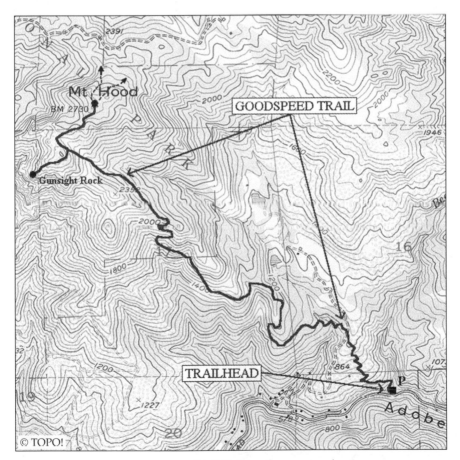

55. Mt. Hood

With Sonoma Creek burbling cheerfully just downhill and right, you descend on the Goodspeed Trail, shaded by California bay, bigleaf maple, and coast redwood. This trail, officially the Nattkemper Goodspeed Trail, honors Clark Nattkemper, a retired biology teacher and an active park docent. Crossing the creek on a long wooden bridge, you enter a lovely, jungle-like area where ferns rise from the forest floor and green moss covers the boulders beside the trail. The forest here includes California and coast live oak, with an understory of hazelnut, wild rose, and poison oak. Downhill and left is Bear Creek, which flows into Sonoma Creek just to the southwest. Both creeks lie at the bottom of steep-sided ravines, and soon you reach a bridge over Bear Creek, which you cross. Now the trail bends sharply left and begins an ascent that alternates between gentle and moderate. As you leave the ravine holding Bear Creek, you rise through a zone of Douglas fir and then enter the realm of chaparral— manzanita, chamise, chaparral pea, leather oak, bush monkeyflower, and rare Sonoma ceanothus, a low, spreading shrub with blue flowers in spring.

A landslide-prone hillside, left, drops steeply to Sonoma Creek and Adobe Canyon Road. On the south side of the road rises Sugarloaf Ridge, a volcanic rampart topped by a series of craggy summits. Your route now becomes very rocky as it passes under a set of power lines and continues a winding ascent. Turning north, you begin to get a view northeast to Bald Mountain (2729') and Red Mountain (2548'), the two highest peaks in the state park. You goal, Mt. Hood (2730'), the crown of Hood

Gunsight Rock, a dizzying perch, offers views south to Kenwood, the Valley of the Moon, and Sonoma Mountain.

Mountain Regional Park, remains hidden. The mountain is named for William Hood, a settler from Scotland who in the 1850s bought a rancho containing the mountain and surrounding lands. The north side of Mt. Hood gives birth to Santa Rosa Creek, and the mountain's south slopes contribute water to Sonoma Creek. Both creeks have runs of steelhead trout, listed as a threatened species under federal law. In places along the trail, you can look southwest along Adobe Canyon Road to the Valley of the Moon and the winery-encircled town of Kenwood. Decorating the borders of the trail in spring are paintbrush and wild iris. Descending now across a steep and rocky hillside, you reach a dirt-and-gravel road just shy of the 1-mile mark. Here you cross the road, turn right, and find the continuation of the Goodspeed Trail, marked by a trail post, a few paces uphill and left.

Still on a single track, you descend via switchbacks through a corridor of trees and chaparral—many of the shrubs here are draped with wild pea and honeysuckle vines. Below you is a boulder-filled ravine, lined with white alder, that holds a seasonal creek, another tributary of Sonoma Creek. This watercourse runs full in spring, its waters splashing over rocks and pouring through channels. When you reach the creek, cross carefully using rocks and logs. Once on the other side, you begin switch-backing uphill over rocky ground, passing under a second set of power lines. Large Douglas firs, and manzanitas so tall they are falling over, line the trail. In wooded areas, the air is still, and the silence is broken only by birdsong. When you reach the crest of a north–south ridge, which may be windswept, you have a fine view southwest to Jack London State Historic Park, Sonoma Mountain, and, on a clear day, the coastal hills near Point Reyes.

Now the trail leaves the ridgecrest and traverses its southwest face. Ahead, on the skyline, is a nearly barren pyramidal hill, topped by a grove of trees. Your route levels and turns northwest, soon crossing another seasonal creek, this one much smaller than the last, nestled in a tree-lined ravine. Emerging onto a grassy hillside dotted with clumps of silver lupine and erupting in spring with wildflowers—bird's-eye gilia, California poppy, bluedicks, fiddleneck, common popcornflower, minia-ture lupine, and blue-eyed Mary—you make a rising traverse that rewards each step with better and better views. Stretching from southeast to northeast is a cirque at the heart of the state park, formed by Bald Mountain, Red Mountain, Brushy Peaks, and Sugarloaf Ridge. To the south are the Sonoma Valley, San Pablo Bay, the East Bay hills, and the Marin shoreline.

Just past the 2-mile point, you enter Hood Mountain Regional Park, operated by Sonoma County. A wooden sign, uphill and right, tells you this trail was built during 1982 and 1983 by members of the Sierra Club. So as you huff and puff your way uphill for the next 1330 vertical feet, you know whom to thank! From here on, the climbing is relentless and often steep. The terrain alternates between exposed grassy slopes, corridors of chaparral, mostly chamise and buckbrush, and wooded groves. Canyon oak is now the dominant shade tree, offering welcome shade on a warm day. Oregon grape and silk tassel may be found nearby. Switchbacks aid your ascent, and your efforts may be noted and commented upon by wrentits, western scrub-jays, and spotted towhees. In some places, the trail is merely a narrow slice of level ground carved from the hillside. In others, it becomes nothing more than a well-worn path over rock steps and ledges.

Fighting against gravity, you clamber uphill over very rough ground to a windy saddle at the 2000-foot level. From here the trail leads onto a northeast-facing slope that is densely clad with bay, manzanita, canyon oak, tanbark oak, and madrone. Shrubs such as creambush and gooseberry form a low, open understory. Spring wildflowers lining the trail, which is on a level grade for the first time since it left the state park, include mule ears, hound's tongue and mosquito bills, also called Henderson's shooting stars. Another saddle provides a vantage point for more wonderful views, mostly to the southwest. Soon the scene changes abruptly, and you enter a grove of knobcone pines, shown on the state park map as Pine Flat. The ground is carpeted with pine needles. This drought-resistant, fire-adapted species has needles bundled in threes and curved, cylindrical cones that taper to a narrow point. In the middle of the grove is a trail post and a junction. Here, a 0.15-mile trail goes left to Gunsight Rock, and the Goodspeed Trail continues 0.25 mile uphill to the summit of Mt. Hood.

Gunsight Rock is a terrific vantage point, and the views from there are better than from Mt. Hood's summit. To reach the rock, you turn left and climb on a gentle grade, soon leaving the pine grove and entering a rocky area of chaparral, mostly manzanita and chamise. Look under the shrubs for heath warrior, a parasite associated with manzanita and madrone. This curious plant, related to paintbrush and owl's-clover, has fern-like leaves and burgundy flowers. When you see Gunsight Rock, the reason for its name becomes obvious—blocks of rock form a notch on the otherwise flat top of a promontory overlooking the steep southwest face of Mt. Hood. There are no guard rails, so use extreme caution. From here, the view extends north to Mt. St. Helena, west across Annadel State Park to Santa Rosa, and south to Kenwood, the Valley of the Moon, and Sonoma Mountain. When you have had your fill of the views from this dizzying perch, return to the junction with the Goodspeed Trail at Pine Flat.

To reach the summit, you continue steeply uphill on the Goodspeed Trail, past volcanic outcrops eroded into weird shapes. Taking root in rocky crevices is common dudleya, a succulent that somewhat resembles a flattened artichoke. Also here is canyon gooseberry, with beautiful spring blossoms, and yerba santa. Nearing the summit, you pass thickets of dwarf interior live oak, a hearty tree adapted, like knobcone pine, to harsh conditions. Soon the trail levels and enters a large circular clearing, the summit of Mt. Hood. Across the clearing, two trails lead downhill through the county park to a trailhead at the end of Los Alamos Rd. Ringed with trees and shrubs, the summit is not as good a vantage point as Gunsight Rock, but there are plenty of views to be had, and, if you search in the shrubbery, you can find a few comfortable rocks on which to sit and rest. When you are rested and ready, retrace your steps to the parking area.

56 Sugarloaf Ridge State Park WATERFALL LOOP

Length: 1.7 miles

Time: 1 to 2 hours

Rating: Easy

Regulations: CSP; parking fee; no dogs, no bikes, no horses.

Highlights: The main attraction of this loop, which uses the Pony Gate and Canyon trails, is a waterfall on Sonoma Creek, best viewed during spring when the creek is full. This is also the time to find wildflowers in the grassy meadows on the upper part of the Pony Gate Trail, or under the towering coast redwoods that border the creek.

Directions: See the directions for "Bald Mountain" on p. 268. At the 2.3-mile point on Adobe Canyon Rd., there are a parking area and a self-registration station, left. Stop here to pay the parking fee, and then go another 1 mile to a parking area, left.

Facilities: None; about 0.1 mile ahead are a visitor center, water, phone, picnic tables, fire grates, toilet.

Trailhead: Southeast corner of parking area.

Shaded by coast live oak, canyon oak, Douglas fir, California bay, and madrone, you follow the Pony Gate Trail, a hikers-only single track that climbs on a gentle grade. In a ravine on the other side of Adobe Canyon Road, right, is Sonoma Creek, whose banks you will walk beside on the return part of this loop. As you gain elevation, you begin to see the looming forested wall of Sugarloaf Ridge, rising just south of the creek. Your trail crosses a few open grassy slopes, beautifully decorated with spring wildflowers. At a T-junction, you turn left, still on the Pony Gate Trail, and drop into a wooded area that holds a creek. Passing a closed trail,

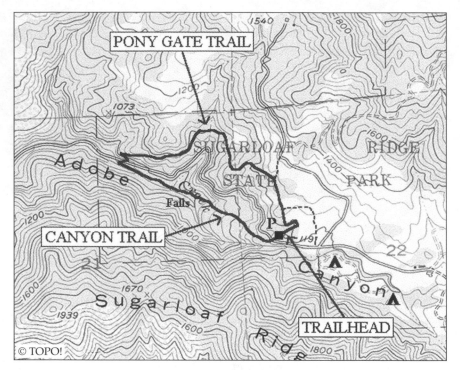

56. Waterfall Loop

right, you continue to descend to another T-junction, where again you turn left. From here to its intersection with Adobe Canyon Road, your route, the Pony Gate Trail, is part of the Bay Area Ridge Trail. Ahead, as it drops into Pony Gate Gulch, the trail becomes eroded, rocky, and possibly wet.

In a dense forest, you reach the gulch, where several seasonal creeks tumble down from the right, creating a beautiful fern-filled jungle. The trail here is lined with snowberry and elk clover, and, as the route bends sharply left, you follow a more substantial creek, which is on your right, downstream. Crossing this creek may be a challenge during wet weather, because you must pick your way across on rocks. Once across, you climb steeply to a junction, where a short trail leads left to a viewpoint overlooking the creek. Continuing straight, your route forges its way uphill, soon merging with a dirt road coming downhill from the right. Veering left onto the road, you pass a trail post, left, with the Bay Area Ridge Trail emblem, and then descend through an overgrown area where bigleaf maple trees tower overhead. In open places, the road is bordered with manzanita, chamise, bush monkeyflower, and poison oak. Turning sharply left at a switchback, you walk several hundred feet to a clearing beside paved Adobe Canyon Road.

After carefully crossing the road, turn right and go downhill about 125 feet to the Canyon Trail, left, a single track. As you leave the paved road, a set of wooden steps helps you descend toward Sonoma Creek, which is just ahead. Suddenly you find yourself in a splendid forest of coast redwood and tanbark oak, with an understory of hazelnut, wild rose, and several species of fern. Look carefully in spring for a tiny white violet, called western heart's-ease or two-eyed violet, growing beside the trail. Nearing the creek, you cross one of its tributaries on a wood bridge, and then walk upstream along a rocky embankment. Across the creek rises a steep hillside carpeted with moss, ferns, and leaf litter. Soon, at a clearing, you catch a glimpse of a fine waterfall ahead, its waters plunging through a narrow, rocky ravine. For a better view, leave the trail where it bends left and begins to climb a series of wooden steps, and work your way across a boulder-strewn clearing to a vantage point near the waterfall's base.

After enjoying nature's fine display, return to the main trail and begin an uphill trek, soon losing sight of Sonoma Creek behind a ridge, right. A seasonal creek, left, may have its own miniature waterfalls to keep you entertained as you work your way to the ridgecrest. More wooden steps aid the steep ascent, but soon the grade eases, and the trail wanders along the top of the ridge until it reaches Adobe Canyon Road. Cross carefully to the parking area where you began this loop.

Johnny jump-up, a violet, appears each spring in grassy areas.

Rosebay, a rhododendron, is found along the coast from the Santa Cruz Mountains to Del Norte County.

Appendix A: Some Other Trails

In addition to the routes described in this guide, there are many other routes in the North Bay worth exploring. Following is a list of some of the trails that I feel are worth including in this guide, but do not require a detailed route description.

Location/Trailhead	Trail Name	Features
Audubon Canyon Ranch	Picher Canyon	Easy hike to view a heron and egret rookery; open weekends and holidays from mid-March through mid-July. For exact dates and hours, call (415) 868-9244.
Golden Gate National Recreation Area, end of Tennessee Valley Road	Tennessee Valley Trail	Easy walk to beach at Tennessee Cove; 4 miles roundtrip.
Jack London State Historic Park	Grave Site and Wolf House Ruins	Easy 1.4 mile roundtrip walk to London's grave site and ruins of his house, destroyed by fire in 1913.
Mt. Tamalpais State Park, East Peak parking area	East Peak Trail	Short but steep trail from the parking area offers 360-degree views from top of Marin County's highest peak.
Mt. Tamalpais State Park, East Peak parking area	Verna Dunshee Trail	Short and easy trail circles East Peak, highest point in Marin County.
Muir Woods National Monument	Nature Trail	Easy, 1-mile self-guiding trail on paved path among towering redwoods.
Pt. Reyes National Seashore, Bear Valley visitor center	Earthquake Trail	An 0.6-mile self-guiding trail straddling the San Andreas fault; also good for seeing and hearing songbirds.

Location/Trailhead	Trail Name	Features
Pt. Reyes National Seashore, end of Pierce Point Road	McClures Beach	For ocean views, birding, and tide-pooling, an 0.5-mile trail from the parking area to the beach.
Richardson Bay Audubon Center and Sanctuary	Terwilliger Nature Trail	An 0.5 mile self-guiding nature trail exploring upland and shoreline.

Tidy tips are composite flowers with yellow centers and yellow rays with white tips.

Appendix B: Selected Reading Material

BAY AREA & CALIFORNIA

Conradson, Diane R., *Exploring Our Baylands*. 3rd ed. Fremont: San Francisco Bay Wildlife Society, 1996.

Gilliam, Harold, and Ann Lawrence Gilliam, *Marin Headlands*. San Francisco: Golden Gate National Park Association, 1993.

Ginsberg, Joanne S., et al., *California Coastal Resource Guide*. Berkeley: University of California Press, 1987.

Griffin, L. Marin, M.D., *Saving the Marin–Sonoma Coast*. Healdsburg: Sweetwater Springs Press, 1998.

Gudde, Erwin G., *California Place Names*. 4th ed. Berkeley: University of California Press, 1998.

Hart, John, *Muir Woods*. San Francisco: Golden Gate National Park Association, 1991.

Hinch, Stephen W., *Guide to State Parks of the Sonoma Coast and Russian River*. Santa Rosa: Annadel Press, 1998.

Lavender, David, *California*. Lincoln: University of Nebraska Press, 1972.

Marinacci, Barbara and Rudy Marinacci, *California's Spanish Place-Names*. 2nd ed. Houston: Gulf Publishing Company, 1997.

Martin, Don, and Kay Martin, *Hiking Marin*. San Anselmo: Martin Press, 1995.

Martin, Don, and Kay Martin, *Mt. Tam*. San Anselmo: Martin Press, 1994.

Martin, Don, and Kay Martin, *Point Reyes National Seashore*. 2nd ed. San Anselmo: Martin Press, 1997

Rusmore, Jean, *The Bay Area Ridge Trail*. Berkeley: Wilderness Press, 1995.

Spitz, Barry, *Tamalpais Trails*. 4th ed. San Anselmo: Potrero Meadow Publishing Co., 1998.

Stanton, Ken, *Great Day Hikes in & around Napa Valley*. Mendocino: Bored Feet Publications, 1997.

Wayburn, Peggy, *Adventuring in the San Francisco Bay Area*. Revised ed. San Francisco: Sierra Club Books, 1995.

Whitnah, Dorothy L., *An Outdoor Guide to the San Francisco Bay Area*. 5th ed. Berkeley: Wilderness Press, 1989.

Whitnah, Dorothy L., *Point Reyes*. 3rd ed. Berkeley: Wilderness Press, 1997.

NATURAL HISTORY

Alt, David D., and Donald W. Hyndman, *Roadside Geology of Northern California*. Missoula: Mountain Press Publishing Co., 1975. ·

Burt, William H., and Richard P. Grossenheider, *A Field Guide to the Mammals, North America, north of Mexico*. 3rd ed. Boston: Houghton Mifflin Company, 1980.

Clark, Jeanne L., *California Wildlife Viewing Guide*. Helena: Falcon Press, 1992.

Faber, Phyllis M., and Robert F. Holland, *Common Riparian Plants of California*. Mill Valley: Pickleweed Press, 1988.

Faber, Phyllis M., *Common Wetland Plants of Coastal California*. 2nd ed. Mill Valley: Pickleweed Press, 1996.

Ferris, Roxana S., *Native Shrubs of the San Francisco Bay Region*. Berkeley: University of California Press, 1968.

Howell, John Thomas, *Marin Flora*. 2nd ed. Berkeley: University of California Press, 1970.

Keator, Glenn, *Pacific Coast Berry Finder*. Berkeley: Nature Study Guild, 1978.

Kozloff, Eugene N., and Linda H. Beidleman, *Plants of the San Francisco Bay Region*. Pacific Grove: Sagen Press, 1994.

Little, Elbert L., *National Audubon Society Field Guide to North American Trees, Western Region*. New York: Alfred A. Knopf, 1994.

Lyon, Richards, and Jake Ruygt, *100 Napa County Roadside Wildflowers*. Napa: Stonecrest Press, 1996.

Lyons, Kathleen, and Mary Beth Cooney-Lazaneo, *Plants of the Coast Redwood Region*. Boulder Creek: Looking Press, 1988.

McHoul, Lilian, and Celia Elke, *Wild Flowers of Marin*. Fairfax: The Tamal Land Press, 1979.

National Geographic Society, *Field Guide to the Birds of North America*. 3rd ed. Washington: National Geographic Society, 1999.

Niehaus, Theodore F., and Charles L. Ripper, *A Field Guide to Pacific States Wildflowers*. Boston: Houghton Mifflin Company, 1976.

Pavlik, Bruce M., et al., *Oaks of California*. Los Olivos, CA: Cachuma Press, Inc., 1991.

Peterson, Roger T., *A Field Guide to Western Birds*. 3rd ed. Boston: Houghton Mifflin Company, 1990.

Schoenherr, Allan A., *A Natural History of California*. Berkeley: University of California Press, 1992.

Stebbins, Robert C., *A Field Guide to Western Reptiles and Amphibians*. 2nd ed. Boston: Houghton Mifflin Company, 1985.

Watts, Phoebe, *Redwood Region Flower Finder*. Berkeley: Nature Study Guild, 1979.

Watts, Tom, *Pacific Coast Tree Finder*. Berkeley: Nature Study Guild, 1973.

OTHER

Darvill, Fred T. Jr., *Mountaineering Medicine*. 14th ed. Berkeley:
Wilderness Press, 1998.

Wilkerson, James A., *Medicine for Mountaineering & Other Wilderness
Activities*. 4th ed. Seattle: The Mountaineers, 1992.

Letham, Lawrence, *GPS Made Easy*. 2nd ed. Seattle: The Mountaineers,
1998.

Appendix C: Information Sources

GOVERNMENT AGENCIES

California Dept. of Fish and Game   (707) 944-5500
PO Box 47
Yountville, CA 94599

California State Parks   (916) 653-6995
PO Box 942896
Sacramento, CA 94296

City of Napa Parks and Recreation Department   (707) 257-952
1100 West Street
Napa, CA 945599

Marin County Open Space District   (415) 499-6387
Marin County Civic Center, Rm. 415
San Rafael, CA 94903

Marin Municipal Water District   (415) 945-1181
Sky Oaks Ranger Station
49 Sky Oaks Road
Fairfax, CA 94930
National Park Service

Golden Gate National Recreation Area (GGNRA)   (415) 556-0560
Fort Mason, Building 201
Bay and Franklin Streets
San Francisco, CA 94123

Sonoma County Regional Parks   (707) 527-2041
2300 County Center Drive, Ste. 120A
Santa Rosa, CA 95403

OTHER ORGANIZATIONS

Angel Island Association   (415) 435-3522
Angel Island State Park
PO Box 866
Tiburon, CA 94920

Audubon Canyon Ranch   (415) 868-9244
4900 Shoreline Highway, Route 1
Stinson Beach, CA 94970

Bay Area Ridge Trail Council	(415) 391-9300
26 O'Farrell Street, 4th Floor	
San Francisco, CA 94108	
Bodega Marine Laboratory	(707) 875-2211
PO Box 247	
Bodega Bay, CA 94923	
California Native Plant Society	(916) 447-2677
1722 J Street, Ste. 17	
Sacramento, CA 95814	
California State Automobile Association	(415) 565-2012
150 Van Ness Avenue	
San Francisco, CA 94102	
Fort Ross Interpretive Association	(707) 847-3437
Fort Ross State Historic Park	
19005 Coast Highway One	
Jenner, CA 95450	
Greenbelt Alliance	(707) 575-3661
North Bay Office	
520 Mendocino Avenue, Ste. 225	
Santa Rosa, CA 95401	
Marine Mammal Center	(415) 289-7325
Marin Headlands/GGNRA	
1065 Fort Cronkhite	
Sausalito, CA 94965	
Mt. Tamalpais Interpretive Association	(415) 258-2410
Pantoll Ranger Station	
801 Panoramic Highway	
Mill Valley, CA 94941	
Napa County Land Trust	(707) 252-3270
1040 Main Street, Ste. 203	
Napa, CA 94559	
National Audubon Society	(916) 481-5332
555 Audubon Place	
Sacramento, CA 95825	
Point Reyes Bird Observatory	(415) 868-1221
4990 Shoreline Highway	
Stinson Beach, CA 94970	
Richardson Bay Audubon Center and Sanctuary	(415) 388-2524
376 Greenwood Beach Road	
Tiburon, CA 94920	

Sierra Club, Redwood Chapter   (707) 544-7651
(for Napa, Sonoma counties)
632 Fifth Street
Santa Rosa, CA 95404

Sierra Club, San Francisco Bay Chapter   (510) 848-0800
(for Marin County)
2530 San Pablo Avenue, Suite I
Berkeley, CA 94702

Skyline Park Citizens Association   (707) 252-0481
2201 Imola Avenue
Napa, CA 94559

Sonoma County Trails Council   (707) 526-9385
PO Box 14483
Santa Rosa, CA 95402

Stewards of Slavianka   (707) 869-91778
PO Box 221
Duncans Mills, CA 95430

The Olmsted & Brothers Map Company   (510) 658-6534
Box 5351
Berkeley, CA 94705

Valley of the Moon Natural History Association (707) 938-5216
2400 London Ranch Road
Glen Ellen, CA 95442

Wilderness Press   (510) 558-1666
1200 Fifth Street
Berkeley, CA 94710

National Geographic Maps/TOPO!   (415) 558-8700
375 Alabama Street, Suite 400
San Francisco, CA 94110

About the Maps in this Book

The maps in this book were created using TOPO! Interactive Maps on CD-ROM from National Geographic Maps. Designed specifically for outdoor enthusiasts, TOPO! CD-ROMS are recognized as the best in digital navigation for backcountry exploration. TOPO! features detailed, accurate USGS maps enhanced with millions of digital elevation points. Powerful tools provide instant elevation profiles, real-time coordinates for GPS users, and extended capabilities for exploring, customizing, and printing seamless topographic maps.

This book was created using TOPO! *San Francisco Bay Area, Wine Country, and Big Sur (2 CD set)*. In addition to the *San Francisco Bay Area, Wine Country, and Big Sur* maps, National Geographic Maps offers interactive maps products for most recreational and metropolitan areas throughout the USA. To learn more about TOPO!, or to find a dealer near you, contact National Geographic Maps at (415) 558-8700. For product information, free upgrades and downloadable trail sets, visit www.topo.com.

For more information, contact:

National Geographic Maps
375 Alabama St., Suite 400
San Francisco, CA 94110
Phone: (415) 558-8700
Fax: (415) 558-9700
E-mail. info@topo.com
Web: http://www.topo.com

Heads Up

Hiking in the backcountry entails unavoidable risk that every hiker assumes and must be aware of and respect. The fact that a trail is described in this book is not a representation that it will be safe for you. Trails vary greatly in difficulty and in the degree of conditioning and agility one needs to enjoy them safely. On some hikes routes may have changed or conditions may have deteriorated since the descriptions were written. Also trail conditions can change even from day to day, owing to weather and other factors. A trail that is safe on a dry day or for a highly conditioned, agile, properly equipped hiker may be completely unsafe for someone else or unsafe under adverse weather conditions.

You can minimize your risks on the trail by being knowledgeable, prepared and alert. There is not space in this book for a general treatise on safety in the mountains, but there are a number of good books and public courses on the subject and you should take advantage of them to increase your knowledge. Just as important, you should always be aware of your own limitations and of conditions existing when and where you are hiking. If conditions are dangerous, or if you're not prepared to deal with them safely, choose a different hike! It's better to have wasted a drive than to be the subject of a mountain rescue.

These warnings are not intended to scare you off the trails. Millions of people have safe and enjoyable hikes every year. However, one element of the beauty, freedom and excitement of the wilderness is the presence of risks that do not confront us at home. When you hike you assume those risks. They can be met safely, but only if you exercise your own independent judgement and common sense.

Index

photo by Ken Kobre

Author and professional photographer **David Weintraub** is a resident of San Francisco and has enjoyed the Bay Area's natural beauty for years. He is an avid hiker, skier, and kayaker. His photographs have been published in many books and magazines, including Audubon, Backpacker, Sierra, Smithsonian, and Sunset. His first book, *East Bay Trails*, was named the best-selling title for several years by the Sierra Club bookstore in Oakland. David is also the author of *Adventure Kayaking: Cape Cod and Martha's Vineyard* and the forthcoming *Monterey Bay Trails*.